Thai Twist

Other Titles by D.R. Ransdell

Fiction:

Campanello Adventures
Amirosian Nights   .

Andy Veracruz Mysteries
Mariachi Meddler
Island Casualty
Dizzy in Durango
Substitute Soloist

Non-Fiction:

Secrets of a Mariachi Violinist

Thai Twist

D.R. Ransdell

Author's Note:
This is a work of fiction. Any resemblance to real persons is coincidental.

Acknowledgements

Many thanks to Elise Ransdell, Sandra Ransdell, and J.T. ("Too many temples!") for their help with earlier versions of this manuscript. A special thanks to Kala Annambhotla for sparking my imagination with the gift of a perfect, purple elephant. Finally, thanks to Lucy Rowell and Ann Cosgrove for helping me visit all those amazing temples.

To Elise Ransdell,

who is brave enough to travel with her fun-loving sister

Chapter One

"Sammy, if it weren't for you, I might quit teaching altogether."

I smiled as I interpreted my sister's between-the-lines praise. Since the ten-year-old Sammy was her only violin student who practiced, Rachel always enjoyed giving him a lesson. He was such a sweet kid that I'd always enjoyed babysitting for him. Maybe I was giving him too much credit. He was blessed with wonderful parents, and ever since they'd moved in down the street from my mom, we'd adopted the whole family.

For the moment, however, I was at my sister's, which was a few blocks away. I was swinging on her front porch swing, waiting for her to finish up. For sisters who were thirteen years apart, we were close, and we usually ended Mondays by going out for coffee. Today I needed her ear more than usual; mine were ringing after a sound reprimand from my counselor. Sometimes I fit the dizzy blonde stereotype more closely than I wanted to, but who said that somebody in her second semester of college should already know her major? Medical field? Too many choices. Law? Possibly. That way I'd have the excuse to stay in school for at least three extra years. High school teacher? I loved the idea of summers off, but what to teach? I'd grown up speaking Spanish, so majoring in the language wasn't enough of a challenge. I'd considered switching to Italian, the domain of my paternal grandparents, but I wasn't convinced I could keep the two languages straight. To be contrary I'd opted to take my mandatory units in French, which was just as confusing.

I was so distracted that I answered my cell without checking the caller I.D. "Hello?"

"We're delighted to tell you that you've won our contest."

"Very funny, Jason. You're a real crack-up." Jason was my sometimes boyfriend, but we hadn't spoken for a week. He was in the doghouse for standing me up at the last minute on a Saturday night, and I wasn't sure I was willing to forgive him for a repeated offense.

"Miss, is this Gina Campanello?"

"Yes?"

"This is Dylan Flores from Tucson Radio Today. Don't you remember? The contest you entered?"

I loved to enter contests: photography, Almanac, word play, you name it. Not for any good reason. Not because I expected to win. But if a man from the radio claimed I'd entered his contest, he was probably right.

"Sir, I'm a bit forgetful. So if you could remind me —"

"The Midwest Envy Contest!"

Then I did remember. I'd correctly guessed January 13th as the night of Tucson's final winter frost for the season.

"You've won a trip for two to Thailand! We're providing plane tickets and accommodations for five nights each in Bangkok, Chiang Mai, and Phuket. Of course, you are free to extend the time if you have a little extra cash."

I'd assumed the prize would be a trip to Vegas rather than something exotic. I knew nothing about Thailand; I couldn't even remember if it was closer to India or Vietnam. I'd been to Mexico at least a dozen times, and Rachel had invited me to visit Greece with her, but Asia? I'd never in my whole life expected to go there.

"We were thinking you would want to leave by early June. If you remember, the only stipulation was for you to write an article about your experiences for publication on our website."

"Wow. That would be great, but, but I can't do it."

"You don't have to write very much. Maybe two thousand words."

"I don't mean the article but the timing."

"We could scoot it back a week. Our travel agent hasn't made the arrangements yet."

"No, I mean, I'll be attending summer school. Both sessions."

I wasn't sure which subjects I needed to be taking; hence the tense situation with my counselor. I was all for goofing off all summer, but my mom and my grandma were getting itchy about my progress. They were afraid I'd never grow up and move out of the house.

"School can wait!" Dylan exclaimed. "I'm talking free trip here! For two!"

"A trip does sound fun." My two best friends, Patty and Maggie, were both doing internships over the summer. They wouldn't even be in town.

"What's your major?" Dylan asked.

"That's just the problem. I'm not sure."

"See? Go to Thailand, and you'll have a chance to think things through. Trust me."

"I'm not sure I'm up to traveling that far by myself."

"That's why it's a trip for two! You don't have a boy-friend?"

"We broke up." Really, I wasn't sure.

"Then get back together again."

"It wouldn't help. He never leaves town."

"Then never mind him! But, oh, wait. Since you're under twenty-one, you'll have to take an adult with you. Do either of your parents like to travel?"

My dad was an engineer in Monterrey, Mexico. He was basically a gringo even though his parents had both immigrated to the U.S. from Italy. My mother was from Durango, Durango, Mexico, but she said that once she'd escaped the rampant machoism of her birth country she was never going back for more than a quick visit. She was plenty happy in Tucson, Arizona, and when Dad took a big promotion to move south of the border, he moved by himself.

"My dad is unavailable. My mother hates to travel." Actually, she liked a trip well enough once she was safely back home, but she hardly ever enjoyed a trip at the time.

"Perhaps another relative?"

"My grandma really hates to travel. And my sister —"

At that point Sammy and Rachel came out on the porch. "Your sister what?" Rachel smiled.

My sister was shorter than I, but she'd inherited the Mediterranean characteristics. That meant her brown hair matched her brown eyes, and she kept a nice tan all year long. She was nearly as dark as the slim boy standing beside her.

"My sister would be too busy to go to Thailand with me," I continued. "In the summer she goes to Greece to play in a bouzouki band because she gets bored playing mariachi music all the time."

"Go to Thailand?" Rachel asked.

"Thailand!" Sammy shouted.

"Give me that phone!" Rachel snatched it from me. "Is this some kind of sick prank?"

She listened for a moment, but then she motioned for a writing utensil. Sammy ran back into the house and found one for her; then he had to race back in to find a scrap of paper.

"Right, right," Rachel said, scribbling as she spoke. "Maybe if we could arrange it for early May …. Yes, yes. I'm not sure two weeks is long enough …. Yes, we could pay for an extra week or so on our own. Do call back when you have a chance."

She handed me back my phone. "What do you mean, you can't find anyone to go with you?"

"Well, I just thought —"

"I'd love to go to Thailand!"

"But since you have to go to Greece —"

"I'll go to Greece from Thailand!"

"Rachel, I know nothing about the country."

"You can add to your elephant collection."

I did not need another elephant. The collection started by accident when Aunt Milena brought me a small souvenir from India. I was eight or nine at the time and easily impressed. The small elephant sparkled with sequins, and I kept talking about how much I liked it. I did like it, but I'd learned the power of brown-nosing, and I wanted her to continue bringing me presents.

My plan backfired. Over the next years, she always brought me elephants from her travels. So did everybody else. My friends and relatives were so happy to find a reliable gift idea that they repeated themselves over and over. I was delighted by the first ten or twenty elephants, but by the time I had a hundred, I didn't have a polite way to say that I didn't want any more. I had elephants made out of glass, clay, wood, onyx, plastic, wax, metal, and crystal originating from India, Pakistan, Japan, Sri Lanka, Mexico, Russia, Denmark, and Africa. Rachel had even found me one in Greece. Although my elephants spanned the rainbow, I even had some that were light green, which was the color of my eyes.

"Rachel, I've got too many elephants already."

"My grandpa and grandma came from Thailand," Sammy said. "Don't you remember?"

Indeed I did. I'd stopped babysitting for Sammy after an elderly relative had gone to live with them, but I could still imagine every inch of the living room full of colorful batiks, mostly depicting elephants and temples, that had come from the Old Country. Kanda Tamarin had only gone to Thailand once, for her honeymoon, but she'd often spoken about her wonderful, romantic visit to the country.

Kanda pulled up in the drive, and Sammy raced over to the car. "Mom! Gina and Rachel are going to Thailand!"

"That's wonderful!"

"It's not for sure," I said. "And I don't know the first

thing about Asia."

"Come over for dinner, and Jim and I will tell you all about it," Kanda said. She waved as she and Sammy drove away.

"Well," Rachel said. "That's settled! We'll have to get cracking."

"What do you mean?"

"Thai is a very hard language."

"Rachel, it's only January. We have plenty of time."

Not even a herd of elephants could have stood between my sister and her newest agenda. So I didn't have my leisurely coffee. Instead of wasting our time sitting, we went straight to the bookstore and snatched up all the material on Thailand.

By the time Rachel and I went to dinner at the Tamarins,' my sister had mastered a dozen phrases of the language. I had learned none. I'd been so pressured by long homework assignments and final exams that I'd accidently told half our friends we were going to Taiwan. Whenever I complained about my time crunch to Rachel, she claimed I slept too much and had no excuse. She'd already completed her bachelor's degree, so what did she care? Even in college she'd never felt the same kind of pressure. She'd never wavered from the idea of majoring in music. I didn't have that option. I wasn't the least bit musical. Despite the fact that my last name literally meant "Little Bell," I, Gina Campanello, couldn't sing in tune.

While Kanda and Jim pretended to sympathize about my lack of preparation, they were delighted with Rachel's efforts. Yes, Thai was difficult, but wasn't that part of the challenge? As if I didn't feel bad enough, when the Tamarins showed us their honeymoon pictures, Rachel identified half the temples by name. In contrast I tried to keep track of basic geography: Chiang Mai was in the north, Phuket was in the south, and the capital was somewhere in the middle. Meanwhile the Tamarins were excited to share their best advice: be sure to visit the Turtle Temple in Bangkok, the ruins of Ayutthaya, and the famous wat—meaning "temple"—on top of the mountain above Chiang Mai. Although I appreciated the helpful hints, from the way Rachel took notes I was beginning to think this had turned into her trip, and I was the one tagging along for the ride.

The trio laughed gaily, but I couldn't match their enthusiasm. What if I didn't like the country? What if I couldn't come up with a decent article for the radio website? What if I should have taken classes all summer after all?

We were nearly through the chicken curry when the old auntie entered the dining room and headed straight to me. The eighty-eight-year-old shuffled slowly because she wore bulky doggie slippers. Since Janjira now suffered from dementia, she floated around the house, disregarding schedules and timetables and even daylight. Kanda had given up on insisting that Janjira eat dinner with the family because she always stood and wandered off. Thin and frail, she was uninterested in food and refused to eat more than a spoonful or two at a time.

She clasped my hand around a small velvet bag. "Go Thailand," she said. "Take lothel!"

"Goodness!" Rachel dropped one of her chopsticks. With a *ping* it bounced off the table and onto the floor.

"I don't believe it," said Kanda.

"Gina, you've worked a miracle," said Jim.

"Auntie really likes you!" cried Sammy.

"Go Thailand! Take lothel!" the woman repeated. Most of her hair had been gathered into a bun, but she ignored the strand that had escaped and now bobbed from one side of her forehead to the other.

"I'm afraid I didn't quite understand," I told the others.

Sammy rushed over and stood behind my shoulder. "Let's see what it is!"

Carefully I unzipped the maroon bag. Inside was a two-inch stone elephant that was dark purple with black specks. The elephant's trunk snaked into the air like a periscope while its left foot stepped forward. The eyes were slender slits. I'd never seen anything like it.

Given my extensive collection, that was saying a lot.

"Take good care," the woman said.

"All right," I said hesitantly. I set the bag on the table and laid the elephant on top of it.

"Thank you for take lothel." Janjira smiled and left the room.

The rest of us watched until she disappeared down the hall. It took us several seconds to regain our composure.

"Now that's a real twist," said Jim. "Janjira hasn't spoken since Valentine's Day."

"It must be the magic of Thailand," said his wife. "That country has all kinds of lovely effects on people."

Jim took another helping of sticky rice. "You must have triggered something locked deep inside, Gina. We've been trying to get her to talk for weeks, but we've never come up with anything that she responds to."

I held the elephant up to the light. "What am I supposed to do with this thing?"

"I'll go ask Auntie!" Sammy bounded out of the room.

"Is 'lothel' a Thai word?" asked Rachel.

Kanda shook her head. "I only know a few words, and that's not one of them."

"I've read that English Rs are so difficult for Thai speakers that they often substitute Ls instead," said Rachel. "Do you think she was trying to say 'brother?'"

"I don't know," Kanda said slowly. "Janjira is not really my aunt. Let me try to explain. She's my mother's sister's husband's brother's wife. She never had any children. After her husband died, she moved in with my mother because she had no other relatives in the U.S. After my mother passed away last year, you might say we inherited her."

I finished my last mouthful of curry. If nothing else I

would look forward to more Thai cuisine. I'd never sampled any Thai food I didn't like.

"So Janjira's brother would be in Thailand?" I asked.

"I don't remember anything about a brother, but yes, any of her relatives would be back in the home country."

"What brought her to the States?" Rachel asked.

"Her husband was a diplomat in Washington."

"Does she often talk about a brother?"

"This was the first time."

"Do you want—" I started to hand over the elephant.

"Keep it," said Kanda. "The way she is now, she'll have already forgotten."

Sammy bounded back into the room and thrust a photo into my hand. A handsome man in his twenties grinned from under a wide straw hat. His teeth were white and straight, but there was a gap between his two front teeth. He was dark and thin, and his features matched Auntie's. He was standing under some green shrubbery, but sunlight danced on his head. He looked so happy that I wanted to reach out and touch him.

"Koon Somchai," Sammy said. "He's an engineer. He makes streets."

I repeated after him, trying to remember. When I turned the photo over, I found squiggles of Thai script.

"Auntie wants you to take the picture with you." Sammy patted Rachel and me on the back simultaneously. "You'll find him, won't you?"

Rachel rushed her hands to her lips, hiding her surprise at such an impossible request. "We'll try, but it might be difficult."

Sammy nodded as if he were already a cocky teenager instead of a kid. "The violin is difficult too, but you always tell me to keep trying." He grinned so winningly that the rest of us couldn't help doing the same.

Rachel was caught in her own trap; she encouraged her students no matter how hopeless they were.

"It's important to keep trying, isn't it?" Rachel asked. "I'll tell you what. Thailand is a big place. Ask your auntie where we should look."

Sammy dashed off again while the rest of us mused about the indomitable spirit of children.

He was gone for so long I assumed he'd gotten distracted, but instead he rushed back to us with a small note written in circles and squiggles--the regular Thai script.

"What did you find out?" Kanda asked.

"Rachel and Gina can find him in Krum Krep."

"Krum Krep," Rachel repeated. "If we have a chance to go there, we'll look for him."

"Thank you!" Sammy cried. "That would make Auntie really happy. I know it would."

The rest of us politely nodded. Sammy was sent off to bed, but the rest of us discussed travel details. Did Rachel and I need to carry bug repellent? What was the range of clothing we would need? Most importantly, how could we travel as light as possible?

By the time Rachel and I stood to excuse ourselves, I felt I was already halfway to Thailand. Rachel held the photo out to Kanda, but I snatched it up.

"Let's hang onto the picture and the elephant too. If we go to whatever town that is, we can keep our eyes open."

Rachel and the Tamarins stared at me.

I couldn't exactly explain my gut reaction, but I had a sense of something left undone, a door that had been opened but needed to be closed again.

"Listen," I said. "If Janjira hasn't spoken for so long, the elephant must mean something to her."

"Tracking down a long-lost relative would be like looking for a monk in a Buddhist temple!" joked Jim.

I knew the odds were against us, but as long as Krum Krep was only a village and Janjira's brother had never moved away from it, we might have a chance.

"I know it sounds crazy," I said. "But we've got to tell Sammy that we tried."

Chapter Two

When we reached the curb outside Suvarnabhumi Airport, we were shoved into the backseat of a cab so fast I hadn't known there was a line for one. Hence I didn't have a chance to protest that our driver wasn't old enough to hold a license since he didn't look a day over fifteen. He shot off into the night as if herds of gangsters were chasing us. Maybe two herds.

When he lurched to avoid the *tuk-tuk*, he sent me careening into my sister. The Thai golf cart scooted over, allowing us to take the lead.

I gingerly removed my elbow from my sister's ear. "See? This is a mistake. If we jump out now, we only have to walk a few miles to return to the airport."

I'd had a twenty-six-hour trip to come up with lots of reasons why we shouldn't be traveling by ourselves through Asia. Getting lost was one of the bigger ones, but I hadn't known enough to put reckless motorists on the list — yet.

Rachel smiled without making eye contact. As we flew down the six-lane motorway, she orientated herself by watching road signs. "Gina, back home you complain that all the drivers are too slow."

"In Tucson half the drivers are snow birds. They value life."

"Here the townspeople are mostly Buddhist. They value life too."

"Not the drivers."

I peered at the ID card taped to the glove compartment, but the name had so many syllables that I couldn't read them as we bounced along.

I wiped sweat off the back of my neck. At ten at night, the air was so hot I could drink the humidity. I could hardly wait to feel the heat of the scorching day that was sure to follow.

"Stupid contest!" I exclaimed. "I only entered because I was bored."

Rachel braced herself against the front passenger seat in anticipation of the driver's next abrupt lane change. "See how well it worked, Gina? You're not bored now!"

No, I was too busy wondering if our speed mobile had brakes. Given the driver's propensity for speed, he didn't need any. He wouldn't bother using them. Evidently he didn't believe in shocks either. The taxi rattled worse than a Fun House at a state fair. We might have enjoyed a more comfortable ride in one of the golf carts.

When we reached a relatively smooth stretch, I hazarded a look out the window. Bright lights flashed by, but I couldn't read any of the signs because vehicles zoomed past on either side. Our driver wasn't the only daredevil; given his contraption, he was merely the most challenged.

"Do you think everyone is trying to race across town at the same time?" I asked.

"This is an enormous city," Rachel said. "Eight million inhabitants. You have to expect a lot of traffic."

"Good you come for night!" shouted our driver. "Too many cars for day!"

Things could be worse during the day?

"This is a madhouse," I complained.

"Eight million," Rachel repeated. "That makes Bangkok half the size of L.A. but roughly the same size as New York City. No wonder it's crazy."

Rachel had read me the statistics a couple of weeks earlier, but the facts hadn't sunk in. I was still imagining Thailand as a gentle country dotted with batik stores run by little old ladies like Janjira, not an Asian New York on speed. I was ready to call Dylan and tell him we unaccepted the prize, but back in Tucson, the time my body was still on, it was seven a.m.

"You go Loyalty Hotel?" shouted the driver. Since he stopped watching the road so that he could turn around and address us, I noticed that he was slightly cross-eyed.

"Royalty," Rachel shouted back.

"As what I say, Loyalty!" He gripped the wheel with both hands as he slid through a yellow light.

"Did you hear that?" Rachel whispered. "He can't pronounce the R."

He'd also substituted "as" for "that's," but I assumed he was merely in a hurry.

"You will likey capital city," said the driver. "Thely thely nice."

"You see?" Rachel continued sotto voce. "Vs are hard too. It's so interesting linguistically."

I did not want a language lesson. Despite Rachel's best attempts to teach me anything, I had soundly resisted. Thai was a nightmare, a tonal language with reverse word order, particles at the ends of words, and curly-cues instead of Latin script. Who needed that much trouble? Besides, nobody learned Basic Thai for a three-week trip. Except for my sister.

Rachel leaned into the wind of the open window as if hoping to catch a better whiff of the air pollution. "Remember Sammy's aunt? Same thing. I bet Janjira can't say a V for the life of her."

Janjira hardly spoke anyway, so it wasn't a fair analogy. I didn't have time to complain because a bump threw me so high that I nearly went through the roof of the vehicle. At this rate I wouldn't be able to deliver Janjira's package because I wouldn't live long enough.

"Look, look!" Rachel pointed wildly as we passed a temple whose white needle shot into the sky. "That's one of the places we're supposed to visit!"

"I can't wait."

Rachel was too focused to catch my sarcasm. She'd spent the flight from Tokyo to Bangkok making lists of things to do, all for the next day.

"Look!" Rachel indicated another temple. "That one is even more beautiful!"

"Only one temple a day," I repeated. I'd told her the same thing twice on the plane, but she hadn't heard me either time.

I ignored the other bright lights. I was much more interested in the red neon sign boasting The Royalty Hotel. When our driver screeched to a halt, narrowly missing a shoeshine boy, the doorman didn't bat an eye.

Our drab gray room contained faded green drapes, twin beds with matching faded bedspreads, a mini-refrigerator stocked with mini-bottles of liquor, an easy chair, and a TV. I dropped my suitcase in the corner. All I cared about was the bed.

"We can flip for who has dibs on the shower," Rachel said.

"Go for it." I sprawled over the closest mattress, dragging my backpack closer to me. Out of an inner compartment, I removed Janjira's velvet pouch and fished out the elephant, but I couldn't get it to stand up straight on the uneven contours of the bedspread.

"Just think. Tomorrow you can start adding to your elephant collection," Rachel said, startling me as she passed by. She wore one towel around her waist while she used another to dry her hair.

I could have sworn that only a moment had gone by, but instead I must have dozed off. "Rachel, I have far too many elephants. I told you that already."

"You can find room for a few more. Not that we have time to waste shopping." She flipped open her notebook. "The Grand Palace and the National Museum are close together, so we can cover them tomorrow morning and visit the Royal Barges Museum in the afternoon."

"We shouldn't schedule more than one museum per day."

Rachel blinked. "I thought that's what you said about temples."

"Right. One per day. That's what Patty said. She went to Europe last summer, but all she can remember are museums and churches."

Rachel tilted her head. "Your friend Patty only cares about boys. There are lots of temples in Thailand, and most of them are famous."

I hadn't done enough background reading to argue. "Two temples then. But only one museum."

I scooted into the shower before she could think of any more arguments. I admired her spirit, but she was too optimistic to be realistic. People needed time to breathe even when they were in a hurry. As I reveled in the refreshing stream, I rehearsed my arguments: If we move too quickly, our memories will consist of blurs; if we walk too far the first day, we'll develop terrible blisters that will slow us down. Rachel wouldn't listen, but that didn't mean I wouldn't try.

By the time I emerged, holding my sweaty blouse as far from my nose as possible, Rachel was sitting in the chair studying her Thai phrase book.

"Listen to this," she told me. "'If you forget to take off your shoes at a temple, someone might shout *mai dee marayat.* That's a mouthful, isn't it? It means 'bad manners.'"

"Never mind that for the moment. What did you find out about Laundromats?"

Rachel squinted in my direction. "We just got here."

"I've worn these clothes since Tucson. That was about a hundred hours ago."

"Not even thirty. Clothes don't get dirty when you're

travelling."

"What?"

"You need to lower your standards." She held her palm to her forehead as if scanning the horizon. "No Laundromats."

"So what do we do?"

She laughed. "Rinse your stuff by hand. It's much easier."

"You're kidding, right?"

Rachel hopped to her feet. "I'm going to spend my time visiting temples, not washing machines! Ready for a walk?"

"Walk? It's midnight! We barely got here! We're jetlagged! We're—"

"If you have that many objections, you're plenty awake for a walk." She threw me my Tevas.

"Grandma wouldn't approve." Our grandmother's list of forbidden activities included walking around after dark.

Rachel dangled the room key and waited for me to slip back into my dirty jeans. "Thanks to you, Grandma thinks we're in Taiwan."

Bangkok was still bustling, but the tuk-tuks were no longer squeezing onto the sidewalks. Instead they could claim space in the regular traffic lanes. Cars passed us briskly, but the drivers were no longer frantic racetrack enthusiasts. Now they merely drove fast.

We turned left once we exited the hotel and passed a row of makeshift sidewalk eateries. Some stands had picnic tables, all of which were crowded with happy diners. At other places customers ate standing up, scooping noodles from their bowls to their mouths in smooth motions. The aromas of roasted meats and fried noodles filled the air.

Rachel caught me lingering as I watched a woman spear pieces of barbecue with a thick toothpick. "Hungry?"

"Impressed. Back home, what's open after midnight besides Denny's?"

"There's *Los Betos*. And *Mi casita* is open until four."

"You know what I mean. Let's keep this area in mind for tomorrow night."

"Right!" Rachel said. "We won't have to worry about cutting our sightseeing short in order to eat."

I was sorry to have given her such a dangerous idea for the very next day. It was bad enough that for each tired step we took forward, we'd have to retrace our steps to get back to the hotel. Or else we could risk our lives again by taking a cab.

An elderly lady passed us carrying a set of dirty tin pots. I watched as she lumbered down the street and disappeared into the night.

"Thinking about Janjira?"

"I can't help myself. Can you imagine spending twenty years in your own country and the next fifty or so somewhere else?"

"Mom has."

"That's different. Mexico is so close that she can go down there whenever she wants to. Janjira must have left her country knowing she was going so far away that she might never return. I hope we can track down her brother at least. That would make a difference to her."

We turned down a long street that ran beside the park.

"Don't get your hopes up," Rachel said. "We don't have an address."

"I know, but Janjira was so excited about giving me the package that I'd really like to deliver it."

"I understand that, but do you remember how Aunt Milena used to get mixed up?"

"Yes." During her last years, my great aunt would talk on and on, repeating the same stories but changing the locales, such that the first time she was followed by a pickpocket she was in Morocco, the next time in Oslo.

"We don't know if this guy was really an engineer," Rachel continued. "We don't know anything for sure."

"I thought you were working with me, not against me."

Rachel kicked a pebble out of her way. "I'm being realistic."

"I know. And Janjira is probably too out of it to make sense of things. But honestly, Rachel, do you know how many hours I've spent at the Tamarins?"

"Kanda set you up for babysitting before Sammy was out of the womb. They practically paid for your first year of college."

"Exactly. So if I can't do this favor for their aunt, I'll feel like I'm letting down the whole family."

"Wow." Rachel stopped walking, and I bumped into her.

"What's the matter?"

She nodded ahead at a red-tiled, golden-tipped roof that shone in the light.

"Is that The Grand Palace?"

Rachel didn't answer. She'd already accelerated. I trailed my sister as she crossed the street. I could imagine what lay beyond the high white walls: the country's most famous temple, former palaces of the Royal Family, and several museums. I'd read just enough about Bangkok to remember that much.

Rachel calculated the distance between the sets of golden tips. "When I studied the map, I thought the main temple would be on the left, but now I'm not sure."

"Speaking of which, where is our map?" We'd pulled it out of the guidebook so that we could carry it easily.

"Back in the room."

"You forgot the map?"

She tapped her cell phone, which was lodged in her pocket. "We can use the GPS if we need to. I didn't want us to look like dumb tourists."

"Sure, Rachel. We blend. Me especially."

She stifled a laugh. During the day I was pale, but at night I was a flashlight. Rachel couldn't pass for a native, but she didn't stand out.

"We can't fool anyone," she admitted, "but I didn't want to look clueless. And I did study the map on the plane."

We traipsed around to the high north wall where we glimpsed the tops of more tall roofs. Their red trim surrounded bright squares of green. Even at midnight I could feel the allure. Over the years I'd spent lots of time with my cousins in Durango, Durango, the capital of a big state in Mexico. Even though I'd attended plenty of events from weddings to baptisms to funerals, any thoughts about the meaning of religion faded into the background. I'd gone through the motions without ever thinking about what they signified.

"Are the Thais mostly Buddhist?" I asked.

"Around ninety-five percent. The other five percent are Hindi or Christian."

"So Janjira would be Buddhist too?"

Rachel stepped over a jagged piece of the concrete sidewalk. "After so many years in the States, it's hard to say. I don't remember the Tamarins ever talking about it."

"Me either. How would you define Buddhism anyway?"

Her eyes widened and she involuntarily took a step backwards. Then she turned away from the palace complex as we started retracing our steps. "You might as well ask what Catholicism is. How would you define that?"

I thought about masses we'd attended, but at the same time I had the image of Mardi Gras drunkards, *The Bible*, the Virgin of Guadalupe, and a postcard Patty had sent from the Vatican.

"Okay, okay, I didn't mean to ask a huge question, but how about the two-minute version? I'm in new territory here, so I have nothing to go on."

"Do you know who the Buddha was?"

"A god."

"Not exactly, or at least not at first. He started off as royalty. Then he realized the world had negative elements."

"Like natural disasters?"

"Like disease and old age. For him it was a big revelation because they didn't use to let him out in public. His parents had been warned he'd either become a prince or a monk."

"Some choice."

"He escaped the palace grounds and saw people who were old, people who were suffering, and, let's see, I can't remember the last one, but at any rate, he decided he needed to reach enlightenment."

"He started to meditate."

"Something like that. When he eventually achieved nirvana, which you might call an extreme form of understanding, he was under a tree. It's in India somewhere."

"Buddhism is based on the state of enlightenment."

"That's the main goal. Plus the peace you feel after you get rid of all your desire."

We waited on the curb as a sudden surge of cars sped by. If any of the drivers were Buddhists, they didn't know much about nirvana.

"So coming to Thailand is a Buddhist act?" I asked.

Rachel studied me, trying to figure out whether I was serious or not. I wasn't, but I knew how to get a rise out of her. After dragging me out so late against my will, I was entitled.

To be safe, she opted for a serious response. "Reaching enlightenment usually takes a few lifetimes plus decades of hard work."

"Can't I be optimistic?"

"Sure, Sis," she said slowly. "Why not?"

Chapter Three

Rachel's concession to jetlag was an extra hour's rest and the promise that a visit to Wat Pho, Bangkok's oldest temple, would be a gentle introduction to the country. Since I'd asked her to choose our first day's activities I couldn't complain, but she hustled me out of the hotel before the coffee took effect. As she hurried us down Maharat Street, I kicked myself again for not trying to recruit a different relative — a much older one — for my trip so that I wouldn't have to hurry around. When we neared the temple, though, the buses in the parking lot convinced me that my slave-driving sister at least knew how to wade through a guidebook and pick out important spots. I was even more impressed when we stepped up to the entrance and noticed that the majority of the visitors were Thai. We weren't at a tourist trap; we were at the heart of the city, a treasured place Janjira would have visited when she still lived in Thailand.

Not even Rachel's enthusiasm had prepared me for the magic that awaited us once we paid our *baht* and continued inside the grounds. First of all I'd expected a single temple. Instead we'd entered a huge temple complex. Each building sprouted decorations the way overdone Christmas trees sprouted lights, each section trying to be more beautiful than its neighbor. Flower buds burst from white walls as toothpaste from a tube. Color exploded in exaggerated hues. The result was a fairyland of imagination that my eyes worked overtime to absorb, a smorgasbord of designs that took the old phrase about too many cooks in the kitchen to the level of architectural madness.

I loved the whole thing. It was a cultural Disneyland that not even the Tamarins had prepared me for, and I felt frozen in time as I tried to take it in. The most outlandish feature was the pair of giants guarding the courtyard. Stretching two stories high, the figures had red legs and huge, gaping mouths that showed their jagged teeth. Crowned with bubbly golden hats, the monster men clutched huge stone swords because they were ready to fight at any moment. Their costumes had so many glittery pieces that I wanted to reach up and break one off as a one-of-a-kind souvenir. The giants were supposed to be fierce reminders of authority; instead they belonged in a graphic novel, one with lots of swords.

The highlight of the visit should have been the room where a reclining Buddha was reaching nirvana, which is where the native visitors bunched up, but I preferred the courtyard full of pointed, rocket-style structures whose mosaic tiles reflected silver bits of sun. I wasn't in another country but in a whole fantastical world. Nearby, a small artificial brook provided the music of running water while a thin brown and white cat darted around the waves chasing bugs. Thai families strolled back and forth among the buildings while anxious teachers herded small schoolchildren lest they get lost among the crowds.

Rachel knocked herself out running around and taking pictures as I stood back, drinking in the view. Despite the traffic outside the temple gates, Wat Pho was a haven recalling an earlier time. Today the visitors carried digital cameras and sported Western clothing, but the temple complex had seen little other change over the past couple of centuries. I was experiencing history. I was standing on sacred ground in Janjira's own footsteps. Which aspect of the complex would she have preferred?

I was heading for a spot in the shade when a group of young teens accosted me. They all wore white shirts that had their school insignia embroidered on the left breast pocket. The girls wore navy blue skirts and the boys navy blue pants. The children bustled with energy, their faces bright from the chance to escape the classroom for the day.

"Do you have one minute for interview?" asked a tall boy with straight hair and a big nose.

I was bewildered until I saw his clipboard. "For English class?"

He brandished his board, and so did his friends. "Please! We need talk you."

The assignment was smart but simple. The students had a list of questions they were to ask five native English speakers. I wished we'd done anything as useful in French class instead of performing mind-numbing grammar exercises week after week. In contrast I'd learned Spanish the easy way, through my mother.

I told the boy to ask away.

"What is your name?" he asked in a loud, confident voice.

Unfortunately, he hadn't heard the name Gina before. I repeated my name three times, and when he still couldn't visualize it, I took the pencil and wrote it for him while his classmates giggled.

"Where are you from?"

"Tucson."

"What?"

"Arizona."

"What?"

"Near California."

He nodded and wrote "California."

"What do you like most about Thailand?"

"I arrived last night, so I can't tell you yet."

The boy smiled politely, but he was puzzled. My response wasn't among the ones they'd studied in class.

"What do you like most about Thailand?" he repeated.

"I came last night."

One of the girls made a rapid-fire explanation, and most of the group nodded. The boy wrote down "she like the night," saying the words out loud as he wrote them.

I made no attempt to alter his perception, nor was I kind enough to tackle third-person "s."

"You come back Thailand more years?"

I let the question roll around in my head before deciding my interlocutor wanted to know if I would return to his country.

"Absolutely." Why shouldn't I make him happy?

"Why you come back more years?"

Why indeed? "I love it here. I can't imagine a better place."

After repeating myself a dozen times, the boy managed to write down both sentences. He and his classmates thanked me profusely before politely turning away to ambush their next linguistic victim. I genuflected, thankful I didn't have to learn Thai.

I slipped into the store that jutted out from the temple walls, a makeshift lean-to replete with chips, sweets, soft drinks, fruit drinks, water, plastic elephant statues, keychains, camera batteries, and extra memory cards. The store did killer business as dozens of schoolchildren spent their extra baht. It didn't do as well with the tourists. Half-melted by the humidity, they didn't have the energy to buy more than water.

I was glad I was from Arizona. I was used to heat.

After I paid for my Coke, I was about to take a comfortable seat in the shade when an older bunch of students, girls, accosted me with questions that were similar to the ones of the first group. The students whipped out notebooks, and once again I failed at explaining that I'd just arrived in their country but claimed I would certainly come back. When they said goodbyes, they handed me a postcard as a way of thanks.

A moment later, when a third group approached me, I wasn't so sure I liked the assignment after all. I became aggressive as politely as possible. "Let me interview you first," I told the leader. The boy nodded his head, his eyes bugging out. I was pretty sure he hadn't understood the word "interview."

"How old are you?"

"Fifteen."

I was surprised. He was so slender and dark I would have guessed him to be no more than twelve. "How many sisters do you have?"

His companions giggled. Then they explained the question to him. After a bit more grilling I learned that Bangkok was his hometown, his favorite subject was math, and he'd never been to Wat Pho before. I relented and agreed to an interview, but I started to invent more substantial answers. I said that I was from L.A., had been in Thailand a week, and my favorite thing about his country were the cheerful people.

The boy happily scribbled my responses before asking me to pose for a picture with him and his friends. They were thanking me and preparing to accost someone else when I finally woke up.

"Wait." I leafed through my backpack to find the photograph I had brought from Tucson. I showed the squiggles to the boy. "Do you know where this town is?"

"Says Krung Thep," the boy stated. His companions giggled again.

"How can I get there?"

The giggles doubled.

"Maybe it's a small town," I suggested.

The giggles degenerated into laughter that rippled through the crowd faster than a wave at a football stadium. The students couldn't talk because they were too busy laughing.

One of the girls spotted the instructor, a slender man with glasses, a worn suit, and a bow tie. Excitedly they grabbed his arms and dragged him towards me, all shouting simultaneously.

The man bowed. He was evidently used to processing

ten separate remarks at the same time. "I thank you for helping my students!"

"They're good students, and they've done a fine job. But I need your help too. Can you possibly tell me how to get to Krung Thep?"

The teacher covered his mouth with both hands. A dozen students grabbing his arms at once hadn't flustered him; one question by me and he was speechless.

Rachel approached, and I felt the sudden need to be rescued from the Land of Oz. "What's the matter?" she asked. "Are you confusing the natives with your American English?"

"I answered all their questions, but for some reason, they can't tell me how to reach Krung Thep."

Rachel gave me a guarded look, the same one she'd used when I'd asked about Buddhism.

"Well?" I asked. "Did I ask something impolite? If so, let me know so that I can apologize. You know how difficult it is when you're in another country. Didn't you tell me that when you spent your first summer in Greece — "

Rachel held up her hand, and I stopped spouting nonsense.

"Krung Thep is the Thai name for Bangkok."

"What?"

"You asked them how to get to Bangkok."

"You're kidding!"

The students' and teacher's heads bobbed in affirmation.

I felt completely stupid, and I worried which shade of red my face had turned. "Krung Thep is Bangkok?"

"Yes," my sister said. "That's it exactly. I thought you knew."

I bit my upper lip, aware that a whole class of children, my sister, and the English instructor were all watching me. They were probably marveling at how interesting it was to meet anyone so naïve.

"Rachel, you couldn't have told me this before now?"

She squinted in the sun. Either that or she was frowning at me and trying to figure out how she could pretend we weren't related. "It's in the first chapter of the guidebook. I read all about it on the plane. I might have mentioned it, but you were dozing."

"I was tired! We were in motion for more than twenty-four hours!"

"Anyway, I don't understand how this came up in conversation."

"Krung Thep! That's where Khun Somchai is supposed to be! Don't you remember? Sammy's great uncle? We were supposed to be looking for him in Krung Thep!"

"Oh, right. I forgot."

At my mention of their hometown, the students giggled all over again.

"Krung Thep same Bangkok," repeated the instructor, bowing politely. "Mean City of Angels."

The boy I had interviewed made a comment in Thai, and all the students laughed.

"He say he angel too," said the teacher, "only today he forgot bring his wings!"

For an English teacher the man was hardly perfect himself, yet I couldn't help feeling silly. I could have sworn my face was still red during the entire walk back towards the hotel. When Rachel and I stopped at one of the outdoor eateries, I turned my back to the street so that nobody could see me. Whenever the waitress came by, I let my sister do the talking.

"It's not a big deal," Rachel said. "We all make mistakes like that. It's normal. The first summer I worked in Greece, my friends laughed at me every night. I was their daily fix."

By now she'd spent three summer vacations on a small island in the Dodecanese, returning to the States with starry eyes and tremendous tans. Even though she performed each evening, I wasn't convinced what she did could actually be called work. She had too much fun doing it.

"You never complained about their joking."

"I got over it. My friends made fun of me, but they were nice about it. Like those kids. They were trying to be polite. All things considered, they did a good job."

Rachel picked up the menu, but I'd already given up on it. Not only were all the words in Thai, but the prices were in squiggles.

"Hey! Give me that photograph of the engineer again!" Rachel compared the back of the photograph to the menu.

"You think Khun was a chef?"

"No, no. But look at this. Those marks are numbers."

She held the photo next to the greasy menu. Several squiggles were the same. She dragged out her Thai phrase book, which included numbers up to a thousand. "Look, Sis. The numbers are seven and two, don't you think?"

I compared the symbols on the photo to the ones in the book. "Seventy-two," I said. "How old do you think Khun is in the picture?"

She shrugged. "Early twenties."

I jotted down the numbers. "Khun would be in his mid-fifties by now."

"You'd think."

Once again I studied the smiling face. "Bangkok, '72, Khun Somchai. It's not a lot to go on."

"You know a lot more now than you did this morning. At least you're making progress."

While we waited for our mystery noodles (we had no idea what we'd ordered), I thumbed through Rachel's Michelin. I hoped to vindicate my naiveté by verifying that our worthless guidebook had hidden a key piece of information, but the Thai name for the capital city appeared at the beginning of the section on Bangkok. The city's official name was so long that the explanation commanded a side bar.

I had no excuse for not knowing where we were.

Chapter Four

The pool was a smart octagon, a modern design that mitigated the waves by allowing water to spill out over the edge. For a hotel pool, it was commendable. I could complete three butterfly strokes before I had to turn around. I swam lap after lap, setting my body in motion while I tried to sort through our experiences.

By the time I pulled myself out of the water, Rachel was sitting near the edge of the pool on a lounge chair. Using a Thai Airways magazine as a clipboard, she'd already written a stack of postcards.

I was careful not to drip on her epistles. "We've only been here a day."

"With what we covered so far, I could write five postcards to each person." She offered me a card of a Wat Pho giant. "Why not write Jason?"

Jason was the last person I wanted to think about. I was pretty sure I wanted to use my trip as a way to get him out of my mind for good. What was the point of having a relationship with someone I constantly argued with? Besides, we didn't have enough in common. He loved to talk about sports and politics, and I didn't care about either one. He claimed to like hiking, but every time I suggested an outing, he found a reason to defer the activity to another time—one that was way in the future.

"We broke up again. This time for good."

"Oh." She resumed writing. She had lousy, nearly illegible handwriting, but she wrote fast.

"That's all, 'oh'?"

Rachel looked up. "You're too young for a serious relationship."

I hadn't expected such an answer. Two of my friends were already living with their boyfriends. A third was in the process of buying a condo with hers. "You think I need to finish college first?"

She put down her pen. "I think Jason is dull." She reshuffled the unwritten cards. "'Dull' is the wrong word. Maybe 'narrow minded.' He wouldn't even go to Mexico with you."

He'd claimed his parents wouldn't let him travel to such a dangerous country, but since he was originally from East L.A., I was sure he could handle Mexico. "You didn't like Jason?"

Rachel looked away, but I could tell she was rolling her eyes.

Silly me. Since Rachel wasn't dating at the moment, I assumed she was jealous of Jason because he commandeered my free time. "Why didn't you tell me what you thought?"

She shrugged. "What do I know? You seemed happy enough, so I didn't want to interfere. And I don't think he's harmful. He's merely typical. He's mostly interested in himself. He doesn't even have hobbies."

"He plays golf."

"I rest my case."

The truth was that Jason and I didn't think along the same lines. He was a business student who played golf because he thought the sport would help him hobnob with the right people. Despite outrageous hinting, so far, he'd never invited me to go along.

"Rachel, the next time I start dating someone you don't like, will you tell me what you think?"

"Probably not."

I lay back against the cushions. I'd only decided to break things off with Jason a couple of nights before, and I hadn't processed the decision. I worried no one else would want to date me ever. I knew the thought was crazy, but it kept nagging me and I hadn't managed to shoo it away.

"Want to hear what happened?"

Rachel started attacking another postcard. "Sure."

"He tried to convince me not to come to Thailand."

She slammed down her pen. She looked at me as if she couldn't understand the language I'd spoken. "When was this?"

"Wednesday."

"He wanted you to cancel two days before your trip?"

He'd made a fine show of enjoying Grandma's pozole, but when we'd gone to sit alone on the back porch, he'd casually mentioned that going to Thailand was a terrible idea. Dangerous. Political unrest. Who knew what might happen, and he wanted me to be safe, didn't he?

I stopped my faded purple swimsuit strap from falling down my shoulder. "He was baiting me. I don't think he expected me to do it."

"By then we had everything arranged: tickets, hotels, airfare!"

Down deep a tiny piece of me wanted to give him the benefit of the doubt. "He was hoping I'd feel guilty about not spending the time with him."

Rachel wiggled her pen at me. "I changed my mind. He's more of a creep than I thought. Thank goodness you're not in love with him."

"What makes you say that?"

"You're not at all upset."

I'd noticed this as well. I'd chalked up my lack of spirit to the intricacies of packing, according to my sister's specifications, with as little clothing as possible.

"At least he had good timing," Rachel said.

"What do you mean?"

She smiled without looking up. "As long as you're not thinking about Jason, you can have fun meeting some locals."

"Oh, that's a great idea."

"Of course it is. How else do you expect to learn about Thailand?"

"Today all the locals laughed at me."

Rachel lay down her pen. "Not at. With."

"I felt really stupid."

"You made a mistake. Big deal. I already told you. That's always what happens when you're speaking a new language."

"I was speaking English."

"But you were operating in a different culture. Give yourself a break. The students were surprised, but think how smart you made them feel. There they were struggling with English, but you were struggling too."

"That was hardly my goal."

"Don't take yourself so seriously."

"I should have known better."

"Gina, it's your first trip abroad! There's a lot to learn."

"You weren't the one they laughed at."

I was irrational because I'd been caught unprepared. The students had been nice enough, but I felt remiss. Worse yet, I was terrified at the thought of running into more of them.

"Think of it as a learning process," Rachel said. "Try to relax."

I regretted the weeks that Rachel had spent studying Thai while I'd been cramming for pointless exams about ecology and popular culture.

"I should have read more about our destination," I said.

"For your next trip, you will. In the meantime, think of yourself as a moviegoer."

"Meaning?"

"You know how you can read the summary of a movie and have an idea what it's about, or you can simply show up and watch it?"

"Right," I said cautiously.

"Think of yourself as being plunked down in a movie called Thailand. Sit back, relax, and enjoy what you can."

"I guess you're right."

"I'm your big sister. I'm always right."

Rather than argue, I dove back into the pool.

That evening I wandered down to the lobby. The night receptionist was young and friendly. Curly black hair bobbed up and down from the top of her head as she smiled. She was one of the few women in Thailand I'd seen without makeup, so she automatically seemed more relatable.

"May I help you?"

"I'm trying to find a guy named Khun Somchai."

She consulted her computer screen. "You don't know the room number?"

"He lives in Bangkok. Do you have a phonebook?"

She whipped out a Romanized directory and turned to the Ss. With her index finger, she scanned the entries.

"No Khun Somchai?"

"Four Khun Somchai. What last name?"

"Somchai. Khun Somchai."

She smiled at me as if I were a five-year-old. "'Khun' mean 'mister.'"

Mister!

"Can also meaning Ms. For man or woman. Is polite way."

A title! For the second time that day, I felt naïve for missing such an obvious detail. I was beginning to think I was lucky I remembered my own name At least the receptionist hadn't called over all her friends to laugh at me. She'd been so well trained to work with customers that she didn't show surprise. She offered the smile out of pity.

I wondered how long I could blame all my mental lapses on jetlag. Then the incongruity finally dawned on me. "You looked up Khun Somchai using the first name?"

"Here we put both. You can find either way if you don't know whole name. Or some people put one." She indicated the page. "I call for you?"

I explained that I was looking for a middle-aged man whose much-older sister had moved to the States long ago. The first Somchai she called turned out to be a teenager. The second had moved without leaving a forwarding number. We left a message for the third. The fourth was too young to be a candidate.

The woman could see my disappointment. "Why no you find last name, come back?"

"Sure. That's what I'll do."

"Whole name, can look for computer."

I marched upstairs. My sister was sitting on the bed, surrounded by three guidebooks that held multiple bookmarks. The Michelin was in her hands.

I planted my arms on my waist and tried to maintain a stern expression.

"Only one wat tomorrow, I promise!" she said.

"I bet you're sneaking caffeine behind my back. No wonder I can't keep up!"

Rachel put down the guidebook. "Did the barbecued chicken disagree with you?"

I took Janjira's elephant from my purse and set it on the TV. "Sammy has sent us on a wild uncle chase." I explained about the name.

"It's not a big deal," Rachel said.

"No? How can we expect to find this guy?"

"You're blowing this out of proportion."

"No, I'm not, Rachel. I'm telling you, we've got to know the whole name! Otherwise we don't have anything concrete to go on, and I might as well dump this stupid elephant in the trash before we leave town."

My sister pushed aside her books. "I didn't mean that finding the last name wasn't important. I meant that it's not a difficult piece of information. Why not text Kanda?"

"She doesn't check her messages for days at a time."

"No worries. Tomorrow we'll call them."

"We've only got a couple more days here in Krung Thep."

"Relax. We'll contact them first thing in the morning before we visit a single wat. Promise."

I crawled into bed while Rachel kept at it with the guidebooks, marking pages and making notes to herself. Suddenly I wished I hadn't made any silly promises so that my vacation in Thailand could be as uncomplicated as Rachel's was.

I slept uneasily, dreaming of phonebooks.

Chapter Five

"What would Janjira have thought of this?" I asked my sister.

"She would have assumed she'd landed in a low-budget sci-fi movie. Then she would have run the other way."

We were seated at Bangkok Noodlefest. Our bar stools next to the open window gave us a direct view of the famous Kao San Road, but the renowned mecca of the ultra-budget tourist was more L.A. than Bangkok. I'd never seen such a parade of strange people all in one place. Presumably they came for the bargain lodging, cheap eating, bars, and Wi-Fi cafés. At ten p.m. there were so many pedestrians that the street was limited to foot travel and scooters. Diners fought for empty tables while street vendors hawked everything from coconuts to sunglasses to imitation disco lights. Friends shouted to one another to achieve basic communication while neon signs blinked for attention.

"This is a little like turning on a light and finding cockroaches," I said. We'd ventured through the area twelve hours earlier, at which time it had been shut tight.

"Fascinating." Rachel was angling to take a picture of a backpacker who carried a surfboard above his head, which was the only way he could get through the crowd without whacking somebody.

"During Janjira's time I bet this was a quiet, residential street," I said.

"Probably. But Thailand has always been a favored tourist destination. Think of *The King and I*."

"What's that?"

"The famous movie with Yul Brynner."

"It was before my time."

"Mine too. I'm just saying that tourism is not new to this country although today's travelers are mostly budget rather than upper class. Think back a hundred years ago. At the time traveling around was a huge deal."

While our long trip had been uncomfortable, it had certainly been do-able. We hadn't spent days on the road to reach our destination. We hadn't gone hungry. We'd merely lost sleep and, thanks to a crazy cab driver, a piece of my sanity.

I imagined Janjira as a young girl walking down a dusty road on a quest to buy vegetables for her mom or walking to school in a uniform like the kind we'd seen so often the day before. "Do you think Janjira grew up wanting to come to America?"

"Good question. I don't suppose we'll ever find out."

"Unless the Tamarins find a diary or something."

"Wouldn't that be something! Although it would probably all be in Thai. We should ask Sammy to look for one. Or for notes. Or for anything. Any shred of information might help us out."

We'd left emails for Kanda, but so far she hadn't replied. The fourteen-hour time difference made it harder to coordinate schedules. Given all the details I wanted to share with her, I didn't want to bother with a text.

"I don't get it," I said. "Even if you fell in love with somebody, really in love, could you love that person enough to leave your country and everyone you knew?"

"People used to do it all the time. They still do." Rachel looked past Kao San Road, and I knew she'd taken a mental flight to Greece. She'd been tight-lipped about details, but during her second summer adventure, she'd fallen in love with somebody. She hadn't dated a single Tucsonan since.

"Should we take bets on how long it takes to get our

bill?" I asked.

We'd finished eating at least forty minutes earlier, but so far the waiters had whizzed by us without slowing down. Given our prime seats, I wasn't in any hurry to leave. More accurately, my sister had spent the day walking my feet off, but as long as I was sitting down, I wasn't in pain.

"I'm not sure they'd notice if we walked off without paying."

The eatery had so many customers that it was more crowded than a Mexico City subway at rush hour.

"Look," Rachel said. Out on the street, a fair-skinned female tourist walked by carrying an entire bunch of bananas. She held them as a prize. "Let's bet how long it takes her to eat all of those."

"Maybe she has lots of roommates?"

"That's Thailand for you," Rachel said. "You're supposed to be able to find anything you want here."

"Anything? "

"I suspect it helps to know what you're looking for. Hey! Watch that guy and tell me if you don't see a genuine devotion to the concept of dinner."

A moped was coming towards us, its driver weaving slowly among the pedestrians. His passenger was perched sideways on the bike slurping noodles from a plastic container.

"I wonder if he's ever lost a meal," I said.

The moped hit a glitch in the road and wavered, but the diner didn't relinquish a single noodle.

"Probably not," Rachel said. "You, on the other hand, need more work. You lost most of your beef, and you were sitting still."

Rachel exaggerated. Almost all the beef made it to my mouth eventually.

"I've never had to use chopsticks before. Give me time."

Rachel shook her napkin at me. "You better start concentrating. I wouldn't want you to starve if we decide to rent a moped."

We gave up on getting the bill and instead set out what we hoped was the right amount of money. We squeezed past busy tables and crowded onto the street, but I automatically headed away from the hotel instead of towards it.

"Let me guess," Rachel said. "You want to check out that dessert place."

When I'd complained to the hotel staff about the slow and unpredictable Wi-Fi connections, the clerks had cited a temporary glitch. The Fabulous Dessert Café, however, boasted fast, free Internet and luscious pastries to boot.

"We wouldn't have to stay long. Besides, it's just up the road."

"Lead the way."

While Rachel had spent time mapping out tourist routes, I'd learned how to reach the café. As we approached, a bus boy was wiping off an outdoor table. The second he finished, we plopped right down.

"Busy place," Rachel said.

"Everything around here is. Nothing like your island on Greece?"

"Amiros is quiet in comparison."

"I like it, though. The bustle, I mean. Something is always happening. It's as if Thailand itself is poised between the old and the modern, and people are running back and forth in between."

The juxtapositions were startling: modern skyscrapers presiding over canals full of old motorboats, fancy restaurants next to hamburger joints alongside simple noodle shops. My grandma always complained that life changed too fast, so I wondered what the older Thai residents thought of their updated capital city. Usually change was hard for people, so maybe it was just as well that Janjira would never be coming back. She wouldn't have to experience the shock of seeing her country transformed into one she could barely recognize.

A handsome dishwater blond scooted over, winked, handed us two menus, and disappeared back inside.

"Are the men in Greece as good looking as that one?" I asked.

"That American, you mean?"

"You think?"

"He was wearing tennis shoes with holes in them. His jeans dusted the floor." Rachel tapped the menu. "Chocolate Satin or Orange Mousse Cake? Or both."

"Both." I was still watching the blond. I guessed him to be a few years older than I was. His chiseled features belonged on a reality show, one set outdoors where he could take off his shirt all the time. He had pale skin and a two-day beard. His orange T-shirt had tiny holes along the seams, and his jeans had three weeks' worth of wrinkles. I was instantly attracted to him, maybe because I wanted to take him home and clean him up. Then I chided myself for having such a silly reaction.

Rachel was correct. The waiter was definitely from the States, but when he came back to take our order, I did all the talking. He nodded as if we'd made the best choices in the history of dessert ordering. Even though I knew he was playing a role, I still enjoyed it. Then I watched as he interacted with some of the other customers: the woman with a small child, two shy teenagers, an older man sitting by himself.

"Okay, then," Rachel said. "Let's get cracking."

"What?"

"You wanted to check email."

I indicated the establishment with a swirl of my fingers. "There's probably a password to get online." What was the rush? The scenery was terrific.

Rachel twisted around and excused herself long enough to interrupt a middle-aged couple who were both typing furiously on small devices. When she asked for the Wi-Fi code, the man jotted it down on a napkin for her.

I knew why she was in a hurry. She wanted to get

straight back to the room and map out our overly ambitious agenda for the next day.

I logged into my account without fooling around, but I didn't have a single message. For the third time I Googled Somchai, but the only websites that came up belonged to a Japanese exercise firm, a medical doctor drumming up business, and a professor of technology from Chiang Mai, the city in the north that was our next destination.

I sank my disappointment into Chocolate Satin.

Rachel let the Orange Mousse roll around in her mouth. "Delicious. Great choice, Gina."

I was too distracted to appreciate our treats. How could we chase after Somchai if we didn't have a decent lead? Rachel told me not to worry, but she didn't mean it. She considered our list of museums more important than the act of chasing after a long-lost man.

"Only two desserts?" the blond asked when we requested the bill. "You can't do any better than that?"

He was playing the game of flattering the customers. It worked perfectly. Given the chance, I would have sat all night trading insignificant quips with him. "Not tonight," I said. "My sister's with me."

"You'll have to come back tomorrow." His green cat eyes darted about. "Not into sweets?" he asked Rachel, who must have been scowling.

She made a clicking sound which meant "no" in Greece but seemed rude everywhere else.

"I don't blame you," he said. "I only allow myself one a week, and I can get the old ones for free!"

"Don't worry," I said. "I'll be back."

He winked. "I know you will be."

"Can we walk slowly?" I asked Rachel once we hit the street. "I never knew that my feet were big enough to get so many blisters at the same time."

"You skipped half the exhibits at the Grand Palace or they would have been worse."

"I saw the Emerald Buddha. That was the most important thing."

"You would have missed the statue altogether if I hadn't pointed it out."

"It's not my fault they keep it so high no one can get close to it." The statue was only a couple of feet high; Rachel's zoom lens got a better view than either of us did.

"The monks want to make sure everyone can see the Buddha even when the temple is as jam-packed as it was today. But never mind. Blisters shouldn't matter. You're not on the ground. You're off in space with that blond."

It wasn't my fault that he had caught my attention. "Admit it. He was cute."

"For a blond."

My sister was prejudiced. Although she had sworn off Latin men, she refused to take a second look at any man who was pale. But our waiter was fair, not pale. There was a difference whether Rachel acknowledged it or not.

"He acts like he's lived in Bangkok for a while," I said. "He can probably tell us tons about the city."

"That's handy."

"Why do you say that?"

"I was afraid you weren't going to come up with an excuse for going back."

Chapter Six

It rained so hard the following afternoon that we had to give up and go to a movie rather than follow through with Rachel's sightseeing tour. I was secretly delighted, but I didn't dare tell her so. She wandered around Siam Center, a well-known shopping mall, as a leopard in a zoo. She kept hoping the weather would shift enough that we could at least get to one more museum, but the sky peppered such thick raindrops that the taxis disappeared. A few extra fares wouldn't be worth the bother.

The weather was so bad that we circled the mall several times after the show before finally hopping on a bus. We sloshed our way to a small restaurant situated between the bus stop and the Royalty Hotel, but the hundred-foot dash left us drenched. Thankful to have arrived at all, we flopped down at a table next to the window and hung our limp jackets over the backs of our plastic chairs. We weren't the only people who were dripping; other foreigners without umbrellas were equally wet.

"What's the matter?" I asked after we ordered. "You don't seem yourself."

"I got lousy pictures of Wat Bowonivet. And we never found the Turtle Temple."

"The rain wasn't your fault."

"Still."

"Tomorrow we could stay in Bangkok instead of traveling all the way to that archaeology thing," I suggested.

We had one more day in the region before flying north to Chiang Mai, and Rachel had planned every moment of it. She had high hopes of reaching Ayutthaya, the ancient capital that was some thirty miles from town. Rachel said we shouldn't miss it, but I wasn't feeling overly enthusiastic. I assumed the site was full of famous temples, and both my feet hurt.

"Skip Ayutthaya?" Rachel stared at me as if she'd caught me shoplifting.

"Okay, okay. I was kidding. But don't feel bad that we didn't see everything on your lists. Nobody else would have seen half this much in three days. Aunt Milena would be proud of you."

"She would have carried an umbrella."

The waitress came out with our selections. I was happy to dig into a plate of noodles even though the first strands slid off my chopsticks before I could get them into my mouth.

"How's the Boar Curry?" I asked Rachel as she blew steam off the top of her bowl.

"A little tough."

We'd debated what the dish would be like. Boar curry turned out to be pork with rinds of fat served in spicy curry and topped with carrots and little branches that dangled tiny hot balls. I'd played it safe with *pad thai*.

"Hot?"

"Warm." She handed me a bit of carrot.

I held the piece in my mouth a few seconds before swallowing. "Hot."

"No wonder the waitress gave me such a funny look. She didn't expect I could eat it."

"Little did Mom suspect her *chiltipines* were training us for Thailand!"

"You can be sure we're more prepared for the food than for the language," Rachel said as she tried another bite. She was frustrated that the clerk at the Siam Center had acted deaf when Rachel asked for the *brá-sah-nee*, which, according to our phrase book, was a post office.

"Language learning takes a long time. You know that."

"I said that word correctly."

"He probably doesn't know what a post office is. He's from the Internet generation."

"You're being way too nice. Luckily for him, I forgot how to say 'bad manners.'"

"Relax. Here the Internet is more common than the phone. Thailand's computerized equipment is relatively up-to-date. Except, as luck would have it, at our hotel."

Rachel put down her chopsticks. "Is that a hint that you want to check your email again?"

"One more time."

"Sammy already said they can't find Janjira's maiden name."

"He also said they would continue looking. You don't want another fabulous dessert?"

"At this rate we would have to swim there." She pointed to the ceiling. Rain was hitting the roof in such sheets that the noise drowned out the conversations of other diners.

I pushed aside the curtain that covered the upper portion of the window. A tiny corner of the sky was gray, but the rest of it was black. "It's letting up a bit."

"How about if you go by yourself?"

"Don't you want to know if Sammy wrote us?"

"Gina, I'm soaked down to my underwear, and I'm going to get soaked again getting from the restaurant to the hotel. You go. Buy a rowboat if you find one. And bring back all the good news. But don't forget about tomorrow morning."

"Are you sure we need to wake up at six?"

"Six-thirty, then. But not one moment later. We've got a big day."

I nodded, but if I accidentally-on-purpose turned off her alarm, what would she be able to do about it? The night was too young for me to worry about tomorrow. As soon as we paid the bill, I sped-walked all the way to the Fabulous Dessert Café.

"No word from the boyfriend?" The blond waiter startled me because I hadn't heard him come up behind me. As if time stood still, he was wearing exactly the same clothes as the day before. The atmosphere inside the establishment, however, was completely different. For the moment I was one of a grand total of five customers.

"Believe me. I wasn't expecting a romantic email."

The waiter smiled before he turned away.

Sammy still hadn't written. I wanted to give him a few more minutes, so I wasted time on Intellicast. Bangkok was supposed to be hot for the next few days, 28-32 Celsius. I was glad I didn't know Celsius well enough to know how hot that was. I didn't look up the conversion to Fahrenheit on purpose. Then, in self-defense, I looked up Ayutthaya. The famous historical park was indeed full of temples, and I could already imagine that Rachel wanted to visit each one. That was the real reason she'd skipped dessert. She wanted to map out the most expedient touring sequence.

The waiter stepped closer. "So tell me what news you were expecting. I'm Thierry, by the way." He sounded genuinely interested, but given the lack of business, he was probably also bored.

"I'm trying to track down a friend's great uncle, but I don't have his full name or a current address." Come to think of it, I didn't have an old address either.

"That's a tough one."

"It's not important."

"I know. Why else would you be trying so hard?" He smiled brightly enough that I didn't feel silly.

"The man is from Bangkok. Since we're right here, it would be a shame not to go say hello."

"How long are you staying in town?"

"We only have two more nights, so it's now or never."

Thierry leaned his elbows on the table. His face was so close to mine I worried that I smelled like pad thai. "How were you going to find this person?"

"I'm waiting to find out his complete name. He might be in the phonebook."

"I hate to break this to you, but the Bangkok phonebook isn't very accurate. Or rather, it's not very complete. At least that's what they say." He indicated the menu. "Did you decide on a dessert?"

Since neither of us had anything better to do, I made him explain about every single option. I wasn't sure whether he was making stuff up or whether he had first-hand knowledge, but it didn't matter. Since leaving Tucson, I hadn't managed an intelligible conversation with anyone besides Rachel. It was a relief to speak English without modifying my vocabulary, and since I'd been dating Jason for nearly a year, I was way behind on flirting.

Thierry's recommendation about the Coconut Cake was an excellent one; each creamy mouthful was more delicious than the last. But maybe the dessert was enhanced by my self-appointed companion. Since he had no one else to talk to, and evidently nothing else to do, Thierry stood at my table the whole time I was eating.

I started wondering about his homelife. Were his parents working in Thailand? And how many Thai girlfriends did he have? Even though the city was full of foreigners, we were both fairly exotic compared to the darker, shorter Thais.

"I'm off soon," Thierry said before I asked for the bill. "Grab a beer with me?"

I was taken off guard. I thought he'd been talking to me to kill time. Before I could answer, my good and bad angels kicked in at the same time. "Go out and have fun!" cried the bad angel. "Six-thirty wake-up call!" cried the good angel.

I gritted my teeth. I was purportedly on vacation, but a

full day of archaeology wouldn't be any fun if I couldn't survive it.

"Tonight I need my beauty rest."

"You look great already!"

"Tomorrow I have travel bootcamp with my sister. I'll need all my strength. Otherwise I'll fall asleep under some monument, and she'll leave me in Ayutthaya."

"Can't have that. You'd wake up with a sore neck and ants crawling up and down your legs. Dinner tomorrow night, then? It's my day off."

Evidently Thierry didn't have a ton of Thai girlfriends after all. Maybe he was merely happy to converse with a fellow American his own age. I considered his offer for half a second before deciding that any hard day of tourism with Rachel warranted a reward.

"I'd be happy to." I would feel bad about abandoning Rachel, but I would recover.

"Bring your sister along," Thierry said.

What? A waiter who could read my mind? "Are you sure?"

"It's no fun to eat alone. Believe me. I know all about it."

Chapter Seven

The famous site of Ayutthaya did not open its arms to receive us. We didn't realize that the archaeological park was at the other end of a modern city. The train station was such a long way from the temple area that we were at the mercy of greedy tuk-tuk drivers to get there. The first one we dismissed when he claimed the museum was closed. The second driver claimed the museum was closed but the park was open. He agreed to take us as long as we paid his exorbitant price. I was afraid Rachel was going to insist that we walk, but a miracle happened; her feet were sore too.

All I really knew about Ayutthaya was that my sister was determined to get us there. Neither of us realized that the site was an entire ancient city rather than a few isolated ruins or that it would be so beautiful. As we approached from the southwest, our first view was fantastic. Small narrow monuments called *chedis* loomed above the tops of tall trees, bricks shone in the sun, and blades of glass swayed below the sky. A few tourists marched down the main road, which was paved, while others whizzed by on bicycles.

I grabbed Rachel's arm and pointed down the street, where Japanese tourists in sets of threes were riding as many elephants.

"That looks fun!"

Rachel frowned. "It's probably expensive. And too touristy."

But it looked grand. What better way to view an ancient city than atop the animal that used to be ridden by royalty? Besides, it was romantic.

I wondered if Thierry had ever ridden an elephant. I also wondered whether or not he was still in bed. I imagined that he was.

When we arrived at the museum, I was thrilled to find that the driver was right; the museum was safely closed. We descended from the tuk-tuk anyway. Rachel felt a strange urge to save face, perhaps because she'd been so rude. Together we walked up to the door and studied the sign.

"Closed Tuesdays," my sister announced. "Thank goodness. We have too much to do as it is."

As usual, Rachel had made an understatement. For the next several hours, I let her lead me around famous ruined temples of the Siamese kingdom's second capital city, but she too was overwhelmed. Though she took a lot of pictures, she insisted on spending a few minutes sitting on the grounds of each site so that she could etch the structures in her mind. Since they all looked about the same, I wasn't willing to work that hard. Instead I watched the other visitors. They were a fascinating array of ages and cultures. While most of us were foreigners, several Thai families had come with children who ran about as if the whole park were their playground.

"I'm sorry I came down so hard on Jason the other day," Rachel said. We were sitting on a grassy patch contemplating a *prang,* meaning a temple tower.

"Why? You're right. He is dull."

"It's none of my business."

"I'm your business! If I remember right, I asked for your opinion. And I already knew Jason wasn't right for me. Call it denial."

She brushed an ant off her toes. "Like I said, I don't think you were in love with him. He still might be fine for a friend, but a boyfriend should be more special than that."

"Being in love sounds so serious. I'm not sure I know what it means."

"If you have to ask, you're not." She pulled a piece of

grass from the ground and toyed with it. "You'll meet someone more suitable."

I shrugged. It was hard to analyze my situation with Jason when all I could think of was hurrying back to Bangkok to see Thierry.

We watched as an extended Thai family strode by: parents, elderly relatives, and a host of kids. They weren't walking quickly, but they weren't exhausted — yet.

"Do you think it's easier to fall in love in a foreign country?" I asked. The question was rhetorical. Whatever happened to my sister in the Aegean never happened in Tucson, but I wanted to see how she responded.

Rachel took a picture of the family unit when she could frame the shot with the prang. "When you're traveling, you're learning new things every minute. You're more open to emotion."

I couldn't help playing devil's advocate, but maybe it was revenge for all the walking. "I have the feeling that it's easy to fall in love on Amiros."

Rachel adjusted her zoom lens and took another shot. "Moonlit nights on the beach help out. And all the romantic songs. The hard part is being in love with someone who's in love with you at the same time. That's what's nearly impossible."

"Didn't you start seeing somebody new last summer?"

After her last trip Rachel had spent two weeks cleaning her apartment from top to bottom and clearing her schedule of everything except for violin students. I was pretty sure she was expecting a visitor, but nobody ever showed up.

"He hasn't texted in months, let alone called. I guess I didn't make that much of an impression."

"Most guys don't pick up the phone. They're too busy doing manly things."

"Such as working at dessert shops?"

I must have reddened because she started laughing. I would have sworn she hadn't been paying that much attention.

"Have we seen enough yet?" I asked Rachel. We had paused in the shade outside the umpteenth temple. My sister was breathing hard, but I was panting. "It must be ninety-three out, never mind the humidity."

She pointed into the distance. "Wat Mahathat is close, so we might as well see it."

"You know that we're well over the daily temple limit."

"These are ruins, not temples." She indicated the landscape. "This is archaeology, not religion."

"It's the same in principle." I faked a stern look, but I relented because visiting another temple was much easier than suggesting to Rachel that we not do something she thought we should. I also wanted her to be satisfied that we'd seen a lot so that we could take an early train to Bangkok. I'd told Thierry I'd meet him outside the café at eight o'clock, and I wasn't sure he'd wait.

"Why is this one famous?" I asked as we trooped towards yet another set of stones.

"There's something about a tree growing around the Buddha's head."

"Sounds great."

She was too hot to notice that I didn't mean it, but Wat Mahathat was as impressive as the other temples. Its symmetrically planned courtyards were filled with not-so-broken Buddhas amidst a peaceful, grassy plain. We saw few tourists; most had been driven off by the extreme temperatures. The afternoon wasn't any worse than a triple-digit day in Tucson, but back home we never exerted ourselves while the sun was out unless we were in a pool.

Rachel grinned as she pointed at the guard. He was dozing in a lawn chair, chin propped on his hand. He wore a brown uniform of long pants and a short-sleeved shirt that was several sizes too large. Maybe the clothes belonged to another relative.

"I don't blame him," I said. "I'm ready for a snooze myself. What are we looking for again?"

"A Buddha head. It must be around here."

The guard's chair faced a huge tree. A short white fence had been built around it. Through the tree's tangled roots peeked the divine head that we'd been searching for. The roots had grown wild around the five-foot sculpture, strangling it.

The sign beside the tree was written in English and Japanese. The English version read, "Please do not stand over the Buddha's head."

"What do you think it means?" I asked.

Rachel read it over several times. "Beats me."

The head jutted out a few inches from the tree trunk it hugged, leaving a shallow, slippery ledge. "Do you think people try to stand on top of this thing?"

"Maybe that's why they have the fence. Daredevil tourists do all kinds of crazy things. Stand there, and I'll take your picture."

I had barely reached the Buddha head's side when we heard three loud claps. The guard hadn't been napping after all. He had jumped from his chair and was sprouting Thai as he hurried towards us.

"What did we do wrong?" I asked my sister.

Rachel backed away from the tree, and I did the same.

The guard turned around and returned to his napping position on the chair.

"Maybe you aren't supposed to photograph the Buddha," I said.

"At the last temple, that's what all the tourists were doing."

"Maybe this one is special." The sculpture didn't seem different from the other ones. Maybe it was special because it was just a head? Because the tree had engulfed it? Because the Buddha had become a forest prisoner?

A pentad of middle-aged female Japanese tourists

passed us, laughing and pointing at the strangled Buddha. They marched straight to the sculpture. Four crouched in front of the image as the last one focused her camera. I wanted to warn them, but I had no idea how. I appealed to Rachel but she held up her hands; she didn't know how to warn them either.

Meanwhile the guard had opened his eyes enough to see what was happening, but he looked on without concern. The woman snapped the shot, and the guard didn't say a thing.

What? We weren't allowed to take pictures because we weren't Buddhist? Because we were younger than the Japanese women? Because the guard didn't like us? What was the matter with this country? I was ready to pout in the man's face, but meanwhile Rachel had raced over to offer her services so that the women could all be in the shot at the same time.

After she took the first picture, the other women all proffered their own cameras. I looked over at the guard, but again, he did nothing. He might have been snoozing already.

In a series of bows and thank-yous, the women reclaimed their cameras and moved on.

I joined Rachel, who was still standing in front of the head.

"Now I get it," she said. "You can't stand so that your head is higher than the Buddha's. Otherwise it's disrespectful."

Suddenly I felt like a small girl reprimanded for getting Grandma's carpet dirty. I never meant to irritate my grandma, and I certainly hadn't meant to disrespect another culture. None of the information from the guidebooks had warned us, however, nor was there a warning on the UNESCO website.

My sister was now taking a picture of the warning sign.

"We were supposed to understand what to do from

'Don't stand over the Buddha's head'?" I asked. "They must be dying for English teachers in this country. No wonder all those schoolchildren kept hounding us."

"English is hard for Thai speakers. We have to remember that."

"I wouldn't dream of forgetting. But maybe the Japanese translation is better. The Japanese tourists knew exactly what to do."

We turned left, heading for the exit. "I think it's cultural," Rachel said. "The Japanese are mostly Buddhists."

Chapter Eight

"I wish you'd go alone," Rachel said as we started for Kao San Road.

For the first time I could remember, I was dragging my sister instead of being dragged by her, and I was enjoying it. According to logistics, we should have been dead on our feet, but Rachel had taught me not to give into anything as mundane as fatigue.

"Thierry insisted we should all go to dinner together," I said. "I think he's lonely for English speakers. He says most of the other Americans who live in Bangkok are computer geeks."

"Promise you won't become one?"

"Rachel!"

"Mom says you live on the Internet."

"That's because my generation doesn't know what a library is."

"I'm not sure that's a good enough excuse."

Not only was Thierry waiting for us outside Fabulous Desserts Café, but he was five minutes early. He'd just showered, and his moist hair gleamed in the streetlight. His black T-shirt was washed, but it had been rung dry so many times that it creased at regular intervals. He greeted us with bouncy hugs that were the product of too much caffeine and thanked us for joining him. We mentioned a restaurant that we wanted to try, but he insisted he'd been in Bangkok long enough to know all the best ones and herded us in a new direction.

Chop Stick was an eatery past the pubs on Kao San Road. On first glance it seemed less than promising. The seats were too low to comfortably accommodate customers who were taller than four feet. The lime-green walls begged for another coat of paint; their only decorations were soccer calendars from random years. The establishment was full of diners, though, and rich aromas tickled my nose. The waiters moved quickly among the tables, shouting orders back to the cook.

Thierry wouldn't let us order. He was so fair that I couldn't imagine him speaking anything besides English or maybe German. When the waiter paused at our table, however, our guide impressed us by spitting out Thai so fast that he sounded native.

Thierry launched into his entire ex-pat story, culminating with how he'd come to Thailand from Minnesota two years ago and found no reason to leave. He made enough money that he didn't have to ask his parents for any, so what else could he need?

"Don't they want you to come home?" I asked.

"They keep asking me about it, but I'm not in a hurry. And I have a younger brother. They can concentrate on him."

"What about college?" Rachel asked.

Thierry hunched his shoulders. "I started it, but they had all these policies about going to class. I couldn't keep up. Too many parties. I'd flunked out by mid-October. The dean told me it was a record."

He twirled a strand of my hair with one hand. "What good is a piece of paper anyway?"

I'd read about people who quit school to run off to exotic places, but Thierry was the first one I'd met. I wasn't sure he made any decisions consciously. Given his disregard for a concrete plan, Thierry was simply in flight. When he ran into clouds, he altered the flight plan without losing altitude.

Thierry halted his narrative for a few minutes to taste the chicken fried rice and lemon grass noodles, but as soon as he'd consumed a few bites, he was back to his story. He'd met all kinds of people thanks to Fabulous Desserts. and a few of them were important. He was waiting for a break, someone to offer him a more important job that would make use of his people skills and pay better. Apart from a sense of freedom, he possessed an inherent optimism that he'd turned into a personal religion. I was ready to sign up.

The longer we talked, the more Thierry surprised me. He claimed to be an expert on Bangkok, but his knowledge was spotty. He knew the eateries within a two-mile radius, but when Rachel asked him about the Turtle Temple, Thierry explained that he didn't do temples. His lifestyle and his selective world was more foreign to me than Thailand, but long before we asked for the check, his spirit had rubbed off on me. I wanted to feel as free as he did to respond to life in my own way and on my own terms. I wanted to surprise myself.

By the time we left Chop Stick, the evening pedestrian crowd was in full swing. The coconut vendors had increased by five hundred percent and the tourists by five thousand. People jostled into one another because there wasn't any other way to make it down the street.

"How about a nightcap?" Thierry asked. "I've got a few beers back at my apartment."

"It's getting too late for me," Rachel said, "but you kids run along."

Rachel was lying. It wasn't near midnight, so I knew she was wide-awake.

"Come over for a while," Thierry told me. "I live around the corner."

"We're flying to Chiang Mai tomorrow morning," I said, "so we have to get up early."

"Who needs sleep? I can show you my CD collection."

I tried to get a reaction from my sister, but she was

studying the foot traffic.

"Maybe I could come over for a little while."

Rachel dug into her bag and rummaged around as if she'd lost an earring. "You better keep a brochure for the hotel in case you get lost."

"Rachel, I won't get lost!"

As she thrust the brochure in my hands, I could feel a package of condoms between its pages. "Just in case," she winked.

I regretted my decision to go to Thierry's as soon as we reached his building. He lived on the third floor of a construction so rickety I felt unsafe using the stairs. When we got to his door, I saw why the stairs didn't bother him. I'd entered a disaster area full of stuff: newspapers, empty cartons, broken chairs, and a bookcase that leaned half a foot to the right. Amongst the junk, he'd created a narrow path from the doorway to the kitchen, from the kitchen to the bathroom, and from the bathroom to the bedroom. As long as we didn't need anything in between, we were safe.

Thierry threw his keys on top of an empty sack of chips, and both sack and keys bounced to the floor. He didn't pick them up. "Don't mind my housekeeping. I don't have the time!"

But he had plenty of time to talk, which he proceeded to do non-stop. As we sat on the bed, the only spot in his apartment besides a section of the floor near the doorway that could accommodate two people at once, I got an earful about why his high school teachers never gave him a fair chance and why he never made the hockey team. Then he told me about the ten different jobs he'd held in Bangkok and why none of them had ever worked out for more than a few months at a stretch.

By the time he tried to kiss me, it was four in the morning, and we were both too sleepy to concentrate. He offered to walk me home, but when I assured him I could make it by myself, he said "goodnight" and reminded me to click the door on my way out. He was snoring before I left the room. I walked to the hotel quickly, wondering what it would be like to be so far from home and so alone.

Rachel flicked on the reading lamp when I sneaked in. "Have a good time?" Her eyes were only a quarter open.

"At least I didn't spend the evening thinking about Jason."

"*Algo es algo.*" Literally the words meant "something is something," but the feeling they gave was "at least you didn't go backwards."

I took off my clothes and folded them on top of the nearest chair. "You didn't care for Thierry, did you?"

"He was all right."

I slipped into my night shirt wondering whether I should have bothered changing or not. It was going to be a short night. "You didn't like his attitude."

"Oh, I don't know. Why should you go to college when you can spend a few years in Asia finding yourself instead? It's quite the career plan."

"Thierry's a free spirit. You're not used to them."

Rachel propped herself up against the headboard. "Half the mariachi players are free spirits too. They steal tips because they're so poor that they feel justified. They steal food whenever the customers aren't looking. They go for months without paying rent and then move when the landlord cracks down on them. You don't have to tell me about free spirits! Thierry is similar. He has no clue as to the real world around him."

"He knows a lot about Thailand."

"He does not. He's been living here for two years, yet he told us Ayutthaya was built before Sukhothai. He was off by a hundred years!" She pointed to her backpack, where her guidebooks were lying in wait. "The island of Ko Chang is not near the island of Ko Samui, as he insisted. Look it up for yourself. They're on opposite coasts!"

I crawled into my bed, which felt surprisingly comfortable given that the mattress was thin and hard. "Thierry hates details. And he's not much of a listener. Do you think I wasted my evening?"

"I didn't say he was boring. As long as you didn't believe anything he said about Thailand, you're all right."

"Thierry hasn't found himself yet."

"He's running out of places to look. He's so set on being rebellious that he couldn't go home if he wanted to."

I poked the stiff pillow, trying to create a reasonable place for my head. "What did you do all night?"

"You don't want to know."

"You made a list of tourist sites, didn't you?"

"Why arrive in Chiang Mai without a plan?"

I pulled the sheet around my ears. "I still didn't get an email from Sammy. Four days in Bangkok, and I didn't come close to delivering Janjira's package."

"You gave it your best shot."

"I wasted the first morning learning that I was in Krung Thep."

"Think of it this way. You'll never forget the Thai name for the capital."

"Sammy will think that's poor compensation."

"If we can't find Janjira's brother, the Tamarins will understand."

I sat up and swung my legs off the bed. "I know. And Sammy will too. That's not the point. Over the years the Tamarins have done so many nice things for us that I wanted to pay them back with something they couldn't do for themselves. Finding one old lady's brother shouldn't be so hard."

"Gina, millions of people live in this city."

I went into the bathroom and came back with a glass of water. "It's like solving a math problem. Logically I should have all the information I need."

"I understand how you feel, but you're not taking cultural or generational differences into account. Even if she were in her right mind, if Janjira were to fly to Thailand today, she wouldn't be able to find her brother herself."

I sighed. "You think I'm being too stubborn."

"I think you're being hard on yourself. You don't have to give up because we're leaving Bangkok. If you find an address, you can send the elephant from Chiang Mai or Phuket. Given the circumstances, that would be good enough."

"I guess."

Rachel yawned and turned off the light. "I'll help you do some more research after we get to Chiang Mai."

"Sure," I said. "Would that be before or after we visit all those temples?"

Chapter Nine

The fact that we arrived at the hotel too early for check-in was Rachel's excuse to march me to several famous temples along the route to Wat Chedi Luang. The temples were all beautiful in their own way, with tremendous elephant statues or Buddha figures or altars full of lotus blossoms, but the artistic details were lost on me because by the second temple the features started melting together. By the third temple I stuck my nose inside to be polite, lost Rachel as quickly as possible, and spent the rest of the time wandering through the temple grounds. As in Bangkok, there were clear indications that the temples had a place in the community, but surprisingly few people were praying. Instead they had come to chat with their friends, supervise young children, buy cheap snacks, or sit and ponder life. The orange-clad monks filtered among them, sometimes greeting them, often bowing, while the apprentice monks, boys from eight to fourteen, scurried from building to building with mops and rags full of dust.

When I finally lost count of the number of temples Rachel had dragged me to, I begged off and meandered back towards our hotel, which was just outside the gates surrounding the old city. The day was so hot that residents left their doors open in a vain hope for circulation, so I peeked inside whenever it wasn't too obvious. In one house a sweating woman ironed as she watched soap operas. In another a man in an undershirt snored on a cot.

I could have napped myself. It was at least ninety degrees and so humid I had sweat through my clothes. I told myself it was all in a day's work, never mind that I was on vacation.

At least Chiang Mai was a sweet contrast to Bangkok. Traffic in the huge capital was overwhelming, but here cars and even bike riders slowed for pedestrians. Chiang Mai's whole pace was relaxed. The city bustled with shoppers and businesspeople, but it hadn't sped up to the clock of the capital or to the modern world. It felt more like Mexico, so I instantly felt at home.

The Internet wouldn't work in my room, but it worked perfectly in the lobby. After an hour's session, I caught up with Rachel at the bar. The area smelled like bamboo, which was the material the builders had used for the walls. Half the customers crowded around the counter while others sat at small square tables. Many were underage Americans drinking as fast as they could raise their elbows.

Rachel sat with a Coke, *The Lonely Planet*, and a frown.

I squeezed onto a barstool next to her. "What's wrong?"

"Nothing."

"Nothing what?"

The young waitress hurried over, but I disappointed her by ordering a Coke rather than a high-priced cocktail.

"Those elephant statues we took so many pictures of?" Rachel asked.

"They were cute. That's my favorite temple so far."

"Well, I have bad news."

The fourteen-year-old returned with a disappointingly lukewarm soda served without ice in a smudged glass. "You likey Chan Beer?" she asked Rachel.

Rachel shook her head, and the girl slunk off.

"She's asked me three times already," Rachel said. "Do I look like a beer drinker?"

"There's always hope," I said. "Anyway, what's the

matter with the elephants?"

"They're fake! Remember the one that was all broken? That's the only original."

"So?"

"We thought they were real."

"We thought they were cute. What's the difference?"

"Oh. I don't know."

I wasn't sure something had to be old or genuine for us to enjoy it. The temple had stood out to me precisely because of the elephants. It was fanciful rather than stern, so it created a positive vibe. I didn't know enough to appreciate the temple's actual age. I'd made several attempts to piece together Thailand's chronology, but the Kingdom of Siam had a long history, and every time I read a little more I seemed to forget half of what I'd read the time before.

"When was the temple built?" I asked.

"In 1441."

"That was nearly six hundred years ago. Why would you expect it to be intact?"

She rotated her glass, which was actually more smudged than mine.

"You're right. I've been spoiled by Greek monuments that are over two thousand years old. Of course, they're mostly broken too. I guess I'm disappointed because I was hoping for authenticity."

"The monks were authentic. And the lotus blossoms."

"I guess."

"Personally, I have lower standards. I'd rather watch the men." I nodded towards a table in front of us. "Check out the guy sitting by himself." He was a tall, fair man with a deep tan and a Thai silk shirt that looked like a bargain item from a night market.

Rachel waited a couple of seconds before turning. "Not bad. Introduce yourself."

"Don't you think he's cute?"

"I'll give you five minutes to flirt with him while I find

the bathroom."

Rachel left, but from a few feet away, I couldn't get the man's attention. He was concentrating on the soccer game playing on the huge TV above the bar. Argentina and Australia were in try-outs for the next World Cup. The man followed every kick. He was rooting for Australia. Evidently the game was the most authentic thing in the room.

While I waited, I fished Janjira's purple elephant out of my purse and set it before me. While I'd seen little elephants in quite a few tourist shops, I hadn't seen anything like this one. Did its age make it authentic? I wanted to think so.

"No luck with Cutie?" Rachel asked.

"I can't compete with a white and black ball."

"Why should you, really?" She tapped the elephant's head. "Any good leads on Sammy's uncle?"

"The Tamarins think the last name is Swoonswangs. They found it written on one of Janjira's letters."

"Terrific! Now all you have to do is check the phone book for Bangkok. Certainly all that information is online."

"I couldn't find a single entry for Somchai Swoonswangs."

"For Bangkok or Chiang Mai?"

"Either place. I asked the receptionist to help me, but she couldn't find anything either."

"Somchai Swoon-what?"

"Swoonswangs. It took me five minutes to learn to spell it. How would you like that for a signature?"

"Personally, I'd write an S and a squiggly line. What else did you find out?"

"By now there are lots of places to study engineering in this country, but most of them have been developed within the last thirty years."

"Before Somchai's time."

"Exactly. Three of the older schools had alumni lists, but no Somchai Swoonswangs. I typed so much my thumb is sore."

"At least you learned something."

"I learned I never want a job as a researcher. It's too disappointing."

"Your efforts are for a good cause."

"The soccer fan would be a better one! Oh, wait. Maybe not." A buxom brunette in a white dress that almost covered her rear slipped into the seat beside him. He acknowledged her without losing a play.

Rachel shook my arm. "Don't feel bad. She won't have any luck getting his attention either."

"She's got more of a chance." I stuffed the elephant back in my purse.

"Tell me about the engineering schools," Rachel said.

"The most famous one is here, Chiang Mai Engineering and Technology. Think there's any chance Somchai attended it?"

"He well might have. Chiang Mai is the second largest city in the country, so it would have been a logical choice."

"I thought so."

"No alumni list?"

"Nothing I could access online."

"Maybe you could drop by tomorrow afternoon."

"Good idea. I'll check out the address later on. What's our plan for tomorrow?"

"Remember? We talked about Doi Suthep."

Doi Suthep was one of the famous spots the Tamarins had told us about. To be on the safe side, I'd done some tourist research myself. The more decisions I left to Rachel, the less chance my feet would have of recovering from my Bangkok blisters.

"You're talking about the temple on top of the hill with the million steps leading up to it," I said. While the pictures I'd seen online showed a pretty complex, they also showed the steps and steps and steps that led up to the site.

"I think there are only a few hundred."

"I suppose it's famous because it's so hard to get to?"

"No. Because the white elephant stopped there."

"Maybe he was tired."

"He died on the spot. Anyway, we'll get a great view of Chiang Mai."

"Sounds cool." But I suspected that despite the scenery and the history it was just another wat, so I was careful not to sound too enthusiastic.

Chapter Ten

By the time we left Old Town, our red pickup truck heading for Wat Prathat Doi Suthep had collected so many passengers that we were smashed together as tightly as racks of keychains in the night market. The truck had been outfitted as a van. It had a roof and two rows of benches. Most of the passengers were Thai, and they didn't seem to mind squeezing right next to one another. We'd traveled for several uncomfortable blocks when we started our ascent to the mountain. Hence we were thrown against one another even more vigorously. I was about to complain when out the window I caught sight of a white sign with gold borders that read Chiang Mai Engineering and Technology in both English and Thai.

I'd had every intention of looking up the address the night before and mapping out the easiest route to get there, but I'd been so exhausted from my short night in Bangkok that I'd fallen asleep with the light on while Rachel was on the Internet down in the lobby. When she'd come upstairs, she'd rescued my cell phone from my clutches and tucked me in.

Some ten hours later, she'd woken me up, and I'd been on my way to Doi Suthep before the coffee kicked in.

"Rachel!" She swiveled and saw what I did: countless students milling through an ornate old gate into the garden beyond.

"Do you mind if—"

"Go!" She pushed on the button to request a stop.

A little too immediately, the pickup came to an abrupt halt, forcing the occupants to make even more intimate acquaintance with one another.

"I'll catch up with you in a half hour," I said as I slithered out.

"Or meet me back at the hotel," she shouted as the truck pulled away.

Liberty. It was a lovely sunny day, and my reprieve from tourism had been sanctioned. At the very least I could enjoy watching young Thai men for an hour instead of traipsing around after my sister. The campus exploded with happy energy. Shy couples spoke in whispers while groups of friends laughed and giggled as they watched members of the opposite sex. Although all the students carried books, I didn't see anybody reading one.

I also learned that English was not the focus of CMET students. The first one I stopped shrugged apologetically when I asked for directions. The next two understood that I was looking for something but couldn't understand what that was. I only managed to reach the administration office through a variety of approximations, wandering through two buildings before I found someone who could direct me.

The sign advertising the office was written in English, but none of the secretaries knew any. They looked up politely, listened while I spoke, and went back to their work.

I stood still, wondering how long I would have to take up space in their office before they tried to assist me. Finally a middle-aged Western woman came along. She wore a crisp green skirt and a jacket made of matching Thai silk. She had reddish blonde hair that curled into a wave, complementing high red eyebrows that she had created with pencil. The right eyebrow had gotten away from her and trailed off into her forehead.

"English speaker?" she asked. English wasn't her first language, but I could easily understand each word.

I nodded as a dog begging for treats.

"Come along," she chirped.

The woman led me down a short corridor. Despite two-inch spikes, her normal walking pace was faster than mine. When we reached a small office, she marched inside, carefully made her way past accumulations of books and folders, and sat behind a desk so massive it reduced her to a miniature. She invited me to sit across from her.

"You want to enroll in our university. We are happy for that, but unfortunately, our classes are full for the next term, so —"

"No, I —"

"You do not enjoy our classes and now you wish your money back?" She wrinkled her nose.

"No, you see, let me explain. It all started with dinner at the Tamarins' house . . ."

Once I managed to explain my story, Madame Lorraine was delighted to help me. She led me to the adjoining office where a clerk was working on an old desktop computer, but the school's list of graduates only went back to the 60s. In clear, measured Thai, Lorraine asked the clerk to research earlier decades. The young Thai woman immediately rose to do so, but she stood before the row of filing cabinets, unsure where to begin.

"We had better go down to the coffee bar," said Lorraine. "No one works well under pressure around here besides me."

Lorraine thrived on good stories. I got most of hers: She and her husband had come from France years ago when he was hired for a hydraulic engineering project. He'd been contracted for six months, but nobody had counted on so many complications. The first two months were wasted because the government building permits hadn't arrived yet. After the project began, workers kept quitting because the days were too long. The company was anxious to make up for lost time but didn't want to compensate for it. Then, after the heavy pieces had been installed, the workers realized that half the parts didn't fit.

The original project took a year and a half to complete, and by then two more projects were pending.

At the time Lorraine was five months pregnant and so ill that she didn't want to travel. In the next months her husband received offers for more work. After their son's birth, Lorraine was so exhausted she had to have help. They hired two maids, one to clean and another to babysit. How could she and her husband possibly afford such things in France? The couple decided to stay until the boy was ready to go to elementary school, but by then a brother had come along. Lorraine and her husband decided to wait until both boys finished school before returning home, but the eldest married a native girl when he was twenty, before the other son graduated, and by now there were three grandchildren. Lorraine and her husband were so used to Thailand that they couldn't seriously consider moving back to France. All of this came out before she finished stirring her coffee. She was more than happy to share her story with someone who hadn't already heard it.

By the time we returned upstairs, the clerk had left the file on Loraine's desk. She donned bifocals that were huge, blue butterflies. She scanned the list for several minutes before pointing.

"Here's the name you asked for."

I was too excited to be coherent, so I looked at her expectantly.

"We have an address but no correspondence for over twenty years."

"Is Somchai Swoonswangs a common name? Do you think it's the person I'm looking for?"

"*Ma chérie*, you will have to do the investigations. A common name it is not, but we cannot assume he is the right person."

"Could you call for me? I don't know any Thai."

She returned to the list. "No phone is listed, but at that time, phones were still uncommon. The good news is that the address is in the center of town, a small street off

Muang Samut. Do you have a map?"

I started to pull out my cell phone, but Lorraine shook her head. "Those little screens are too hard for me to see." She rummaged for a moment in her desk and pulled out a paper map. She spread the whole thing over her desk, careful not to knock anything over. Despite ragged edges, most of the street names were legible. Lorraine expertly traced through the city's main lines, pointing with a pink fingernail. Muang Samut was by the river. Rachel and I had wandered near there to visit the night market.

"Why don't you try dropping by?"

Lorraine made the situation sound easy, but suddenly I had qualms. I had visions of some little old man who couldn't speak any English chasing me off his property, probably with a weapon. "Maybe he wouldn't want to be disturbed."

"To receive greetings from his sister? Nonsense! He would like nothing more."

"What if he's passed away? I'd hate to bring the family sad memories."

Lorraine shifted in her chair, slowly nodding up and down. "After so many years, that is a sad possibility. But Thais take family seriously. I believe his descendants would be delighted to find out any scrap of history, especially something about a long-lost family member."

As she wrote the address on my map, we heard a shy knock.

"Yes?"

A male student entered. Despite the heat he wore long pants and a short-sleeved shirt. He was dark and thin, like most of the natives I'd seen. He addressed Lorraine in soft Thai. She asked him a quick question before turning to me.

"Phom is one of my best assistants. He has finished his work for the day, so he will go home. Muang Samut is on his way. He could escort you if you would like."

The student smiled brightly. I wasn't sure if his expression was fake or genuine, but given the context he seemed perfectly safe. Now that I had a real lead, I had to seize it.

"I'd hate to inconvenience him," I said softly, as if I hoped no one would hear me.

"It is no problem. Go with Phom." She hugged me before handing over a business card. "I wish you luck. Please send me an email so that I know the rest of the story."

Phom grinned as he led me out to the parking lot. No matter what he thought of me, he seemed pleased to be doing a favor for Khun Lorraine. After passing rows of tired cars, we reached a dated sedan. The door on the driver's side was broken; Phom had to crawl through from the passenger side to reach his seat. I was embarrassed to be escorted by a stranger with whom I could only communicate through hand signals, but Phom seemed unconcerned, as if he took strangers around all the time. Given Lorraine's cheerful disposition towards bewildered foreigners, he probably did.

As he headed towards downtown and away from Doi Suthep, I felt a pang of conscience. Rachel was probably lingering at the famous temple, taking extra photographs, and waiting to show me around. If I texted her that I was following a lead, she would reply that I should visit the "most fabulous temple ever" first and follow the lead second.

Instead I turned off my phone. If questioned, I could claim the battery was dead. In reality Rachel was good at enjoying temples. She didn't need me in the least.

I expected Phom to dump me along Muang Samut, but instead he escorted me to the side street in question. We couldn't find 205/1 Sorasak, just 204 and 219. How could a number disappear? Phom offered to help me look, but I was afraid we were chasing wild geese, so I waved him on and motioned that I'd mosey around myself.

I had no idea what to do. I walked up and down the block as I tried to think up a decent strategy. In my cousins' town in Mexico, addresses were sometimes renumbered. Typically street crews painted new numbers on the wall, ignoring the old numbers that were no longer valid. During the day visitors could easily choose the correct ones. At night they made mistakes. Possibly a similar system existed here. I knocked on the gate at 219. No response. I tried 204. Inside, a dog barked. Finally an old woman opened the front door. She scrutinized me as if I were an alien.

"Khun Swoonswangs?"

She watched me, so I repeated myself more loudly. I had Rachel's phrase book in my bag, but I didn't have time to dig it out. Nor did I have time to turn on my phone and wait for a data signal. Instead I smiled, and she smiled back. Then she went inside.

At the third house another woman came to the gate. She frowned as if disapproving of my mismatched blouse and Capris. I didn't like the combination myself, but all my other clothes were dripping dry on the balcony outside my room.

"Khun Swoonswangs?"

She shook her head, crossing her hands in front of her body. She watched me as I turned around and started in the opposite direction. I couldn't tell if she was being honest or trying to get rid of me, but I felt uneasy. I knew I was out of place, so why did she have to remind me?

I tried one more house. This time an older man answered. He seemed to know the name but pointed over his shoulder and kept repeating "Mae Nam Ping." Maybe Mr. Swoonswangs had moved? As soon as I was out of sight, I wrote down the sounds I thought I'd heard; I knew they wouldn't stick in my mind for more than a few seconds. I searched for Mae Nam Ping on the map, but I found nothing in the immediate area. Google Maps couldn't find the term at all.

Following the man's general direction, I headed towards the river. Annoying rock music I would never listen to back home boomed from a riverside café. The songs blasted the dwellings nearby, but their inhabitants didn't seem to mind. Many of them lounged on their front porches, fishing. The river was so muddy it was black. I wondered how much of the town's seafood supply came from the river and told myself to avoid fish.

The sky had darkened. I headed south, roughly in the direction of the hotel, and came upon a huge flower market. From stalls and the beds of pickup trucks, pinks, reds, blues, violets, and yellows sprouted like a fantasy sequence in an animated film. As long as I couldn't find Somchai, I might as well enjoy beauty. The blooms were so breathtaking that I could hardly believe the sellers outnumbered the buyers. A couple of vendors beckoned to me, but I kept moving.

I came across a stall whose occupants sold lotus blossoms. Here I dared to linger because a line of people waited to buy Buddha offerings. I overheard a transaction. Fifty baht a bunch. I whipped out a bill. A little help from the Buddha couldn't hurt in my search for Somchai.

I continued on, trying to decide which temple should get my pretty white blossoms, when I spotted huge dragons snaking up a column. Rachel and I had read about a Chinese wat and put it on our list of "should sees." This temple was a candidate for the foreign wat, but it wasn't marked on my map. Unlike the wats in the Old Town, it didn't have the benefit of a helpful English-language sign.

The ornate door was jubilant, midway between silly and tacky. I wandered inside. From murals on either side, jungle animals leapt in relief. They seemed as out of place in a temple as I had been on Sorasak Street. No wonder I liked them. They had learned to embrace their incongruity.

Cautiously I took a few steps forward. Behind a desk on the right side of the temple, a monk paused from reading his book and waved me forwards. I proceeded cautiously. Ever since the episode Rachel and I had with the Buddha head, I hadn't trusted my instincts. Worse, when I reached the altar, I wasn't sure what to do. The several flower vases were already filled with other lotus blossoms. The monk came up behind me, stepping so quietly I didn't hear him until we were side by side. I worried I had committed yet another cultural gaffe, but again he smiled. He pointed to the full vases. When I tried to hand him the lotus blossoms, he shook his head. He reached for the closest vase and shoved its stems to the side, making way for mine.

"Thank you," he said. "Good for pray Buddha."

I smiled back. Evidently there was always room for more lotus blossoms. I was so pleased that he'd recognized and appreciated my intentions that I wanted to rush right out and buy more flowers. No wonder Thailand was such a gentle country. The spiritual emphasis was on gratitude and beauty.

Before I had ventured one step outside the temple, the sky opened with a thunderclap. Flanked by dragons, I watched the downpour from the temple's doorway. I wondered how long ago the Swoonswangs had moved, and why, and where they had ended up. I'd been hopeful when I'd met Lorraine, but how could I think up any new leads? And how much would I regret never visiting the famous Doi Suthep?

Twenty minutes later there was a break in the deluge. I exchanged a final wave with the monk and hit the street, stepping over the biggest puddles and smelling the freshness of the air. As I felt the water between my toes and the lingering drops of rain on my face, I thought about Janjira. In a place as dry as Tucson, how much did she miss her native rain?

"Anyway, you saw a new part of town," Rachel said. It was early evening, the rain had finally stopped, and we'd headed off for dinner. She was disappointed I'd skipped Doi Suthep, but she was trying not to show it. She could see that I was even more disappointed by the day's venture than she was.

"At least the French lady was interesting," she continued.

"And unique." I felt a raindrop.

"She was sincere about wanting you to email her back. You made a new friend."

"I'll probably never hear from her."

"Maybe something will pan out."

"Yeah." We felt a host of brisk drops. We picked up our pace as we hit the main drag that led to the market district. Both Westerners and Thais hurried towards their destinations. We all knew what was coming. "Tell me about Doi Suthep."

Instantly she changed from concerned sister to enthusiastic tourist. "It's wonderful. Around the temple is a wide balcony where you have a view of the town. Then you walk into a courtyard which is the temple area, and you see statues of Buddha in different positions, one for each day of the week, and two for Wednesday, although don't ask me why. There were gold chedis that glimmered in the sun, and a pregnant cat that kept inspecting all the visitors."

She would have gushed out more, but she had to stop and catch her breath.

"Lots of tourists?"

"The place was crawling with them, but there were lots of natives too. You could tell it was a big deal for them because they got so excited when they neared the entrance. They bubbled inside the main entrance like Catholics visiting the Virgin of Guadalupe."

I'd only visited the famous basilica in Mexico City one time, but the memory was vivid. Crowds stood in an impossibly long line waiting to go inside and say their prayers to the Virgin. My cousins and I had contented ourselves with waving to the image from outside the church and dashing into a nearby ice cream parlor. "Is Doi Suthep the main temple in Thailand?"

"In Northern Thailand. People travel here specifically

to make a pilgrimage to the top."

I grinned. "Did you enjoy the climb?"

"It wasn't that bad. Suthep is actually the name of the mountain. From the parking lot, the temple is only about three hundred steps."

"Only?"

"You should have heard these ladies behind me. British, I think. They were fuming because they didn't realize there was a funicular until they were on their way down."

We heard thunder. I was hoping the afternoon downpour would satisfy the storm gods for the day, but they'd sent in fresh recruits.

"What did you say the temple was famous for?"

"It houses a relic from Buddha."

"And a relic is—"

"A piece of bone or something." She caught my expression. "Right. It's pretty hard to determine the validity of a relic."

"What did Aunt Milena say about St. Francis, or maybe it was St. Peter? Didn't she visit his relics?"

"She used to say there were so many churches that claimed to have pieces of St. Peter that he must have been quintuplets."

A thunderclap rocked the sky overhead, and the rain started pouring.

"Darn it," Rachel said as she started jogging. "I already got soaked once today. I'm completely out of dry clothes."

"Where's the restaurant you wanted to try?"

"It's up ahead several more blocks."

I turned 360 degrees, hoping to spot a store we could visit. "Look! There's a travel agency on the corner."

"Run! We can pretend we want a tour."

A large filing cabinet and a desk with a desktop computer dominated the tiny office. The space also contained a small sofa, a coffee table, and a big poster with destinations and explanations of the fourteen tours the company offered.

Before the desk, three U.S. tourists were agreeing on a full day's tour to Chiang Rai while the polite Thai agent copiously recorded their names and hotels.

At first I merely pretended to be interested. Rachel abhorred guided tours because she complained that you were always carted around like a piece of luggage. I didn't have anything against such tours — yet.

"What about Number Seven?" I asked her, pointing to the poster. Jungle Trekking promised an elephant ride, tribal villages, a waterfall swim, and a bamboo raft ride. "Doesn't that sound cool?"

Rachel shrugged. The rain was still pouring. "We could ask about the price."

One hundred and six dollars bought a full day of touring. "There aren't any convenient ways to reach the elephant places," I said. "I checked a bunch of websites." Some of the tourist places advertised eco-tourism where no elephant riding was allowed, but didn't elephants have to earn their keep? Ever since Ayutthaya I'd set my heart on riding one.

"I'm sure there are lots of ways to arrange for an elephant ride," Rachel said. "You don't need to tie up the whole day."

Again I indicated the poster. "This is convenient. It's quick."

"You would be overpaying, you know. You could visit all these sites much more cheaply by tuk-tuk. Usually on a tour you spend the whole day visiting junk stores where the guides earn a commission."

"We haven't had time to do much shopping."

Rachel frowned. "It's too early in the trip. You don't want to lug a suitcase of souvenirs down to Phuket, do you?"

We discussed the tour's possible merits until the rain stopped and foot traffic resumed outside. Then I convinced my sister the easy way, by offering to pay for both of us.

Chapter Eleven

"So this is a go-go bar," I said, half asking and half answering. We'd read about the type of establishment where hookers openly awaited clients. The guidebooks were in favor of such bars. The girls wouldn't steal their clients' wallets because the customers knew where they worked.

This particular locale featured an outdoor area populated by picnic tables. Inside was a bar counter hosting a dozen stools and a pool table currently surrounded by five teens from Singapore. From the ceiling hung a small TV on which a nature program showed the beauty of forest frogs.

From our seats at the picnic table, we studied the waitresses. All three were striking. The most beautiful seemed to be the youngest. She had long black hair, perfectly rounded features, and a voluptuous body that she'd poured into such tight clothes I wondered how she would get out of them without ripping the fabric.

The eldest of the three, the cashier, ran the show. We deduced that she was the boss because every time the old Eagles tape reached the end, she was the one who rushed to turn it over. She wasn't as pretty as the other girls, so she made up for it by being more businesslike.

The middle waitress, whom I placed in her late twenties, sat at the end of the counter with a man three times her age. The man's most prominent feature was his big, noisy mouth. I'd spotted him at the market the night before shouting what sounded like German or maybe Dutch. His Rudolph-Reindeer nose protruded between red cheeks. He drank beer from a twenty-four-ounce mug; her glass held half a can.

While the man laughed at the forest frogs, he slid his fingers down the woman's waist, but she guided his hand back up again.

"Looks like a go-go bar to me," Rachel said. "Otherwise they would have thrown that old fart out an hour ago."

"Let's hope he's rich."

"Let's hope she's not a university student."

We'd both been stunned by an article in *The Bangkok Post* proclaiming that "University Students Fund Studies with Prostitution." It was a vivid reminder that we were in a third-world country where people made desperate decisions so that they could get on with their lives. The contrast was especially vivid when I reflected on my fellow university students who used trust funds to pay for sorority initiations.

A cue ball bounced past my foot, but I was too slow to catch it. The young waitress swooped it up as if she trapped balls all evening long. She probably did.

"Maybe later we can shoot a game of pool," I said.

"We're hardly the preferred customers."

Rachel and I had both ordered Cokes, which we proceeded to nurse, but the members of the Singapore quintet were downing shots of whisky. From the volume of the teens' laughter, they were downing a lot of them.

"Excuse me." A local guy my age leaned over from the next table where he and some friends drank Singha beers. He had dark skin, straight black hair, and wide-open eyes. "You are from the U.S.?"

Our accents had given us away. I didn't mind; he seemed friendly rather than intrusive. "Arizona," I said.

"That is U.S.?"

"Next to California."

"Can I asking you questions?"

He wasn't hitting on us or practicing his English. His older brother was heading for a language school in Oregon at the end of the month. The family was concerned because the most they knew about Oregon was that it lay north of California. Unfortunately, that was the most we knew too.

"Are you a university student?" I asked.

My new friend nodded. "I almost done."

"How many years have you completed?"

"Seven."

"Seven! Are you studying medicine?" I asked.

"Finance."

"School must be a lot harder over here," Rachel said. "Back home most people earn that degree in four or five years."

"Here too! But I am activist for Burmese people. I don't always go class."

"Burmese people?" I asked.

"Now is called Myanmar."

I addressed Rachel. "Didn't the Burmese destroy that town we visited?"

"Ayutthaya," said Rachel.

Nopporn, as he introduced himself, shook his head. "Is long ago. Don't worry for that anymore. People here is think Burmese all bad. Not give chance."

He tried to explain the philosophies of what he called the new generation, and between his broken utterances, we tried to complete the picture.

"You should finish school," Rachel said.

"I know," Nopporn replied. "Maybe for next year."

"I understand," I said. "I don't much like school either."

"Problem no for no like school. No like for studying accountant."

"So why do it?"

Nopporn set down his beer mug. "My father accountant. My grandfather accountant."

"Your brother?" I asked.

"He go Oregon for be English-speaker accountant."

"Do you have to do the same as your father?" I asked.

"That's terrible."

"Is tradition. We do everything same way our fathers."

"And had you been a girl?" asked Rachel.

"My small sister, she study for be —"

"Accountant!" Rachel and I called out.

Silently I thanked my mother. My father had wanted me to study engineering as he had, or at least business, which he saw as more practical than Rachel's studying music. When I told my mother that I wanted to try computer programming because my high school teachers said I had a knack for it, she urged me forward. "Always try to do what you're good at," she'd advised. "Makes your life easier. And if it doesn't work out, change your mind." Unfortunately for me, programming was so tedious that I'd already changed my mind several times over. I just hadn't settled on anything else.

"My sister finish first year university very high grades," Nopporn confessed.

"You'd better watch out," said Rachel. "Otherwise she'll finish before you do."

"Is true. And if I not careful, she take job in my uncle's company he promise for me."

"Your family sounds a bit difficult," I said. "Maybe you can look for work outside Chiang Mai."

"No can. My parents is here. My brother and my sister is here. I don't leave." He handed me a homemade business card. "You come back to Chiang Mai in five years, ten years, twenty years, you find me here. Father's house."

Nopporn stood to leave, thanking us for the kind information. We wished his brother good luck in Oregon.

"Talk about following tradition," Rachel said. "This is worse than Mexico. Of course, it would depend on the family. I'm sure some aren't so conservative."

"Nopporn's family might be an extreme, but I feel sorry for him. I don't think he'll ever be a good accountant."

"At this rate I don't think he'll be an accountant at all. Or an English teacher."

The cue ball bounced our way. I stopped it with my foot, and one of the teenage pool sharks raced over for it.

"Sank you, sank you!" She raced back to her friends.

I turned to Rachel. "The date on Janjira's picture was '72. And in the picture Somchai looks — what, twenty-five?"

"Something like that. So?"

"Let's say he had children when he was in his twenties."

"All right."

"By now his children should be in their twenties too. Guess what they would be studying."

Rachel smacked her temple with the palm of her hand. Once again we'd managed to overlook an obvious clue. "Engineering. Of course. But what kind?"

"Sammy said that he made streets."

"Civil engineering, then."

"Most schools have some kind of email directory," I said. "I can't imagine there are thousands of Swoonswangs, can you?"

"Even if there were a hundred, that would still give you a lead."

"It's a long shot, but I don't mind sending a few emails. Chances are that Somchai's kids would be in school here in Chiang Mai even if they weren't attending his alma mater."

Rachel reoriented the drooping flower arrangement that decorated our table. "One problem. Somchai could have had daughters who married and changed their names."

"Most women finish school before they marry, don't you think?"

Rachel nodded towards the cashier-waitress. "We could ask. But since we know Somchai was at CMET, why not write all its current civil engineering students and describe Somchai in your email?"

"Better than that, I'll send his photo as an attachment."

"Congratulations. You've got another lead," Rachel said.

"Just what I needed."

"Exactly."

We never shot any pool. The Singapore kids kept drinking, laughing even more loudly as they rocked into one another, but they stayed on their feet. No matter how often the cue ball skidded off the table, the waitresses retrieved it cheerfully. By now the old guy had secured his hand around his companion's hips, a Brit was flirting with the youngest waitress, and the Eagles were crooning "Hotel California" for the fifth time. I left Rachel talking to the cashier about women's education in Thailand and headed back to our lodgings. I was back in business.

By the time I returned to the room, Rachel was lying on the bed eliminating the unfocused pictures she'd taken that afternoon. Despite her best efforts, she'd found it nearly impossible to take any decent pictures from on top of an elephant.

"How'd it go?" she asked.

"I didn't come up with anything. No Swoonswangs became civil engineers, at least as far as I could tell."

I lay on the bed beside her, and she handed me the camera. The boy leading our elephant had taken a crooked but focused picture of the two of us on Honeysuckle, our faithful elephant.

"This is the best shot we have. I need more practice at motion photography."

Our elephant ride had lasted an hour as Honeysuckle slowly made her way up the jungle path. Since she continually paused to eat a leaf or sniff at one, the journey was unpredictable. Each time she leaned down, Rachel and I felt so unbalanced that we giggled at the thought of falling off.

"You didn't find a single lead?" Rachel asked.

"Nothing. Maybe I'm going in the wrong direction."

Rachel turned off the camera and slid the camera battery into its charger. "Why don't you try researching the computer engineers?"

"What?"

"I was thinking about Somchai. It's a good theory about having the same profession as your father, but consider this: In Somchai's days, computer engineering didn't exit."

I rolled over to mask the disappointment I felt at not recognizing this possibility before my sister did.

"You think Somchai's offspring might have studied computer engineering?" I asked, pretending the notion was far-fetched.

"If it was a hot new field, why not? Even if Somchai hoped his kids would follow in his footsteps, he probably wouldn't have stood in their way of pursuing a similar profession."

As I watched, a fat beetle marched across the ceiling. "You think I should email the computer engineering students?"

"And alumni. If you want to take the time."

Rachel started reading me sections of the guidebook that pertained to her ambitious list of the next morning's activities, but I wasn't listening. I was composing emails.

Chapter Twelve

Rachel and I sat across from each other at the go-go bar. This was an accomplishment because she had surrounded us with mountains of purchases. Since we were flying south in the morning, my sister had spent the last few hours searching for bargain presents at the night market. She was determined to take advantage of what everyone had assured us were the best prices in Thailand. She'd loaded up on elephant purses and silk ties because they were easy to pack and didn't break. She'd also found children's clothes for a pregnant cousin, a sleeping wooden cat statue for Mom, and a woven bracelet for Grandma. Rachel had also bought bookmarks, decorated pens, and little wooden animals, especially elephants, that I knew she'd be tempted to keep herself instead of giving away.

I'd spent the last hours emailing computer engineering students a short note explaining that I was a friend of a Thai woman living in the States and had a package to deliver to her brother. I'd included the image of Somchai, but so far I didn't have any leads. I worried I'd misspent my time and wondered if Rachel would sell me one of the little purses. They each had a main zipper compartment and two smaller ones. The black velvet rectangles depicted sequined elephants in bright pinks, purples, blues, golds, and greens. The purses were too wild for daily use, but I could envision one hanging on my wall.

"Don't feel bad," Rachel said, referring to my search. "You've done your best. You've gone a lot farther than the proverbial extra mile."

"The father-offspring engineering link seemed like such a good lead."

"It was. It still is — who knows? Not everybody spends all afternoon on the computer."

"Computer engineers do."

"They have to eat."

"Usually with one hand on the mouse." I'd received a bunch of emails right away. Interesting, several students wrote, but I don't remember anyone by that name; you might try the Thai Engineers Website (I did immediately, to no avail); I had a friend who looked somewhat like him, but the hair is all wrong. The responses were kind, but no one recognized the man in the picture.

"I hate to disappoint Sammy's aunt," I said.

"It's his great-aunt and only by marriage. She won't know the difference anyway."

"That's not the point. Maybe I feel responsible because she reminds me so much of Aunt Milena."

Rachel swigged on her Coke. "I wished you'd known Aunt Milena when she was in her prime. By the time you were old enough to hold a conversation with her, she was a little wacky. She'd had so many adventures in so many places that she couldn't keep them straight. Besides, I think she exaggerated."

It was a sad fact that, genealogists aside, nobody had enough time to keep old histories alive. If only Aunt Milena had written journals about her travels! Instead we had inherited boxes of slides with minimal labels. Mom kept trying to throw them away, but I'd prevented her from doing so — so far. Janjira's situation was somewhat similar, but we had even less information to go on.

"Janjira had such a visceral reaction when she heard about our trip," I said. "She must think about her brother a lot."

"True. But by now she can't share her thoughts about him."

The real tragedy was that Janjira would never benefit from my efforts. Sammy was too young to understand what a challenge he'd asked of us, but at least the Tamarins wouldn't be upset that I'd failed. "I went overboard on my research. I should have known it would be impossible."

"You're just disappointed."

"I feel like I let you down, making you go off by yourself, not going to Doi Suthep."

"You brought me to Thailand! I forgive you. Here's the good part. You have the perfect excuse to return to Chiang Mai someday since you missed its most important temple."

Another trip to Asia would be far in the future, such as after I finished college and worked a professional job for a while. I suddenly had a mad urge to be hurrying up those three hundred steps that would have taken me to the famous temple. I'd missed out on something important, and I would regret the omission until I made it back.

"I'd be happy to return to Thailand," I said. "Everybody's friendly here. The people are laid back. They may have low wages, but they seem content."

"I've felt at home as well, but there's only so much you can take in on a first trip. Consider all the temples right here in Chiang Mai! The city has around three hundred of them. We didn't make a dent. And it's good to switch gears. Tomorrow at this time we'll be drying off after a day at the beach."

Phuket was a prime tourist destination for young people who wanted to party and have fun, not study architecture. Then for our final destination we'd chosen Krabi, whose beaches were supposed to be the finest on the mainland. As long as I kept my tablet in my suitcase, I'd be able to enjoy the rest of my vacation without getting hung up on lost causes.

"It probably doesn't make sense to you, doing this email stuff and everything," I said.

"You probably can't figure out why I go to Greece to work on my language skills every summer. What kind of crazy challenge is that?"

"I thought you were going for the men."

"Ha! Given the times I've been stood up, broken up with, or merely disappointed, that's not a good enough reason."

I shifted my legs too fast, sending a sack full of silk ties from the table to the floor. We both stooped down to pick them up.

Again I regretted my lack of shopping. Not only would my friends be disappointed I hadn't brought souvenirs, but Rachel would make me look bad at Christmas. She'd bought extra presents for Mom and Grandma too.

"I took on delivering Janjira's elephant as if it were a mission," I said. "I couldn't resist the idea of finding a long-lost relative." I'd also wanted to prove that I could navigate a foreign landscape. Wrong.

"You made progress," Rachel said. "A week ago we didn't know what kind of needle we were looking for, and we hadn't chosen a haystack. You got really close."

"Close only counts—"

"I know, I know. In horseshoes or bocce ball." Rachel indicated the empty pool table. "Come on. Let's shoot a game before those Singapore kids show up and outdrink us."

I played really well, beating Rachel four games out of five, which was the reverse of what usually happened. I attributed my winning to high concentration. I couldn't find a Thai engineer in the middle of the country's second biggest city, but I could hit the cue ball in a straight line every single time.

Rachel caught me sneaking out of the room early because I rammed my foot into the bed so hard that I cried out. She scrambled for her watch to check the time, worried she'd overslept and missed our flight. Then she relaxed and squinted at me through half-closed eyes.

"Afraid they won't have any Internet connections on Phuket?"

"Since we don't have to leave for the airport for at least another hour . . ."

"Go." She rolled over.

The lounge was ghostly quiet at seven in the morning. The girl at the reception desk was so sleepy she didn't see me. I appreciated having the space to myself. I plopped into the most comfortable cushioned chair and waited impatiently for the Wi-Fi to kick in.

I had a total of eight new messages. Four had been returned because the addresses were no longer valid. Two writers apologized that they didn't recognize the picture. Another wished me good luck. Then I came to the final message, which had been written five hours earlier:

> *Dearest Gina,*
>
> *I am quite sorry that I was unable to respond more quickly. I was called to Bangkok on business and will not return to Chiang Mai until tomorrow evening. I do not wish to make too hasty a judgment, but I very much believe the man in your picture to be my grandfather. I will look through my family albums to find similar photos, but the smile and the stance, as well as the gap between the front teeth, seem identical.*
>
> *Although my grandfather is still alive, his eyesight is poor and he suffers from dementia. Last year he had a stroke and no longer speaks, so even if his memory were accurate, he would not have any way to communicate his thoughts. Your details do indeed match my grandfather's biography. He left Bangkok when he was a young man and studied to become a civil engineer in Chiang Mai. However, my grandfather's sisters did not leave Thailand as far as I know. I will call my aunt this weekend to find out more information,*

but as she is often busy with her family, she is difficult to reach by phone.

Grandfather and I live near San Kamphaeng, which is on the outskirts of Chiang Mai. How long will you be staying in the area? If the man in the photo is my grandfather, I would be most delighted to meet with you and retrieve this package although if it is not monetarily valuable, perhaps you would prefer to send it through the post so that it will not take up your time. I will be happy to cover the cost of this process. Thank you for taking so much trouble over someone else's family history. Your message to me was fantastic.

Sincerely,
Sompong Swoonswangs Osuwan

I read the message three times. Then I read it again, slowly. I pinched myself. I was the only person in the lounge, or I would have shown it to the nearest person to make sure I hadn't dreamt it.

I was off by an entire generation. There was still no guarantee I had the right Somchai Swoonswangs, but there was a strong chance that I did. To top it all off, I had written something fantastic.

But our flight was leaving in less than three hours. Why did I have to receive the most important email in my life half a day too late? The sensation was as bad as learning you'd earned 89.4% in your college chemistry class or meeting the most handsome man ever the night before his wedding. I couldn't turn back the clock because my wheels of motion had been set. Murphy's Law had ruled against me.

I trudged up the stairs. I had a five-minute window before our prearranged cab would be arriving to whisk us away from a dream.

Rachel was doing a final check to make sure we'd packed everything, including all the new purchases. "Good timing!" Rachel thrust my bag and backpack into my arms and herded me back into the hall. She didn't notice my demeanor until we were out on the street waiting for the cab.

"Bad news?"

"Not really," I said.

"I can see it in your face."

"Good and bad."

A taxi pulled up, and a middle-aged driver popped out. "Lachel Campanello?"

"Did you hear that?" Rachel whispered. "No Rs!"

"Lachel Campanello?"

"That's us!"

The man deposited our bags in the trunk while we climbed into the backseat, our bulging carry-ons between us.

"Airport?" he asked.

"Airport!" Rachel exclaimed.

Although the driver was going at a moderate rate, the town walls whizzed right by us. Above them peeked the tops of unidentified wats, which Rachel was no doubt categorizing for future visits.

Once we passed Old Town, we only had another couple of kilometers to go. The airport was moments from the heart of the city.

"So tell me," Rachel said once we passed the historical walls.

"You won't want to hear it."

"It's that bad?"

"It's that late." I showed her a screenshot of the email.

Rachel scanned the message and handed it back. "There must be some mistake. The man in that picture wouldn't be old enough to have grandchildren."

I shrugged. "The guy who wrote me wasn't sure it was his grandfather."

"But he lives near Chiang Mai?"

"If we can believe what we can read."

The cabbie turned into the airport. "Very modern," he

said, "but small. You like."

Given the circumstances, I was sure he was wrong.

Rachel paid our fare, but instead of rushing into the airport, she pointed to a large, laminated map of the city that was on a post nearby. Together we scoured it until we found San Kamphaeng. The area lay to the east beyond the town limits.

"The guy won't be back today anyway," Rachel said. "Why didn't you leave the package at the hotel? He could have picked it up there."

"I considered doing that."

I'd rejected the idea within seconds. How could I leave a package for an anonymous stranger without the pleasure of seeing a brother and sister spiritually reunited?

Rachel checked her watch. "The airport is only seven kilometers from our hotel. You have time to run back, leave the package, and still make the flight."

I shuffled my feet.

"Seriously, take a cab, make him wait outside while you dash in and—"

"That's okay."

Rachel nodded. "You're afraid to leave it at the desk in case the clerk steals it."

"I hadn't thought about that. But what if we have the wrong person?"

Rachel nodded. "You need more proof."

"I want to be sure."

We nosed towards Thai Air and joined the line at the counter.

"If What's-His-Name finds out more information, you could always send the package from Phuket."

"I was hoping to meet Somchai in person."

Rachel set her heavy backpack on the floor and scooted it forward with her foot. "Do you want to ask about changing the ticket?"

I must have looked as dejected as I felt. "That's okay."

Changing the ticket was precisely what I wanted to do, but how could I admit to such a crazy thing?

"It might not cost that much. We could find out."

I felt like I was in a bad production of *Hamlet*. The man might have been the right one, but I didn't have proof. And thus I hesitated.

"We have hotel reservations on Phuket, and Mom was going to call tonight," I muttered.

"I'll go on to Phuket. You can join me later."

Despite the temptation, invisible strings held me back. How could I make such a big decision on a moment's notice? Besides, at the rate I was going, any efforts to defy fate would backfire. "It's a silly thing anyway. And I don't want you to have to fly south by yourself."

"I don't mind."

Rachel was being completely honest, but I felt intimidated by the thought of being alone in Chiang Mai. Rachel didn't speak much more Thai than I did, but she knew how to navigate.

We took a few steps forward as we neared the ticket counter. "Maybe it's better like this."

"You're saying that," Rachel said, "but you don't mean it."

I did and I didn't. I had a plane ticket in my hand, and then suddenly I had luggage that was checked through to my final destination. I thought of a video game flashing the urgent message of "Game Over."

We were the last passengers to board the plane. Rachel gave me every possible second to change my mind, but I was too angry to make choices. I was mad at everything: email, my timing, Murphy and his damned law.

An hour later I picked at my dessert. The fruity pudding was rich and creamy, but I felt so sorry for myself that I couldn't enjoy it. Somchai's grandson and I had come so close to connecting.

"Take one," Rachel said sharply.

The poor airline attendant had proffered the bowl of

hard candies for several long seconds, and Rachel knew I wouldn't purposefully pass up chocolate mint.

"For landing," the attendant smiled.

I selected a candy, but I could sense Rachel's concern for me. "I couldn't hear over the engine," I explained, turning back towards the window.

I had to use such force to liberate the candy from its wrapper that it flew from my hand and rolled down the aisle. A small boy picked it up. Before his mom could stop him, he shoved it in his mouth.

Chapter Thirteen

Ko Phuket is an island off the southwest tip of Thailand's main peninsula. The zone had suffered from a tsunami over a decade earlier, but by now the hip tourist destination had camouflaged any disasters. Rachel and I were staying in Patong, the island's most popular hangout, where the wide beach stretched from one edge of town to the other, the water was generally calm, and the sand provided a soft cushion for sun-worshippers. A row of tall palms divided the beach from the commercial buildings behind it. We heard wisps of traffic, but at least we couldn't see any cars. We weren't even burdened by fellow beach bums. The height of the tourist season had given way to extreme temperatures that were the prelude to heavy rains. Thus we could relax and bask in the beauty of nature without so many distractions.

As an alternative we lounged around the hotel's clover-shaped pool. The lush surroundings were carefully curated. Tall trees provided spots of shade. Flowers hung from baskets fashioned out of coconuts. The deck was filled with white plastic chairs whose blue pillows and umbrellas invited lazy catnaps. In the distance, balconies laden with bougainvillea offered dots of pink or purple. Pool boys in khaki uniforms drummed up snack orders while hungry cats followed them, eager for crumbs. Waiters tooled around on tricycles, balancing their trays as they pedaled.

Rachel alternated between the pool and the beach, but I preferred dipping in the pool's clean blue water. I wasn't used to swimming in salty ocean waves.

The sea reminded me of childhood trips to San Diego, where the water was always cold, and I always managed to swallow unpleasant mouthfuls of brine. I wasn't much used to the sun either. In Tucson I stayed out of it. I took after my dad, who couldn't tan either. Instead we turned red.

After dinner each night Rachel and I hit the streets. Patong was famous for its wild nightlife, but luckily the parties didn't extend to the low season. There were enough fellow travelers to prevent us from feeling lonely, but we didn't have to wait for a table at any restaurant or a stool at any bar.

My reaction to the city was neutral. The endless rows of carbon-copy shops and neon-lit eateries didn't enhance Patong's appeal, but when we got fed up with shopping strips and exuberant hawkers, we strolled along the beach. Vendors haunted us there too, but our ragged towels and weather-beaten bags kept them from trying very hard.

Tuk-tuks were plentiful, but the drivers were less ag-gressive than in Chiang Mai or Bangkok. As Rachel and I walked past, the drivers would ask where we were going without pursuing us, almost as if they were hoping we wouldn't offer them any work. The whole island was as somber as if everyone had a relative who was terminally ill. The end of the tourist season meant the end to easy money, and the effect was a universally lackadaisical demeanor shared by everyone from receptionists to merchants to waitresses to clerks. Rachel called it tropical lassitude.

"It's like this on the Dodecanese islands too," she ex-plained. "As the low season approaches, everything grinds to a halt. The locals become depressed because they know they'll have to live on their meager savings until the follow-ing year."

"I suppose Phuket can't hope for much business once the rainy season hits."

"Once it starts raining, they say it doesn't stop."

The sky had been so clear that we didn't worry about

the weather. Despite the pessimism of the locals, Rachel enjoyed each moment of each day on Phuket, whether lounging in the sun or swimming lazy laps in the water. I was restless. I took long walks by myself and nosed through bookstores. I comparison shopped for elephant statues, but none were as pretty as the purple one lording over my nightstand back at the hotel. Our room was well wired, but I left my tablet in my suitcase and tried to forget about it, lamenting the fact that my most important message had arrived too late.

By our third day on the island, Rachel said she couldn't stand me any longer. As soon as we'd breakfasted on fresh oranges and pastries, she marched me up to the room, shoved the tablet in my hands, and said to use the damned thing.

"I thought we were going to start the day with a long walk on the beach."

She added her Thai phrase book to her backpack and pointed in the direction of the pool. "I'll wait for you downstairs."

I had a dozen messages. Mom wanted to know why we hadn't called or written. Two friends reminded me to bring them silk. Two wrong Swoonswangs explained that they didn't recognize the man in the picture.

Sompong had sent three lengthy messages. He started with apologies; he was awfully sorry if he'd missed us in Chiang Mai but wanted us to have his address: Wattana Road, Soi 6. His next email consisted of strategic planning. In case we'd already left his city, he suggested an alternative. He assumed we were scheduled to fly home from Bangkok. Could we meet him there? His grandfather was too ill to travel easily, but Sompong could fly down for the day himself. In the third email, he explained that he could arrange for free standby tickets, courtesy of an uncle who worked for the airlines, if we would come all the way back to Chiang Mai.

I was flattered by his attention but flabbergasted at his

outlandish suggestions. He had no solid proof that his grandfather was the Swoonswangs I was looking for. Most of the details sounded right, but he hadn't found a picture that was similar to mine nor had he found a photo of his grandfather wearing a straw hat. Although Sompong had worked his way through a box of old family records, he hadn't uncovered any information about a sister who had gone to America.

I drafted my email over and over, each time detailing pros and cons to his suggestions and always ending with the same conclusions. It would be futile to meet in Bangkok because Rachel and I only had an hour's layover. I couldn't accept Sompong's offer to return to Chiang Mai because I wouldn't be able to dislodge my sister from the beach. Once she'd given up temples for ocean dips, there was no turning her back.

I wrote Lorraine because I'd promised to keep her posted about my findings. She happened to be online at the time, and she immediately replied: "You found the man?!! Return to Chiang Mai. Do not end your quest now. I have a good feeling about this."

I wrote back explaining the situation, but Lorraine didn't care about my lack of solid proof or my sister's love of water. Lorraine told me to go back to Chiang Mai alone, that Rachel's adventure might be Greece, but spiritually I was linked to Chiang Mai. "Seek your destiny!" she wrote in our final exchange. "Don't expect destiny to come to you. It's too busy."

The last email I read was from Sammy. Hadn't I met his grand-uncle yet?

I found Rachel lounging under a palm tree, so absorbed in her book that I startled her when I sat down.

She bookmarked the page. "You must have heard from What's-His-Name."

"Sompong. It's a variation on his grandfather's name. How did you know I'd heard from him?"

"When I checked on you half an hour ago, you didn't notice."

I wished I weren't so easy to read.

"Let's have it," she said. "Tell me about this mysterious man."

"He seems nice."

"That's all? The ocean is nice. Our accommodations are nice. The whole country is nice. Can't you do better than that?"

"Okay, he's a soulmate who is my exact other half. He's gentle and friendly and has a sense of humor. He's already been through school and has a good job as a programmer. He's not married, he doesn't have any children, and he spends most evenings at home. How's that?"

"Much better. Is that all?"

She was partially kidding, but by now I was ready to take on the challenge. "His written English is good. I would suspect that he uses it a lot at work or with foreign acquaintances."

"At least the two of you can communicate. What else?"

I sighed. "He spends his free time assisting his grandfather. They have a live-in maid who helps with caretaking, but, ironically, Sompong almost never leaves Chiang Mai. He sounded genuinely sorry that he missed us, but he's there and I'm here. He's not going to be flying to the States any time soon, so I probably won't ever have a chance to meet him."

Three young American guys went by wearing only swimsuits and flip flops. They had towels draped around their necks as if they were making fashion statements. They were exactly the kind of men I didn't want to meet.

Rachel watched the trio, probably thinking that we'd wasted too much morning beach time and calculating how many afternoon hours she'd have to enjoy the waves. "You're sure this is the right guy?"

I carefully adjusted my chair so that I could lean back. "I'm pretty sure. Sompong thinks it is. He has some pictures of his grandfather as a young man, and the faces are a strong match. This afternoon Sompong is going to look for a photo with a straw hat. That might give us a better idea."

"To me a lot of the Thais look similar. Why didn't Sompong email you some attachments so that you could judge for yourself?"

"He said he would as soon as he had time."

"Or maybe he's stalling."

"Maybe."

"Gina, your picture is dated from '72. That would make Somchai around 55."

I sensed the trap but couldn't see the bars. "Yes."

"How could this guy who wrote you have a grandfather that young? Mathematically it doesn't make sense."

The thought had occurred to me early on, but then I had conveniently forgotten about it.

"Gina, what if this is some kind of scam? What if he's some ten-year-old kid putting you on?"

I crossed my arms, petulant. At times like this, Rachel reminded me of Mom. It wasn't fair. They were both a lot older, so naturally they were more realistic. They'd already had a lot more things go wrong in their lives, so they were prepared for obstacles. "It feels right. It's a gut instinct."

I knew that I sounded childish. I wasn't sure which was worse: not finding my fantasy man or having to admit that my intuition was faulty. I'd held on because I wanted something to believe in, something that was mine.

Rachel handed me the Thai language book. "Read the box."

I took out the bookmark and read the words in the gray area on the margin of the page: "'The Western style of calendar dating is becoming more popular, but the older population still calculates the years using the Buddhist Era, or BE.'" I lowered the book. "Buddhist Era?"

Rachel retrieved the guide. "This is almost as bad as not recognizing the Thai name for Bangkok." She flipped to a blank page at the back where she'd made chicken scratches. "If your picture is dated in Buddhist Era, it's 543 years ahead of the Roman year. A picture from BE 2472, abbreviated to '72, would be our 1935."

I calculated using my fingers, lost track, and calculated again. "If Somchai had been twenty in 1935, by now he would be in his eighties."

"Yes."

"Making him a lot closer to Janjira's age."

"Right again."

"And he could easily be Sompong's grandfather."

"That's what I'm thinking."

"Then it's him." The idea sunk in slowly, like ginger ale in a dense carpet.

She shrugged as if we were discussing answers for a crossword puzzle. "Good chance."

"We actually found him!"

"We might have."

"This is proof!"

"Not quite."

Images rocked my mind: an ecstatic Sammy hugging a delighted Janjira, an old man's toothless grin, and the sincere thanks of a tall, dark, handsome man named Sompong. Then I wondered if I'd watched too many made-for-TV movies and needed to have my head examined. "If this is him, we have to return to Chiang Mai. We can't give up when we're this close."

"What do you mean, close?" Rachel asked. "We're miles away. Several hundred."

"You know what I mean. At least we're still in the country. We're a lot closer now than we'll ever be in Arizona. We have to fly back to Chiang Mai. We have to meet him!"

"Him? Are you talking about the grandfather or the grandson?"

My sister had caught me again. Too many movies.

"You promised to accompany me to Krabi," Rachel

continued. "What if this Sompong guy is a nut?"

Krabi was a town on the mainland, across from Phuket, whose beach was rumored to be even better than Patong's. My sister had been salivating ever since she'd seen pictures of it. She'd taken care of the accommodations herself. She'd devised a schedule that would allow us to see both of the nearby national parks before we shot back to Bangkok. Skip Krabi? The idea was ludicrous. But no matter how wonderful, the beach wouldn't compare to connecting with the Swoonswangs.

"We have to try!"

"We?"

"If we've got the wrong guy, or if he's weird, we'll immediately hop on a bus, return to Bangkok, and spend our last days at a seaside resort south of the capital."

"Krabi has a four-star beach. All the guidebooks say so."

I didn't care about the ocean. At the moment I wasn't even sure I cared about Rachel. She traveled all over the world, so she could take of herself. But this was my one chance to do something special. Winning a trip to Thailand had seemed random at first, but then along came Kanda inviting us over, and then Janjira suddenly springing alive. My whole life had somehow been leading up to this very moment.

"Beaches are important, Rachel. I know that. But family is more important. If you were Sompong, you would feel the same way."

"You want us to skip Krabi."

"Yes."

"Where we already paid for the room."

"Yes."

"And planned our schedule."

They were Rachel's activities, not mine, so they didn't count.

"What if I want to go to Chiang Mai more than I've

ever wanted to do anything?" I felt like a child, but I couldn't help myself. I might have been the kid on Christmas Eve stubbornly waiting for Santa Claus to come down through the chimney. "We have to try!"

Yes. I was channeling a nine-year-old.

Rachel planted her chin on her fist. "You could go by yourself."

"Dylan said I had to go with an adult."

"The radio is only paying through Phuket. In Krabi we don't have any rules."

I didn't want to abandon Rachel, though, and I certainly didn't want to make a fool out of myself pretending I could speak any Thai. Instead I decided to pout. I'd been practicing for years, so I was pretty good at it.

"You promised Mom you'd watch out for me. I overheard you one night when the two of you were sitting in the kitchen. You promised Grandma too."

Rachel stretched her arms up above her head and arched her back. "I have confidence in you. You're tough. You can take care of yourself."

I wanted to think that she was right, but Rachel handled travel details much better than I did. Despite linguistic setbacks, she was fearless. When she needed something, she found a way to ask for it. I wasn't sure I could do the same.

"Krabi is supposed to be the best of the southern beaches," Rachel said slowly.

"You'll be in Greece soon. All the beaches you want. And all the Greek men. You don't seem the least bit interested in the guys around here."

"I haven't met the right one yet. But I return to Greece every year. This might be the only time I make it to Thailand. I have to see the best of the best."

"You're choosing geography over family."

"I know what I like."

"Krabi is like Patong," I said. Actually, I wasn't sure. "There won't be a noticeable difference in the quality of the beaches."

"Who told you that?"

I took a deep breath. How different could two beaches really be? "They're on almost the same latitude. Instead of going to see another beach, we can meet Khun Somchai Swoonswangs and his grandson. How cool is that? You said yourself we needed to talk to more natives."

She waved her hands through the air. "You don't see any natives around here?"

I gripped her arm. "Come back to Chiang Mai with me. I know it's crazy, but lots of things are. You won't regret it. We'll have an adventure."

She finished her last sip of Coke and crushed the can. "You have no idea whether I would regret it or not. What if I don't want to be a third wheel?"

Again Rachel surprised me. I hadn't given her permission to read my thoughts, so how was she managing such a feat?

"Our visit probably won't be anything like that."

"You're hoping it will be."

For a few seconds we listened to the kids shouting in the pool while I reviewed my wild romantic notions. Sompong was devoted to his grandfather, so certainly he was a wonderful person. His grandfather was a handsome man; naturally Sompong would be even more so. Thanks to his extensive training in English, he would be well educated and open-minded. Best of all, he would like me.

I didn't want to be unfair to Rachel and her own ideals for a vacation, but my conscience had given me the go-ahead. Letting herself be pried from the beach would entail a personal sacrifice on Rachel's part, but we could book a hotel with a small pool. As soon as Rachel reached Amiros, she could spend all day, every day, on the beach. The taverna where she worked didn't open until nine at night. That gave her more than enough time to swim laps during the day.

All Rachel needed was a push, so I played my trump

card. "Sompong offered us plane tickets."

Rachel nodded. "Is he rich or bored?"

"His aunt's husband is a pilot for Fly Thai."

"Hmmm."

"Otherwise we'd have to book tickets on the overnight train. The trip takes about seventeen hours."

As a cobra raising its hood, Rachel prepared to strike with objections, so I offered my other trump card. "We won't have any expenses because Sompong also said we could stay at his house."

She stared me down. "Staying at a guesthouse would be more appropriate."

A guesthouse was a smaller, homier version of a hotel. More importantly, it was significantly less expensive.

I'll even pay for it," I said. "Eventually."

Rachel took her Greek worry beads from her bag and twirled them. This was her fallback whenever she was trying to think things through. "I understand why you want to go to Chiang Mai. I'm afraid you might be disappointed."

"I'd be more disappointed if we didn't try. Sometimes you have to take a chance."

She twirled harder. She'd taken plenty of risks herself. That's how she'd gotten herself to Greece. But she never talked about the starry eyes.

"I need to do this. I don't know why." I patted my stomach. "Something in here is telling me that I have to go to Chiang Mai even though I don't understand the reasoning myself. And yes, I could go alone, but I need your help. Come with me."

Rachel put the Thai phrase book back in her bag. "We've already paid for tomorrow's excursion to Phang-nga. We can decide what to do after that. All right?"

I could hardly complain. Given our successful elephant adventure in Chiang Mai, I was the one who had insisted on the excursion.

"Fair enough. We'll decide tomorrow. Shall we take that walk on the beach now?"

She popped to her feet. "I thought you'd never ask."

From her cheerful response, I knew Rachel was leaning in my direction. All I needed was one more good argument. As we walked up and down the beach, that's exactly what I tried to think of.

We were unsure about the wisdom of buying tickets to FantaSea, a gala show held at an amusement park a short distance from town. The Las Vegas-style brochures promised way too much, but we liked the humor of the Frommer guide writer who'd labeled the venue a "guilty pleasure." The company's free transfer out to the park tipped our decision.

FantaSea turned out to be a perfect fantasy theme park without the rides. Its shops, eateries, and theatre blinked against a backdrop of neon lights. The van deposited us an hour before the theatrical show, the main feature of the evening, so we had plenty of time for shopping. I succumbed to a small stuffed elephant; it wouldn't break on the long trip back to Tucson.

The theatre offered a commanding façade of stone elephants that shot water into a vast pool. Tourists, including some Thais, scrambled for the best vantage points to take pictures of themselves against the wall. To the left, live elephants were posed for picture opportunities. For a few hundred baht you could climb an elephant and have your friends take your picture. Other tourists, mostly Asian, had rented traditional Thai dancing costumes with brocaded hats and gilded vests. They dashed around to the most picturesque spots, trying to snap as many shots as possible before they had to relinquish their costumes and go in for the show.

Inside the theatre lurked a final tourist trap: a photo opportunity with baby tigers. Two trainers were handing them off, bottle and all, to anyone who wanted to invest their ten bucks to take a picture with them. We watched as sets of American and Japanese tourists took turns.

"It's probably not good for the tigers," I said. "They're being handled by dozens of people in a short period of time."

"Right," said Rachel slowly. "But unless you're a talk show host, how often do you get to hold a baby tiger?" At the first chance we rushed to grab them.

A few minutes into the performance, I understood the reviewer's sense of a "guilty pleasure." FantaSea's sense of spectacle was enormous: plastic tree branches sprouted from the wall to create a jungle effect, leaves fell from the ceiling, elephants paraded through the aisles. The flimsy storyline made the weakest Broadway musical a master-piece by comparison, but the conceptual idea of "show" didn't apply. The focus of each moment was a fleeting im-age designed to stimulate the senses like a series of pin pricks. Chickens and goats and water buffalo ran past lav-ish sets, a couple sang in Thai, dancers and acrobats vied for attention, and politically incorrect Siamese "twins" told jokes. Overhead, trapeze artists swung from glow-in-the-dark neon cords. Baby elephants prepared the audience for the finale with eighteen of their elders.

While not on the scale of Disneyland, the venue re-minded me of the California attraction. I tried to imagine how such a lavish project had ever gotten off the ground. Investors might have argued that the venue was too inno-vative, too speculative, too difficult, too Thai. Yet someone, or probably someones, had come up with a vision. They'd had the courage to carry their adventure through to the end. Elephant statues spouting cascades of water? Why not? A show with eighteen of the biggest animals in Thailand on stage at the same time? Who said such a thing couldn't be done?

It was important to fly in the tired face of convention. The world needed creative leaders who accepted a chal-lenge. Sometimes their successes were long in coming. Sometimes they never came. Was that a good reason to give up before you started?

Walt Disney hadn't enjoyed instant success either. No one thought that an amusement park on the scale he envisioned could possibly be a financial triumph. Who had money to enjoy such silly things? On the other hand, who could afford to pass up a dream? The year I was an annoying fifth grader, I'd begged and begged to go to Disneyland. "It's so close by," I argued. "All my friends have gone!" I mapped it out for my mother and proudly showed her that Google maps calculated the driving time as only seven hours. What was the big deal?

In retrospect I understood my mother's hesitations perfectly. My father had just left for Monterrey, essentially abandoning us so that he could follow his dream job. Mom worked a clerical position at the university, but initially she feared we wouldn't make it on our own. My childish rants about Disneyland were silly and selfish, and my mother wisely ignored them. A few years later Rachel took me to Disneyland herself. I was in high school by then, but I appreciated the amusement park all the same. Remembering the disappointment I'd felt as a child, I appreciated my sister five times over.

By now I considered myself a responsible person. I helped Mom with household chores, took each college class seriously, and avoided credit card bills. I'd made mostly wise decisions. But not everything in life needed to be logical and practical. Every so often people needed confirmation that a trip through a haunted house could fuel the imagination of a lifetime. Dreams motivated people to take action and gave them hope. Not every dream came true. Most dreams didn't. But they couldn't come true if they were murdered before planting season or squashed before they had a chance to bloom. I'd been granted a special dream of my own, and it was my obligation to chase it.

As balloons fell from the ceiling to celebrate the end of the show, I made my decision. We still had another week and a half in Thailand. I'd spend one more day with Rachel on Phuket. All day long I would give her my best arguments for returning north. Then, even if I had to go by myself, I'd head back to Chiang Mai.

Spiritually, I didn't have a choice.

Chapter Fourteen

Travel agencies around Phuket offer endless package tours of the vicinity. Because local transport is complicated, Rachel had agreed to a tour for Phang-nga, pronounced "panang," site of the James Bond movie *The Man with the Golden Gun*. I wasn't sold on Roger Moore, but the promos showed intriguing mountainous rocks snaking out of the sea. The tour promised a bird's eye view of natural wonders, including a canoe trip among the area's prized limestone cliffs.

By eight a.m. we were in the mini-van heading northeast for our sixty-mile trip with a Malay couple, two brothers who were college students from Guadalajara, a male driver, and a young female guide named Darana. Neither Rachel nor I felt like talking. I was too busy thinking about Chiang Mai, plus we were both studying the ominous clouds that lurked outside. The Malay couple read; the Mexicans lightly snored. Up in the front seat, Darana chattered incessantly at the driver. I wondered if he appreciated the banter or whether he hoped his co-pilot would fall asleep. The prospect was unlikely.

The famous limestone cliffs of Phang-nga can only be reached by boat. When we arrived at the loading dock, we donned once-orange life vests and transferred to a long-necked fishing boat. The wizened boatman seemed oblivious to the light rain, but Rachel and I gazed into the mist. Long drops of rain shrouded the random cliffs in romantic mystery that was more gothic than Bond. The air was balmy; I wasn't sure it would stay that way.

A few minutes later we came to the fishing village of Phang-nga. Surrounded by natural beauty, the village was famous for being Thailand's most faithful Muslim outpost. All our guidebooks featured Phang-nga's picture. Now that we'd seen it, we could pretend to be seasoned tourists.

A mosque rose from the north end, symbolizing protection, but the village was either peaceful or dead. We passed rows of docks leading to restaurants before we saw a sign of life: a lone boy sweeping the wooden walkways. When we pulled alongside the final restaurant, another boy came running out. The boatman had brought him supplies. Tourists would swarm the area in the early afternoon, and the kitchen staff would need all morning to prepare.

Once past the town, the fishing boat transferred us to the tour's base camp, which was a ship with wide rubber canoes tied to the aft. We were supposed to adjourn to the canoes to take a closer look at the cliffs surrounding us, but the rain had increased to a pour. Darana ushered us into a sheltered portion of the ship's upper deck, where we took turns pouring ourselves cups of stale coffee.

"Can we wait for the rain to die down?" I asked. The day's program, which included a visit to a Buddhist temple and a "traditional lunch," didn't allow much time for the canoeing segment. I was afraid that if we didn't get started right away, we'd miss our chance.

"Sure. No problem."

She spoke so quickly that I didn't trust her.

"I thought the rainy season wasn't going to start for another two weeks," said Rachel.

"Can start early," said Darana. She pointed at the blackening sky. "Maybe start for you."

My sister frowned. "It probably did. Hey, they're getting ahead of us!"

The brothers, having stripped to shorts and life vests, were piling into one of the canoes, determined to ignore the rain. Their native escort, a young boy, seemed equally enthusiastic. Rachel looked on wistfully.

"Can skip canoe," said Darana.

We ignored her. We were too busy trying to squeeze inside the awkward rain ponchos we'd bought in Patong. Rachel's was bright blue and mine was orange. We could be spotted in the dark three miles away.

The escort waiting to paddle for us looked about sixteen. He wore long shorts and a blue T-shirt that said "Phang-nga Canoes" in Thai and English. A plastic sack covered his head. So what that it was raining? Water surrounded us anyway, so why shouldn't it be coming down?

"Come on," the teen said. "Today everybody James Bond."

We rushed into the sturdy rubber canoe and set off behind the Mexicans. The Malay couple was not far behind.

"James Bond never had to put up with this," Rachel said as we neared the closest cliffs. She was trying to take a picture from underneath the hood of her poncho.

Our escort laughed and paused under a protected cave so that Rachel could take some hurried shots. Then he took us around the cliffs' edges and the cavernous overhangs made of barnacled shells. He played "duck" with us, guiding the canoe under low stretches such that we had to lie on our backs to avoid crunching our heads into the rocks. He submerged his paddle to show that the water was only a few feet deep. When I stuck my hand in the sea, I was surprised to find that it was warm.

By the time we pulled into a tiny islet alongside the other two canoes, the rain had stopped. The Mexican brothers immediately jumped from the canoe to wade in the water. Then they started a water fight.

"I can't stand this," said Rachel. She threw off her poncho, never mind that it had actually kept her dry, and joined the guys in the water. The polite Malay woman seemed surprised, but finally she and I were swept up in the moment. Despite our efforts to ward off the rain, we now submerged ourselves.

While Rachel and I tread water, the Malay man took off rowing, and the Thai boys dared the brothers to perform back flips off the canoes. The Mexicans wouldn't budge.

"The water isn't deep enough," Pedro said.

To prove him wrong, his rower did a back flip with a twist, grinning the whole time.

"Come on," Rachel told the brothers. "Don't tell me you're worn out!"

Sheepishly, they admitted that they were.

"Sis!" she called out.

I nodded. I'd read her mind. We each climbed onto a canoe. In tandem, we did awkward back flips off the ends. The water was so shallow that I hit my knees on the slimy bottom, but the ground was too soft to be painful, and the applause was too loud for me to admit to any miscalculation. "Girls is number one!" our paddler cried. The other natives roared.

We'd started drying off when the rain hit again, this time in such big cold drops that we weren't sorry to hurry back to the base camp. But our commune with the rain had barely started. We transferred to another long-necked boat with another boatman who was oblivious to the rain or to the falling temperatures. He hadn't unrolled the plastic awnings that could be used as a shield, so we shivered all the way to James Bond Island.

"Twenty-five minutes!" Darana shouted cheerfully.

We assumed she was kidding. Even with ponchos, we couldn't enjoy sightseeing because the water was cascading in sheets and the temperature had plunged accordingly. The only refuge was the lid of a wide cave, where an army of Japanese tourists already huddled. We rushed to join them, bypassing vendors who were even more disappointed than we were. They had bravely covered their rows of shell trinkets with plastic, still hoping for sales, but the rain had made us all purposeful. We were here to see the vertical mini-cliff that the Bond film had immortalized, capture it on film, which we did with great difficulty by shielding our cameras with our ponchos, and then find a high dry place to stand so that we wouldn't feel as miserable.

"That was the entrance to the bad guy's hideout," Rachel shivered, pointing to the cliff. "An antenna rose from the peak."

I hadn't seen the film. "Did the bad guy live in a cave?"

"It was more elaborate than that. Then he and James Bond chased each other all around these limestone cliffs."

"In boats?"

"I think. Or maybe in planes." She shivered again.

"How much of the movie takes place here?"

"About ten minutes."

She looked so pathetic that I didn't complain.

The van driver was as glad to head back to Phuket as the rest of us were. We didn't have to ask him to turn on the heat; he did so automatically because our teeth chattered in unison. As the strength of the rain alternated between heavy and heavier, the windshield wipers flapped with loud, dull slaps.

I was almost asleep, my arm curled uncomfortably into the fold of the van's armrest. In the background I listened to Rachel and Darana. My sister had asked a single question, but our guide had plunged into her life story. She'd reached the part about moving in with her boyfriend's family a few months earlier.

"His mom doesn't mind if you live there?" Rachel asked.

"Why she mind? I make good money during tourist season. Now season over, but can't help for that."

"Over?"

My eyes opened.

Darana tapped the front window. "For rainy season, we take tours one, two days a week."

"That's all?" I asked.

"You saw. Today is so and so. When real rain comes,

we cannot take canoes. Tourists takes pictures from big boat and return early Phuket."

"That's not much of a tour," Rachel noted.

"That's why tomorrow we already cancel tour. Forecast big rain. Rain all week."

I sat straight up.

"On all of Phuket?"

"All of peninsula."

"Both sides?" asked Rachel.

Darana nodded with her head, neck, and shoulders.

"Krabi?" I asked.

"Same rain as here."

At the edge of Patong, the driver slowed to a crawl. The streets had disappeared into the downpour. Water had overtaken the curb, running into the open-door shops whose keepers sloshed about in sandals as they fretted about the lack of sales. The usual line of tourists had been reduced to a few drenched souls who'd given up trying to use umbrellas.

"This is incredible!" I exclaimed.

"No," Darana replied. "Is the nature. Same every year."

Alongside the van, a drunk American did a poor imitation of Gene Kelley, pretending to enjoy himself as he sang to streams of water.

"I hate the rain because bad business, but it keep Phuket beautiful," Darana said. "So what you can do?"

The driver let us off at our hotel. As soon as we stepped outside the van, water raced up our legs. We dashed to our door within twenty seconds and then stood on the porch while water dripped from our backpacks.

The rainy season. A true godsend.

A few phone calls and ten hours later, Rachel and I were on an early morning flight to Chiang Mai. Rachel sat by the window, saying goodbye to the beaches.

Luckily, it was about to rain.

Chapter Fifteen

We stumbled off the plane dazed because we'd fallen asleep during the last minutes of the flight. As we staggered towards the baggage claim, my carry-on slipped off my shoulder, and half the contents spilled onto the floor. By the time we were watching swirls of suitcases glide past on the carousel, I was ready to fall asleep again.

Rachel tapped my shoulder. "I thought you were going to call Sompong after we reached the guesthouse."

"That's what we decided last night. Why?"

"I think that's your man," Rachel whispered.

She was studying a native who looked more dazed than we did. He was a little taller than my five-feet-seven and no longer slender. His nose was a little too big for his face while his eyes were round and wide. A gold bracelet adorned his right wrist. A necklace, barely visible, lay between his black shirt and white cotton undershirt. Even though it was at least ninety degrees, he wore jeans and loafers. Everybody sported shorts and sandals.

"Sompong?" I asked as I approached. When he nodded, I held out my hand. A clammy one clasped mine as the man smiled.

This was Sompong, the man I had been imagining. I was sure his awkward smile matched mine. Neither of us could think of what to say, so we stared at one another instead. His skin was a beautiful dark brown. His curly black hair, parted in the middle, waved up and over his head on either side. I wanted to pat down the strands of hair that had broken rank.

"I'm Rachel!" She thrust herself between us so that we wouldn't turn into statues. "Nice to meet you. My sister was so excited to get your emails."

"I was excited to receive hers." His voice was soft and sweet like a chocolate bar, as if he only spoke of pleasant things.

"Sompong," Rachel continued, "what are you doing at the airport? I thought we were meeting you tonight."

"I knew you would be tired from your journey, so I thought you might appreciate a ride."

Chivalry alive? Up until now, I'd only read about it.

"I hope you do not find me presumptuous, but since I have a car —"

"Thanks so much," Rachel said as she retrieved our bags from the conveyer belt.

"I will take those." Sompong pointed sideways with his chin. "I have left the car out that way."

"This is a wonderful surprise," said Rachel. "It's extremely kind of you."

"It is not a problem. I had nothing important to do this morning." He led us out to an old Nissan Sentry whose white roof had faded into blotches. The vehicle was newer than my '96 Toyota, and it had been recently vacuumed. "I apologize for my ancient vehicle."

"It probably runs," said Rachel as she scrambled into the backseat. "Besides that, who cares?"

We pulled away from the airport and headed towards the walls of the old city. Sompong drove us past the fancy hotel we'd stayed in during our previous visit and started down a *soi*, a narrow lane.

"How's your grandfather?" I asked.

Sompong drove carefully, making constant use of the rearview mirror to anticipate the assortment of scooters and bicycles that approached on either side. "He is almost always the same. In the morning he walks slowly in the garden. That is his best hour. After lunch he takes a long nap. In the early evening he revives for a short period of time."

"Would you rather take us to see him now?" Rachel asked.

"You need the chance to relax after your trip. Then, tonight, we can share a pleasant meal at our house."

Sompong turned down another soi, passing several other guesthouses before pulling up in front of Baan Jan Come, where he had made arrangements for us.

"May we bring something to dinner with us?" Rachel asked. "We don't want you to go to a lot of work."

"Please, you have come many kilometers as a favor. I would not ask you to do more than that."

The proprietor of the guesthouse, a lanky man with a tiny moustache and quick eyes, met us at the curb and exchanged quick words in Thai with Sompong. "I have good room for you," the man said. "You like here."

We stepped inside a reception area while the man went to doublecheck on our room.

"Your friend?" Rachel asked Sompong.

"A friend of friends. But all the foreigners who stay here enjoy this place."

I understood why. It was cozier than a hotel and more personal. The guest rooms were upstairs while the main floor served as the family's house as well as the reception lobby. The open-air space contained couches, a bookcase of abandoned paperbacks, an aquarium, several sets of dining tables, potted plants, and a bar counter with high stools. In the far corner stood a drum set. Atop the bar, a TV announcer shouted local news. For a moment I felt like I was at my cousins' house in Mexico, which had a similarly open, disheveled, well-lived look.

"May I come for you at seven?" Sompong asked. "That should give you enough time for a nap."

Rachel checked her watch and nodded. She was happy to get rid of Sompong, but she had no intentions of napping when there were unvisited wats nearby.

"That would be great," I said. I was still stunned he'd

shown up at the airport and that Rachel had identified him so swiftly.

He shook our hands and waved goodbye.

Rachel rushed upstairs, never mind that she was carrying an increasingly heavy bag. I followed behind, trying to keep up. I knew that if I didn't want to go "watting" with her, I'd have to act dead on my feet. But how could I pretend to be tired when all I could think of was how hard it would be to wait for seven o'clock?

I stood before the full-length mirror in our room and stuck out my tongue.

"You look fine," Rachel said.

I'd bought a silk skirt on Phuket. The red design was simple, but I felt silly wearing a piece of cloth with a gold border. "I look like a tourist. The kind that buys local stuff and doesn't know what to do with it."

Rachel motioned for me to turn in a circle. "It's flattering because it fits so well."

"You mean it's tight."

"It shows you off."

I started to untie the cloth strap that substituted for a zipper, but Rachel shook her head. "What else could you wear? One of your size XXX T-shirts?"

After two weeks of drip-drying, my entire wardrobe had stretched into cotton tents. "I don't know what to wear."

"Sis, it doesn't matter! We're not going to a dinner party for fashion models. There's me, Sompong, and an old man who won't remember what you wore."

"I don't want Sompong to think I'm too ...."

"What?"

"Too I don't know."

Rachel patted her dress shorts. At least her blouse hadn't gone limp the way all my cotton garments had. "He's a computer engineer, right?"

"Right."

"And he designs websites."

"Right."

"How often does he see females?"

"Rachel! That's not fair."

"How many women take computer classes?"

"Quite a few."

"In Thailand?"

On the campus of CMET I'd seen far more men than women. "I'm sure there were some women in his classes."

"Right. And now he's employed by a company, but he mostly works out of his house so that he can care for his grandfather. He doesn't have dating material coming out of his ears."

I tugged on my skirt, centering it. "Okay, not."

"So don't worry about your skirt."

I kept staring at the mirror. "I'm so pale. Do you think makeup would help?"

"Did you bring any?"

"No."

"So don't worry about that either. Perfume might be nice."

"By accident I applied it twice."

Rachel smiled. "Remember when you went to your first high school dance?"

"I try not to." I'd spent hours getting ready. Finally Mom tired of listening to my anal questions about shades of fingernail polish and called in Rachel. Characteristically, my sister traipsed into my bedroom, took one glance, pronounced me ready for a beauty pageant, and went to raid the refrigerator. By the time my date arrived, an hour late, he was so drunk he couldn't see straight. He acquiesced when I suggested that we take my car to the dance, but within fifteen minutes, he'd passed out in the school bathroom. I never asked how he got home, but it wasn't with me.

"Do you have the elephant?"

For the eighth time, I checked for the velvet bag inside my purse. "Yes."

"It's five to seven," Rachel said. "Let's go downstairs so Sompong doesn't have to wait."

He was already waiting. He was sitting at the family dinner table, chatting with the proprietor's wife, two maids, and a small child.

"Good evening, you—" Sompong's words got stuck somewhere between his throat and his mouth. For a bad moment I was afraid I was inappropriate, but then his eyes twinkled. "You look so nice," he said as he whisked us off.

We passed the night market and the Mae Nam Ping River, which so far had been the eastern limit to our own version of Chiang Mai. It was exciting to be heading to a different area of town.

"I'm sorry you had to come so far out of your way to fetch us," I said.

"It is not that far. I live just past Shinawatra."

"What's that?" Rachel and I asked in union.

Sompong's eyes didn't leave the road, but he swallowed a laugh. "You are not shoppers."

"Not especially," said Rachel. She picked lint off her "dress" shorts, the ones she'd bought on sale from Target at the end of the previous season.

"Shinawatra is a famous silk store. Many people come to Chiang Mai to visit it."

"Can't they buy the same thing in Bangkok?" asked Rachel.

"Very nearly." Sompong turned onto a highway. "But the finest silk, and the best tailors, well, how can I say? I have no silk suits, but every day I pass Shinawatra and there are busloads of shoppers. I have seen the advertisements my whole life. The company is very popular."

Moments later we spotted signs for Shinawatra, Legend of Thai Silk. The biggest sign, well lit, boasted free parking, but now the lot was filled with Shinawatra vans.

"I guess they deliver," Rachel said.

"All day long, their drivers bring people to the store and then take them back to their hotels. It is big business."

"I've never heard of such a thing," said Rachel.

"Special Thai service," winked Sompong. He turned onto a small soi lined by modest houses on either side. Again I thought of Mexico.

"We have arrived home," he said quietly.

Chapter Sixteen

After pulling into a narrow driveway, Sompong got out of the car so that he could slide open a metal gate. He drove past a spirit house, which was a miniature wooden house designed to offer shelter to homeless spirits, and continued to a carport surrounded by shade trees and coarse grass. Beside the carport, men's shirts danced on a clothesline.

The house consisted of two stories distinctly marked by color. The bottom floor was white. The brown wooden trim around its windows matched the color of the second floor. I liked the odd contrast. In our neighborhood back home the houses might be pink or green or blue, but most were painted all one color. Sompong's house was more unusual.

The bright porch light that hung from the balcony gave the home a friendly look. We heard dogs barking from all directions, but only one, a medium-brown mutt, rushed to greet us. Sompong pet its ears before leading us inside.

"Grandfather?" Sompong called out in Thai as he kicked off his shoes.

A woman replied from the kitchen.

"*¿Quién diablos es esa?*" *Who in the devil is that?* I asked Rachel. I immediately felt silly and possessive. Why wouldn't there be a woman in the house?

"*A lo mejor la criada.*"

Of course. He'd told me there was a maid; he needed someone to stay in the house whenever he was away.

Sompong led us through the hall to the living room.

The area was dominated by a large vinyl couch. Its cushions were decorated with sequined elephants. A coffee table stretched before the couch, its coasters swimming on the smooth teak surface. A glass ashtray with "Chiang Mai" printed on it weighed down a Thai-language newspaper. An easy chair held its ground between a knickknack cabinet and a metal stand holding a small TV.

"Sit down, sit down," Sompong told us. We did so while he disappeared into the room beyond. He returned with a girl in tow. "This is Nui. She has been helping with Grandfather."

Nui was probably older than the seventeen that she looked. She was short and thin, and her long straight hair clung to her blouse. She greeted us in Thai and disappeared into the kitchen.

"We will have dinner soon. May I offer you a drink?" Sompong asked.

We didn't answer.

"Whisky, Singha beer, Chang beer ...."

"Today was a scorcher," said Rachel. "Could we start with cold water?"

He seemed surprised but nodded and disappeared.

"¿Y ahora que hacemos?" I whispered. Now what do we do?

"Relájate. No te apures." Relax. Don't worry.

I knew she was right, but my umpteen-thousand-mile trek from Tucson had been leading up to this very moment, and all I could think about was how strange the situation was. We were seated at the house of a man we'd barely met on a mission from a woman we couldn't talk to in a strange country where we could barely say hello in the native tongue. We were at an unusual disadvantage.

Sompong returned with three crystal glasses filled with water that he carried on a black wooden tray painted with golden leaves. The glasses shook as he walked. "Please, sit back and relax."

We complied as much as possible. We made small talk about how warm the day had been. When Sompong asked if we'd had a restful afternoon, I laughed until Rachel explained the names of the three wats she'd dragged me to see. While he and Rachel exchanged tidbits of knowledge about the city, I imagined what the house had looked like fifty years ago. Probably very little had changed.

Sompong sat on the edge of the easy chair as if he might need to dash to his feet while Rachel kept the dialogue going by asking about current events. I followed the banter, glad I didn't need to jump into the conversation. For once I preferred to sit quietly and listen. After a couple of weeks in hotels, it was a luxury to be in an actual house again, especially when enticing aromas hinted that dinner was moments away.

More importantly, though, Rachel and I had finally reached the Swoonswangs. I wanted to text the Tamarins, or better yet Skype them. Instead I forced myself to contain my excitement.

Rachel downed her glass and set it back down on the tray. "Where's Somchai?"

Wait, I wanted to tell Rachel. *Don't be impatient. Savor the moment.*

"He is resting. Soon I will go for him."

In the meantime the innocent little purple elephant burnt a hole in my pocket. I took a deep breath and reached into my purse. "This has waited long enough." I pulled out Janjira's bag and handed it to Sompong.

"This was given to you at the house of your friend?"

"With strict instructions," I said. "See what you think."

With gentle, slender hands, Sompong removed the elephant from the bag, turning it to catch the light much the way I often did. He considered the trunk and the sparkles, testing the statue's weight by holding it in one hand. Finally he stood the elephant on the coffee table. "It is finely made, but you can find many such things in Thailand."

"You agree that it's Thai workmanship, then?" I asked.

"We've looked all around, but we haven't found any similar pieces."

"Everywhere they sell elephant statues in this country, but I have not paid much attention. Grandfather has some." Sompong crossed over to the cabinet. He opened the glass door, disturbing a collection of dust. The middle shelves displayed colored plates and temple replicas. The top shelf displayed jungle animals — mostly elephants.

None of us were tall enough to see clearly, but Sompong reached up into the cabinet and took down some statues. "Let's put them on the table so we can take a good look."

Somchai's collection wasn't fancy or valuable. It was cute and touristy, like mine. One elephant was made of small sea shells, two of glass, and several of porcelain. Others were made of wood or stone. The largest elephant, made of red silk, bore a tag from Shinawatra.

"My grandfather has always liked elephants. I am not sure why."

"We rode one the other day," said Rachel. "It was great!"

"Yes, your sister told me in her email."

"Have you ever ridden an elephant?" I asked.

"Many times. My grandfather's friend worked for a trekking company. Grandfather and I used to visit him every Saturday, and he would always let me take a ride."

Rachel picked up a black elephant decorated with pieces of glass and beads. "You have fond memories."

"Oh, yes. I am very grateful. Grandfather did everything he could for me."

I'd gotten details over email. Somchai, Sompong's widowed maternal grandfather, raised him after his parents had been killed in a car accident. Sompong had two aunts on his mother's side, but they had families of their own.

"I am sorry that now, when you meet him . . ." He sighed with his whole chest. "He is old now. It is not his fault. When he sees me, or Nui, or his dog, his face lights up, but we do not think he understands."

Sompong lowered his head, and for a moment I thought he was praying. Then I realized he was hiding his pain. I tried to hide my own disappointment. We'd discovered the right old man, but we'd arrived several years too late.

If only we'd known to come sooner.

Nui called to Sompong from the other room. He excused himself, and we heard the clattering of heavy dishes. Then Nui appeared and motioned us into the dining room where settings had been prepared: soup bowls, plates, napkins, and silverware.

Sompong carried in a steaming dish. "We have made curry soup. I hope you enjoy it."

We started to sit down. "And your grandfather?" I asked.

"He is still asleep, but he will wake up soon. We let him do so of his own accord. We have considered putting him on a schedule, but in the end we do not bother."

"It's not like he has to go to work in the morning," said Rachel. "I wouldn't worry about it."

"No," said Sompong. "We have plenty of other things to worry about. When someone is sick, you quickly learn to change your priorities. That is one benefit, I guess you could say."

It wasn't much of a benefit. Sompong tried to sound positive, but I couldn't imagine the burden. Worse yet, he didn't seem to have anyone to share it with besides the maid.

"Eat, eat," Sompong said.

We were happy to comply. For days Rachel and I had dined on delicious meals at a variety of restaurants, but the homemade dish used richer oils and a greater variety of spices. I took the time to smell each bite. I doubled my vow to dine on Thai food at least once a week after I returned to Tucson.

When Nui brought out a salad of cucumbers, lettuce, onions, tomatoes, and spicy beef, Rachel got brave. *"Takiem ka?"*

Nui looked at her blankly.

"Takiem ka," Rachel repeated decisively.

Nui turned to her employer and shot out a string of incomprehensible words. After Sompong quietly replied, Nui brought in a set of chopsticks.

Rachel thanked the girl with a frown. "So much for Thai lessons. No matter what I try to say, no one understands me."

"What you said was fine," Sompong said gently. "You are doing splendidly to attempt any Thai words at all. Please give yourself some credit."

"How can I? A month of study and I can't even say a simple word correctly."

"Your pronunciation was reasonable. The problem is that since so few Westerners learn Thai, we are simply unprepared. When you utter a Thai word, we cannot imagine that we have heard right."

"That's not very comforting."

"You have noticed yourself that Thai is a difficult language."

"Oh, yes."

"That is why our tourists rarely trouble themselves with it. Not that I blame them." He pointed to the new pot that Nui had set on the table. "Please, eat heartily. Nui has worked hard to prepare some special dishes for us."

Rachel didn't trust Sompong's explanations, but she refocused her attention on the vegetable dish and bowl of sticky rice that now awaited us. When Rachel tried to serve herself some of the rice, it stuck to the container. She used so much force that half of the bowl's contents flew across the table. Her obvious embarrassment sent us into such peals of laughter that all four of us were crying by the time Somchai slowly worked his way into the room.

He looked completely different from the smiling young man in the photograph. The current-day Somchai was a small, wrinkly man with a kind face but a vacant look in his eye. He wore lose workout shorts, an old short-sleeved shirt with blue stripes, and soft moccasins that protected his feet. He propelled himself forward through mini-steps, left foot first. When he saw Sompong, he smiled with a grunt. Sompong stood and kissed him. He and Nui helped Somchai into a chair because he had little control of his legs.

"These girls have come to see you," Sompong said. The old man considered us for a second before motioning at the food, or perhaps he'd been simply staring into space.

With great care Nui prepared the old man a plate, cutting all the vegetables into small bites while Sompong spooned them in. They didn't need to talk because the pattern was well established. Their own plates were abandoned while they helped Somchai.

I finished my own meal with a lump in my throat. I was too young to remember much about my maternal grandfather, but Rachel spoke vividly of the way he'd suffered through Alzheimer's. The rest of the family had suffered as they watched him grow steadily weaker, but they had all taken turns to help out. No wonder Sompong needed an assistant; caring for Somchai would be a full-time job.

As soon as Somchai tired of eating, Nui and Sompong led him to the living room and sat him down on the couch. Rachel and I followed behind. After the man caught his breath and situated himself, he noticed the elephants on the table. He reached for them one at a time, considering each briefly before setting it back down.

"The girls have brought a gift for you all the way from America," said Sompong. Eagerly he presented the velvet pouch to his grandfather.

Somchai's demeanor changed. He stared at the pouch as if he wanted to stare through it. Time stood still for him as he focused his attention. He brought the pouch closer and closer to his face until his eyes flickered. Then his hands started trembling. Sompong caught the pouch as it fell from his grandfather's hands.

"Look, Grandfather." Sompong pulled the elephant out of its case, and the old man reached for it, mumbling. He grasped it sharply with his right hand and kissed it. Tears filled his eyes as he made a final unintelligible sound. Clutching the elephant to his chest, he took labored breaths before slumping forward. Sompong was fast enough to break his fall but not prevent it. The man fell into the coffee table, scattering the elephants, and then landed on the floor, his thin body slipping between the table and the couch on the way down.

Sompong dove to the floor, examining the man's head. He shouted at Nui, who ran for a phone. Then he glared at me. "How dare you come here to hurt my grandfather!"

"But—"

Sompong's eyes had grown wide. As he spoke, he did arm circles. "You have caused him a heart attack! If he dies now, it will be your fault!"

Our host had gone out of his mind.

"All I did was bring a present!"

Sompong switched to jumping jacks, and at any minute I expected some ninja kicking. "You brought a curse!"

We had not. If anything, we'd brought a peace offering from an earlier time period. I glued my hands to my hips. "You don't know what you're talking about!"

"A curse!"

I couldn't believe what I was hearing. We'd brought a simple elephant as gifted from a long-lost sister. A curse indeed. What an idiot! Didn't Sompong realize I'd spent nearly two weeks looking for him? That I'd wasted my vacation hunting him down? That all my interest in Thailand was tied up inside that one velvet pouch?

Rachel tapped my shoulder. "Time to go. Grab your purse."

"You represent evil!" Sompong yelled. "You have brought darkness! Leave this house at once!"

A stone elephant had sent Somchai into a frenzy. What was he imagining?

"Thanks for dinner," Rachel said, pulling me behind her. *"Korp Khun ka,"* she called to Nui, who was too unnerved to use the phone she held in her hand.

Rachel dragged me to the front door even though I protested the entire time. I wanted to shake Sompong and tell him to get ahold of himself. He should have been delighted that his grandfather had shown any reaction at all.

We exited the house and stumbled down the driveway while our eyes adjusted to the dark. Sompong had locked the metal gate behind him, so we climbed over it, racing into the street, ignoring neighboring barking dogs that seemed as angry as Sompong.

"Shit," said Rachel. "I forgot my jacket."

While I stood trembling she climbed back over the fence and raced to the door, but instead of entering the house she turned around and rejoined me.

"What happened?"

"Nui and Sompong are yelling at each other. It's an old jacket anyway. Maybe it'll fit Nui."

"So now what?"

"Now we're on our own."

We'd traveled all the way from Phuket to deliver a package that we should have dumped along the way. Our evening was ruined, our trip was tarnished, and worst of all, I was wearing a stupid skirt that would have been more appropriate for Halloween.

Chapter Seventeen

We ran down the soi until we hit the main road. Rachel pointed left. A big road sign read Lamphun 23, Doi Suthep 23, but there weren't any indications for Chiang Mai.

"Didn't we come from this direction?" she asked.

"I don't remember." I hadn't paid attention to our surroundings. In the middle of a country I knew almost nothing about, in the car of a stranger I'd barely met, I hadn't had the sense to keep my eyes on the road. During the whole drive to the house, I'd been stealing glances at Sompong.

As we hurried along, cars whizzed by at dizzying speeds, their lights balls of white fire against the black night.

Rachel pointed to a pink neon sign. "Shinawatra. From here we go straight."

I followed behind, disoriented. We'd gone from a comfortable home to a swirl of engines and exhaust fumes. The contrast took me off guard.

Suddenly Rachel grabbed my hand and drew me behind one of the Shinawatra tourist vans that our host had pointed out to us earlier. "Sompong!" she hissed.

As I peered around the van, the Nissan roared past. Nui was in the backseat fanning Somchai.

"They must be on their way to the hospital," Rachel said.

"Do you think he'll pull through?" I asked.

"That old guy is tougher than he looks. He got excited and lost his breath. He wasn't having a heart attack."

"You're sure?"

"Pretty sure. Naturally, at his age he's so brittle that any fall could be a bad one, but I don't think he got hurt."

We scurried along the road while cars passed uncomfortably close and fast. There wasn't any sidewalk; we were pedestrians on a highway, not tourists strolling around a residential area. Every time a car got too close, I involuntarily shuddered.

"Are you doing okay?" Rachel shouted without turning around to check.

"I can't walk fast in this stupid skirt," I shouted back. But that wasn't my biggest problem. I'd dragged Rachel on a goose chase that hadn't turned out to be fun. I wanted to punch Sompong for thinking ill of us when our intentions had been practically angelic, but instead I hadn't stood up to him. More immediately, since I was wearing nice shoes instead of rubber sandals, my feet hurt worse than they usually did.

We reached the end of a block, huddling together before attempting to dart across lanes of traffic.

"How far are we from Chiang Mai?" I asked.

"You don't want to know."

"Are you sure there's no Uber in this country?"

"It was banned. If we worked at it hard enough, we could figure out how to call a taxi. Or just walk."

Walking seemed like the smartest option until a few minutes later when we reached a sign that said Chiang Mai–9 Kms. That meant we were roughly five miles from town.

We reached the parking lot of a commercial establishment where we could walk side by side for a couple of minutes without worrying about traffic. "I'm so, so sorry I got you into this mess. You were right; Sompong is a nut. I should have listened."

Rachel kicked a rock, which I knew was her usual sign of high irritation. "It's not your fault. But can you actually believe I'd be happy to see a tuk-tuk?"

Instead not a single one was in sight.

"I would pay for a cab even if the driver was as crazy as the one we found at the airport," I said.

"Right. This is exactly like New York City. Cabs on every corner."

We kept trudging, walking single file to stay as safe as possible. At first I'd felt upset that Sompong had misjudged us. Now the thought made me angry. We'd done so much for his grandfather, but instead of showing the least bit of understanding, he'd jumped to conclusions and made the stupidest assumptions. I tried to put myself in his shoes: What if someone had come with a package that upset my grandma? But there was no reverse side. Grandma knew all hundred or so of her relatives.

With each step I felt angrier. Sompong hadn't given us a chance to explain. He didn't even know what had happened to his grandfather. What if for one brief moment the man had felt tremendous happiness? Given his current quality of life, would it be a tragedy if he passed?

I started kicking rocks myself.

We'd trudged about a mile when a dusty old pickup carrying a bed full of pineapples paused alongside us. A dark, middle-aged woman poked her head out of the passenger-side window; a plump man smiled from his spot behind the wheel.

"Chiang Mai?" Rachel asked hopefully.

The woman nodded and indicated the truck bed. Rachel ran to the back end, placing a foot on the bumper to scramble up. She made a place to sit by moving a few pineapples out of the way and then reached to give me a hand.

Two women out alone in a foreign country hitchhiking at night? I could imagine Grandma having a fit at the thought of it. I wanted time to consider our options, but Rachel was gesturing wildly.

"Hurry!"

I hiked up my skirt until it was almost around my

hips. Then I stepped on the bumper, grabbed Rachel's arm, and flung myself over the tailgate.

"Ouch!" I'd sat on a pineapple. "You think this is safe?"

Rachel had turned so that the wind kicked her hair. "Safer than walking all night on a busy road in a country where pedestrians are viewed as obstacles. Besides, I've really got to go to the bathroom."

Inside the cab, our hosts chatted as if it were normal to pick up two stranded *farang*. From the way she calmly watched the scenery on either side, Rachel acted as if it were normal too. I wondered what was wrong with all three of them while I tried to imagine the worst-case scenario: the couple demanded more money than we had, pineapples went through our soft brains during a collision, we fell asleep and woke up in Laos.

We rumbled down the road while other vehicles zoomed by. As soon as I'd found a sweet spot among the pineapples, I relaxed enough to be thankful to be heading in the right direction. It was one thing to ruin my own evening and my own vacation, another to ruin my sister's. I closed my eyes, letting the wind whip tears off my face.

The pickup slowed when it reached the point where the Mae Nam Ping River bordered Chiang Mai's night market. The man called something over his shoulder.

"I can't understand where he's going," said Rachel. "We better get out right here."

She nodded and pointed, and our kind rescuer pulled over to the side. We crawled over the tailgate shouting *"korp Khun ka, korp Khun krup"* several times over. The couple nodded and drove on, seemingly unaware that they'd done us such a tremendous favor that we couldn't properly thank them for it. Even if they'd understood English, we wouldn't have found a coherent way to explain.

Chiang Mai was oblivious to our plight. The city was still in the midst of its evening bustle. Restaurants boasted groups of diners while barstools summoned partiers. Tourists carrying packages in large plastic bags filled the streets, laughing as they compared notes on their bargains. Idly waiting for new fares, tuk-tuk drivers lounged in their cabs.

"Lazy bums," I said. "They'd make a lot more money if they searched for stranded tourists."

Rachel ignored my humor. "Stop for a drink?"

She pointed to a bar called Western Rangers that sported a tacky façade that imitated the U.S. Southwest and a row of empty bar stools in the patio area. We perched ourselves where we could watch the street. Although my sister suggested that what I needed was a real drink, we ordered Cokes instead.

Guilt choked my throat. "Rachel, I'm so sorry I dragged you back to Chiang Mai."

"Are you kidding? Tonight was more fun than a *telenovela*. A really good one."

I thought all the Mexican soap operas were bad, and I'd certainly never expected to be featured in one. "I'll buy you a new jacket tomorrow. I'm sure we can find one."

Her attention wavered as her eyes followed a good-looking Asian man down the street until he was out of sight.

"Who needs extra clothing to carry?" She pinched her arm. "This is perfect weather. It's hardly ever been cold enough for a second layer."

"At least now I won't have to carry around that stupid elephant." I wondered where it was by now. On the floor? In the old man's room? In the garbage after being crushed to pieces by a mad grandson?

No. The elephant was stone. It was uncrushable.

Well, perhaps it would succumb to a hammer.

"Check out that combination!" Rachel whispered. A Western man walked by in a plaid shirt and striped pants. "Either he's out of clothes or he dresses badly to get attention."

The man's clashing patterns drew stares from half the

passersby. In my tourist skirt and dress sandals, I stood out even more than he did. I was certain a pineapple had ripped my fabric in several places, but I hadn't bothered to check.

"Do you think Somchai recognized the elephant?" I asked.

Rachel rearranged herself on the bar stool. "I'd say it reminded him of something he hadn't thought about for a long time."

"So he's not completely out of it?"

She shrugged. "I don't know that much about dementia, if that's what he has. But he did seem to have a genuine response. Maybe he has sensations, like when you go to the other room to fetch something, but once you're there, you can't remember what you wanted. You're left with the odd notion of something half-remembered."

"Then why the violent reaction?"

"What if you lost track of me for fifty years, thought I was dead, and then I suddenly resurfaced? That would be enough to spook anybody."

"Why wouldn't Janjira have contacted him earlier?"

"Maybe they had a fight. It could be like Grandma and Uncle Jaime, only more extreme."

Our grandmother spent half the year on speaking terms with her brother and the other half too mad to talk to him. Rachel and I had never figured it out, and we'd given up trying. Since Uncle Jaime lived in Tucson, the situation was awkward. Mom kept track of their feuds somehow, skillfully inviting Uncle Jaime to dinner on occasions when Grandma was spending the evening playing canasta with her lady friends.

Rachel swiveled on her stool. "Here's another thing. Let's say they didn't want to communicate for a while, and by the time they did, they'd lost one another's addresses. Janjira was so far away she might not have had any sources to turn to. People didn't used to travel so much, and it was harder to send letters. Think how hard it's been for us to track down Somchai even with the benefits of modern technology."

"True. Still, it's odd that she suddenly wanted to make contact."

"If Janjira senses she's near the end, she might be anxious to make amends."

"That sounds reasonable," I said, "but are you sure Janjira is coherent enough to sense anything?"

Rachel answered by slurping her Coke. Then I helped her analyze the fashions of all the passersby.

It was one a.m. before we returned to Baan Jan Come. The guesthouse lobby was dead quiet. A dim nightlight between the couches led us to the stairs.

I paused at the door to our third-floor room and blew dust off our patio chairs. "I'll sit outside for a while."

"I'll rinse off," said Rachel. The temperature had only dropped to eighty-five. In lieu of air conditioning, a lukewarm shower was better than nothing.

I sat in the dark and listened to the bats flying in circles overhead. Rachel had done her best to distract me, but I needed time to process. I couldn't believe the evening had really happened. Although I had imagined many outcomes of a meeting with Sompong, fleeing from his house was not one of them. The more I remembered the Internet searches to find him, our email exchanges, and the events of the evening, the higher my temperature rose. Instead of learning about Thailand, I'd chased some silly fantasy as a child on an Easter egg hunt. At least little kids got to find the eggs, and half the time they were full of chocolate.

I was still cursing myself when Rachel joined me outside wearing a fluffy white towel as a bathrobe.

When I tried to apologize again she cut me off.

"At least we had an unusual evening. No package tours include what we got."

"I'm so angry."

"Try not to be. Sompong reacted out of fear. His grandfather is a big responsibility that he's managing by himself. Why don't Somchai's daughters take care of him?"

"They live out of town."

"It seems odd that they've abandoned their father, especially in a traditional country."

"I think it used to be more like Somchai taking care of Sompong, but by now the tables have turned."

"There's always a story behind the story. Never mind. Here's the thing: If taking care of this man is all on Sompong's head, you can't take his reaction too seriously. He's doing his best to handle a difficult situation. His grandfather is getting sicker and sicker, and there's nothing either of them can do about it. I'd be frightened too."

"Poor Sompong and all that, but he still kicked us out of his house."

Rachel swatted a bug. "He was in shock. Don't analyze it."

I couldn't imagine myself as a family caretaker, but I'd never had such responsibility. I barely managed to take care of myself. In fact I didn't. All I had to do was concentrate on getting through classes that I took at a university not three miles from my house. Whether Mom cooked dinner or not, she made sure food was in the refrigerator. I didn't have to worry about the electricity bill or the gas or the utilities. At home everything was automatic, yet I was spoiled enough to complain when I had two tests on the same day.

A dog's bark brought me back to reality. "Rachel, my intuition said to complete this mission. I worked hard to do so."

"Hard work is supposed to be good for something."

"My efforts turned into a disaster. How am I going to muddle my way through life if my intuition is worthless?"

"You were wrong this one time. Don't take it so hard. After all, you accomplished what you set out to do. Janjira asked us to deliver the elephant. We did! That's it."

"It never occurred to me anything could go wrong

once we found the right Somchai."

"What went wrong? We left before dessert, that's all. I don't know about you, but I'd already eaten plenty."

"By now Sompong hates me. He thinks I'm a witch or something."

"He probably thinks we both are! So what? Maybe this whole thing isn't about you. Some good may come of it. We can't pretend to know the final result."

"We'll never find out."

"Not necessarily. My bet is that Sompong will be on our doorstep tomorrow, apologizing."

I shook my head.

"If not tomorrow, because he might be tied up with a doctor or something, then the day after that."

"You really think so?"

"He's smart enough that he'll realize how much he overreacted. Watch and see."

A bat flew in our direction, barely missing the wall behind us.

"Maybe we should find a new guesthouse. Or leave town."

"Let's not move that fast," Rachel said. "We don't have to overreact just because he did. You might want to speak to Sompong before we head elsewhere."

"No."

"Never say never."

"I thought that was a James Bond movie."

Rachel shrugged off my criticism. "Let's get up early and take a day trip to Lamphun. We can make more extensive plans tomorrow night."

I didn't share Rachel's interest in Lamphun's famous temple, but the journey would keep us busy for the day. "Okay."

Rachel stood. "Coming inside?"

"Pretty soon."

Softly she shut the door behind her. I sulked in the

dark with the bats. I knew what was in store for me: a day of touring one super famous temple followed by visits to at least a dozen lesser ones. And given the mess I'd gotten us into, I wouldn't be able to complain.

Chapter Eighteen

When I woke up the next morning, Rachel was already making Greek-style iced coffee, meaning that she mixed instant coffee with sugar and water in a plastic shaker. At home she added ice; on the road she didn't bother. The result was awful. I tried it once and barely managed to spit it out instead of gagging. Rachel would have argued that her homestyle frappé was an acquired taste. I was glad I hadn't acquired it.

"Good morning!"

"Right," I answered without moving.

A guidebook lay face down on the dresser.

"Is there a train soon?" I asked.

Rachel shook her caffeinated concoction. "There are trains all day. I didn't expect you up for a while. You went to bed pretty late."

"I couldn't sleep. I'm afraid you're right, that Sompong might show up, and I'd rather leave before we have to talk to him."

"I'm ready when you are," said Rachel. She was already wearing her zip-off shorts and the blouse she'd rinsed the night before. After the previous evening's melodrama, she was fresh and relaxed, ready to pounce on the next touring challenge. After the way I'd screwed everything up, I was a perfect victim to her worst whims. If I were lucky, maybe lots of schoolchildren would want interviews, and I could skip most of the temples.

Quickly, I threw on dirty walking shorts and a purple tank top that now showed streak marks from sweat.

Minutes later we were locking the door behind us. We'd descended one flight of stairs before Rachel stopped short. I stumbled into her. We would have fallen down the stairs if she hadn't grabbed the rail.

"Sorry!" I called out.

"Shh!" She pointed to her ear. She was listening to voices.

I don't know why I hadn't noticed; maybe I wasn't awake yet. We crept down the next flight as if we were jewelry thieves at a gem show and peered over the railing. Sompong sat at the counter of the guesthouse bar, calmly chatting with the proprietor. Rachel's jacket lay on the stool beside him.

"Shit," I whispered. "What the hell is he doing here?"

"He's come to apologize."

I was stunned, but not so incapacitated that I didn't remember all my anger from the night before. "He should have thought of that last night! Now what do we do?"

The proprietor's wife bustled down the stairs, nearly sweeping us away with her broom. She smiled politely. She had pretty, soft features, and even early in the morning, she was alert and friendly.

"Man wait you!" She eagerly pointed downstairs.

I shook my head until it hurt.

"Man wait you!"

The woman started towards the bottom floor, but Rachel gently took her arm. "Bad man!" Rachel whispered. She pointed at me and mimicked crying. I vehemently nodded. "Go Lamphun, no man!" Rachel continued.

The woman must have had plenty of practice with foreign women to understand us so accurately. She nodded as she appraised us, chose gender over nationality, and motioned for us to follow. She led us back upstairs and down a service hall that led to another staircase that took us behind the reception desk and out to the main street through the garage. When we thanked her, she winked.

I hated Lamphun because by late morning I felt guilty about our escape. I could have been a little friendlier. I could have said hello rather than slipping out like a coward.

"Don't be upset with yourself," Rachel advised as we made our way into a small eatery.

"How do you know I'm upset?" I snapped.

"I just hauled you through three temples, and you didn't complain."

"Maybe I'm getting used to them."

"Mostly you're upset."

"I liked the lions." Lamphun's main wat was guarded by Burmese beasts. Rachel had me pose in front of them, but I kept my sunglasses on in case my eyes were still red. The site contained a huge golden chedi whose bright shine hurt our eyes. Other than the lions and the golden dome, the wat didn't distinguish itself from the host I'd seen in Chiang Mai other than that I was more miserable while walking around it.

Rachel had diligently consulted her guidebook at every step of our tour, pointing out key features that made each wat "a true treasure." She couldn't even take a mental lunch break. While loading her chopsticks with noodles, Rachel filled me in with back stories about the Mon kingdom, which had dictated the city's history. Even though she could tell that I'd tuned out, she kept slinging information at me as if she were the announcer from a public TV station. She wasn't trying to convert me into a Thai history buff. She was hoping for a sign of life.

When I finally did smile, it was because a full bunch of noodles slipped off Rachel's chopsticks and splattered broth all over the table. She wiped a drop off her cheek, chiding herself to be more careful. The show was for my benefit. She knew she couldn't cheer me up, but I appreciated the fact that she was trying.

Her next strategy was to remind me about all her worst boyfriend stories, most of which I already knew.

Then she started in with her friends' stories. By the end of the meal I felt as if I'd been through a war zone, especially since I knew she was barely exaggerating. I'd had my share of disappointments as well, such as my entire relationship with Jason, but most of my heartaches were short-lived emotions based on even shorter-term relationships. Sompong had caused me more trouble than all my previous boyfriends put together, and we hadn't even managed a date. Suddenly I missed Thierry. He was egoistical and self-serving, but I hadn't needed a psychologist to see where he was coming from.

In the afternoon I followed Rachel through the market and trudged through another couple of wats. Rachel dawdled on purpose to delay our return to Chiang Mai. When we found streets we liked, we walked up and down them a couple of times. At the more verdant temple grounds, we stopped for ice cream and watched children chase each other with joyous shouts. Because we'd miscalculated connections, we had to wait an extra two hours for a train back to Chiang Mai. I sulked my way around the station while Rachel busied herself with making plans. She'd asked for my input, but every time I said the same thing: "I don't care where we go, but get us out of Chiang Mai."

During the train ride Rachel found some travelers who had been to Si Satchanalai, another ancient Thai capital, and she pumped them for details. How did the site compare to Ayutthaya? Were the ruins distinct enough to warrant a visit?

As we walked from the train station to the guesthouse, Rachel cheerfully outlined our plans. If we left early enough, we could cover Si Satchanalai in one day. Then we could work our way south to Bangkok in preparation for our flights out of the country.

I didn't listen to a word. All day I'd alternated between feeling sorry for myself, being angry at Sompong, and imagining the limited world of Somchai.

When we reached our soi, I slowed down so much that

Rachel stopped to see what was wrong.

"Did you want to grab a midnight snack or something?"

"No. I was just thinking. What if Sompong is at the guesthouse?"

"Sis, it's after midnight. We left the Baan Jan Come seventeen hours ago."

"He could have gone away and come back."

To be on the safe side, we approached slowly, listening for conversation. The reception area was silent and dark except for a small night light in the shape of a tortoise and the bubbling sounds made by the aquarium. Even though I knew it was stupid to feel that way, I couldn't help being disappointed.

The next morning we were up by seven. We quickly packed our toiletries and headed to the lobby with all our luggage.

Usually the proprietor or his wife sat near the cashier's desk, but for the moment the spot was vacant. We meandered towards the bar, looking for someone to pay.

Rachel and I saw Sompong at the same time. Fast asleep on the couch, he was breathing laboriously. His shoes were tucked beneath the couch and his watch lay on top of them. He'd curled himself into a semi-ball and seemed perfectly comfortable. He'd unbuttoned his striped shirt but left it on. His white undershirt spilled over the waistband of the black dress pants while his gray-white socks had slid around his ankles as if trying to work themselves off.

Part of me cheered, part of me regretted being so standoffish the day before, and the rest of me was simply astonished. I wondered what god-awful hour of the morning he'd arrived and how long he'd been asleep. Wordlessly, I asked Rachel what to do. She tapped her fingers together in a sign for "talk." I tried to nod "yes" and "no" at the same time. The movements cancelled each other out.

My instinct was to flee, but I was too unsure of myself to do anything.

Rachel took off her backpack, which thudded when she set it on the floor. She sat on the edge of the couch next to Sompong and shook his legs. "Ever heard the term 'lounge lizard'?"

Surprised, Sompong braced himself to avoid falling off the couch as he struggled to sit up. "Gina! Rachel! I didn't want to miss you."

I sat across from him, at the safe distance of ten feet, my arms folded tightly across my chest so that he wouldn't see how hard I was breathing.

He looked between Rachel and me, assessing damage. "I am so, so sorry for the other night. I will tell you the truth. I was terribly frightened. I overreacted at your expense." He spoke rhythmically and softly; he'd rehearsed.

For a moment we didn't reply, and his eyes moistened. I didn't doubt his sincerity.

"How is your grandfather doing?" asked Rachel.

"He is—as usual. That night, after you left, we rushed him to emergency, but before anyone could attend us, he revived. We took him back home."

"We were worried sick him," Rachel lied pleasantly. "Thank goodness he's all right. Thanks for letting us know. When people reach that age, they're delicate."

"I knew you would be concerned." He didn't know how to continue. He was as bad at social situations as I was.

After several awkward moments, Rachel gave up on us. "It's nice that you stopped by. In fact you barely caught us. We're leaving town."

Sompong stood. He pressed his open palms together and touched his fingertips to his lips. "Gina, I admit that I acted horribly. But please let me ask you to forgive me."

Sompong's gentle curls glistened in the morning light. For the moment he was as vulnerable as I was.

"I was wrong," he said. "Everything was my fault. But you must forgive me."

Must?

"You kicked us out like stray dogs," I said.

"I deeply regret my actions."

"We might have gotten run over."

"I am quite happy to see that you are all right."

"Would you like to know how we got back to Chiang Mai? We hitchhiked!"

The proprietor came in from the street carrying the daily newspaper. As he returned to his post at the cashier's desk, Rachel scurried over to pay the bill. She chatted gaily about the lovely guesthouse and the lovely city and the lovely everything while leaving me to face Sompong on my own.

"Your behavior was despicable. We never tried to harm you."

"I know, I know! I have been praying you would give us another chance." Sompong hung his head. "That is the best I can do."

My resistance wasn't weakening; it was vanishing. In the morning light, Sompong's skin was a beautiful milk chocolate brown that made him seem even more tender than normal.

I stood and came a little closer. He wasn't much taller than I was, so we faced each other squarely. "How are we supposed to give you another chance?"

"Come and stay with Grandfather and me for a couple of days. Both of you, of course."

Come and stay? Scenarios flashed through my mind. Dinners served by the maid. Walks along Sompong's pleasant lane. Evenings sitting complacently in his living room. Racing from the house if Sompong and I had another terrible misunderstanding.

"Really, Gina, you must. I promise to be the perfect host."

"As opposed to the kind you were the other night?"

"Absolutely."

I already wanted to say yes. What was one more mistake after so many that I'd made in the same two-week time period? But I didn't want to make a decision for Rachel; I wanted her to make it for me. My intuition was a betrayer, and I wasn't objective. I wasn't even logical.

"I'd have to ask my sister."

"You must convince her!"

"Rachel?" I spoke loudly enough for her to hear me and stood motionless until she joined us.

"The bill is squared away," Rachel said cheerfully. "Sompong, you picked out a great guesthouse for us. We enjoyed staying here. The accommodations were excellent, and the people could not have been friendlier. The location was convenient for everything we wanted to see."

Neither Sompong nor I spoke.

"What's up?" Rachel asked.

"I have been begging your sister to give me another chance. Please tell her to do so!"

"Oh?" Rachel feigned surprise, but I knew it was an act. "You tossed us out of your house. How can you top that?"

"I can beg you to be my guests!"

Rachel pretended to clean her ear. "Really?"

"Sompong wants us to stay with him for a couple of days," I said.

"He does, does he? Is that what we want to do?"

Rachel had thrown everything back in my lap. I wanted to talk to her alone but didn't have a skillful way to do so. Instead I attacked. "We're too dangerous. We're evil, remember?"

As Sompong shook his head, his thick hair bobbed in several directions. "I cannot take back what I said. I acted very badly. Please understand that when I lose my grandfather, I will be all alone. He is all I have."

"What about your aunts?"

"They are of little consequence."

I couldn't imagine such a sad situation. Not only did I

have my immediate family, but I had plenty of backups. While I wasn't close to all of my Mexican relatives, at least I had dozens to choose from. From my dad's side I had cousins in Texas, Rhode Island, and Oregon. If I wanted to spend time with relatives, I had plenty of ways to do so.

"Rachel, what do you think? You already had today all mapped out."

"This is correct. Sompong, we don't have much time in your lovely country, and there are more monuments than we could cover in a couple of months. What did you think we would do, sit around your house all day doing nothing?"

"I'm happy to take you wherever you would like to go!"

"Si Satchanalai, for example?"

"Yes, of course. It is only three hours from here."

"Three and a half," Rachel said. "Unless you drive way over the speed limit."

"I would be more than happy to take you there."

"And your grandfather?"

"Nui cares for him excellently when I am not present."

"Very good," Rachel said. "But perhaps we shouldn't risk your grandfather's condition."

She pretended to be stern, but I had heard that schoolteacher's voice countless times while waiting for her to finish violin lessons.

"I have considered my grandfather's health very carefully. I do not think he is at risk," Sompong said softly. "Gina?"

"We delivered the package, and it was unwanted. You don't have any need to see us."

Sompong ran his fingers through his hair. "Grandfather does."

I shifted my feet. "Oh?"

Sompong nodded, his eyes wide.

Rachel sat down. "Let's hear the whole story."

Sompong sat on the edge of the couch. I did the same.

From across the room, the proprietor listened as well.

"Since yesterday, he has been shuffling around the house singing," Sompong said.

"So?" I asked. "A lot of people sing. Even when they shouldn't."

"He has been singing to the elephant you brought."

For the first time since we'd been kicked from the Swoonswangs' home, the sky brightened up enough to let in a ray of light. "Does he usually sing to things?" I asked.

"Never. Somehow this elephant represents great happiness."

I sat back, crossing my legs. So the elephant might have meant something after all. But I wasn't content to sit back and relax, not yet.

"How do you know it's the elephant?" I asked. "I would imagine your grandfather has his good days as well as his bad ones."

"He has not been so content in many months. The elephant must bring back favorite memories."

"You don't even know which ones they are."

"That is why I need your help." He looked between us to make sure we were both listening. "If I can recover Grandfather's past, I can recover a bit of my own."

Even Rachel's eyes flickered. I understood why. Up until now she had been happy to toy with Sompong's emotions, but we'd reached a new level. Here was a man who had lost his parents tragically when he was young and lived alone with a nice but crazy old man. Sompong no longer had access to the main parts of his own history, but he had worthwhile questions. I would have been looking for clues myself, and I would have clung onto any possible strands of information.

The proprietor's wife whizzed into the room carrying stacks of clean sheets in her arms. When she saw that we were speaking with Sompong, she set the sheets on the coffee table. She said a few words to Sompong that made him smile. When he nodded agreeably, the woman pointed to a table that had been set for breakfast. "Time eat," she said, winking.

I wanted to catch Rachel's attention to make sure we agreed about our best course of action, but my sister wasn't paying attention to me. She had immediately headed for the table, thanking the woman as she passed by.

The woman smiled as an accomplice.

Sompong and I joined Rachel at the table. We had reached an uneasy truce, but we had the prospect of a quiet breakfast to work out details.

The guesthouse owners seemed to understand exactly. The woman disappeared for only a few moments before emerging with a pot. Without asking if we wanted any, she poured us cups of rich, hot coffee.

It was a lot better than Rachel's crappy frappés.

Sompong's yard was cheerful in the morning light. Blades of grass swayed in the breeze while the sun danced on the potted plants until they sparkled. Laundry dangled on the line, and the dog stopped biting at the shirttails long enough to greet us.

The house itself seemed soft in the natural light. Its dusty atmosphere was quaint, suggesting that a thorough cleaning would erase its history and leave it naked. The intricately carved wooden furniture was decades old. The walls had faded to a cream color. The rugs were frayed, and years of footsteps had beaten them flat.

We might have been walking through a museum.

Sompong led us through a corridor to a bedroom that was clearly his own. A computer dominated the desk while old programming material filled a bookshelf that stretched from floor to ceiling. The faded bedcovers on the twin beds depicted cartoonish biplanes flown by baby elephants.

"You will sleep in here," he said, depositing the bags next to the beds.

Rachel immediately inspected the bed covers, leaning in closer for a better view of the artwork.

"I am sorry for the childish covers," Sompong said. "They were a present from my grandfather, so I haven't yet replaced them."

"Please don't," said Rachel. "They're too charming. If you're not careful, I'll take them with me!"

I patted the bed. "Don't worry, Sompong. They won't fit into her suitcase, so you're not in danger."

"Thank goodness for that! I would have to chase after you all over again!" He flung open the light green curtains that covered the two small horizontal windows that looked out into the garden.

"It's not fair for us to kick you out of your room," Rachel said. "You don't have a guest bedroom?"

"We have no guests! Nui has a small room upstairs. Once in a while my aunt Kai comes, but she is busy with her family. Anyway, I insist you take my room. I will sleep on the couch."

"I hope it's more comfortable than the one back at the guesthouse," I said quickly.

Sompong laughed heartily. "That is what I like so much about you, Gina. You have a wonderful sense of humor."

Humor? I was trying for sarcasm, but by now the mood seemed inappropriate. Sompong was doing his best to please us, and we'd accepted the challenge. Now I had to convince myself whole-heartedly to embrace it.

"Wait till I'm really trying to be funny," I said. "You won't be able to stop laughing even if you want to. But enough of this suspense. Where's your grandfather?"

"In the mornings Nui takes him for a stroll around the block. He seems to enjoy it. They must be out walking now."

Sompong opened the sliding glass door and scooted us onto a small veranda with a view of the backyard. A card table was surrounded by four chairs, and the dog raced among them.

"Here we can sit comfortably while we map out the day's plan," our host said as he pet the dog. "Perhaps we should have some tea?"

"What's his name?" asked Rachel as a wet tongue licked her leg.

"Chubby! By now he is quite normal, but when he first came to live with us, he looked like a little ball."

"I need a pet," Rachel said. "The problem is that I travel too much."

Rachel acted as if we were having an everyday conversation, but I wasn't as convinced. "Are you sure you can take the day off work?" I asked.

"I assure you it is no problem. I can take you anywhere you would like to go.

"And tomorrow?" Rachel asked.

"Tomorrow too. I will clear my schedule while you are in Chiang Mai. It is the least I can do."

If I'd been a little nicer, I might have warned Sompong about what he was getting himself into. Instead I kept quiet. This was his penance for treating us like criminals. If he could survive a couple of days with my sister, he would have paid the price several times over.

"So would you like a cup of tea?" Sompong repeated.

"One quick tea, but then we have to get going," Rachel said. "We have a lot of temples to see."

"I will hurry! The temples do not stay open all night, so you are correct. We should not waste any time."

While Sompong went off to the kitchen, Rachel and I sat in the shade and took in the greenery. The day was a perfect temperature so far, but it would grow hot later on.

"Sompong thinks you were kidding about the temples," I said.

She threw a stick, but Chubby became too engrossed in his tail to pay attention. "I noticed that you didn't warn him!"

I rested my feet on a spare chair. They would be getting yet another workout, so I needed to pamper them while I had a chance.

"He'll find out about your evil tourist ways soon enough," I said.

"Ha! Now you sound like an accomplice yourself."

"Let's not put it quite that strongly." I kicked off my Tevas for a little extra comfort. I wasn't willing to turn into my sister, but I could feign a morning's enthusiasm. My hip was still sore from sitting on a pineapple.

Chapter Nineteen

Under Rachel's directions, Sompong drove us to the wat-filled city of Lampang, a hundred kilometers southeast of Chiang Mai. During the time we were on the road, Sompong was perfectly cheerful, pointing out landmarks and making suggestions for side trips we could make on another day.

As we neared the city Rachel explained her list of top sites we needed to visit. Sompong was familiar with Rachel's first objective, Wat Prathat Lampang Luang, and remembered visiting the temple as a child. Thanks to good signage, he was able to drive straight to it. However, he couldn't remember why the temple complex was famous. Instead he had to listen as Rachel pointed out the Buddhist Wheel of the Law, the 19th-century murals, and the bronze bells of the Buddha Viham. I feigned interest in each detail.

The poor man damaged his credibility even further by first claiming he could easily find Wat Pra Keo Don Tao (he had to resort to his GPS and three natives) and then being oblivious as to the temple's cultural importance: It had once housed the Emerald Buddha that Rachel and I had visited in Bangkok.

By the time Rachel was ready to visit Wat Pa Feng, Sompong asked her to lead the way. He listened patiently while Rachel told us all about it. He lucked out that Wat Chong Khai was along the same street, so he didn't have to lose face trying to find it. I'd already decided I liked Sompong again, but I wasn't ready to let on.

Instead I marched through these third and fourth temples, keeping right up with Rachel, while Sompong lagged a few feet behind. Then a few yards behind. Then, though he tried to mask it, he started panting.

"You're not tired are you?" Rachel asked. "Perhaps you didn't sleep well last night?"

Sompong ignored her question. "Such lovely artwork. I am thankful to be learning about my own country."

"We could take the train back to Chiang Mai if you're tired," Rachel said.

"No, no. I am perfectly fine."

Rachel gave Sompong the look she usually reserved for violin students who swore they would practice their scales but never ever did. She knew he was lying, but she pretended to take his words at face value. But weren't the temples marvelous? she asked. Weren't they all splendid in different ways? He said they were amazing. He had no idea so much beauty existed in one town. Since it was relatively close to Chiang Mai, he could hardly believe he hadn't come more often.

I sensed the trap but carried on. Normally I would have made noise about the temple limit, but when Rachel suggested Wat #5, I agreed before she could finish the sentence. Rachel won in the end, of course. At the entrance to Wat Pong Sanuk,   Sompong gave out. He reminded me of the story about the tired elephant who had walked and walked until it expired on Doi Suthep. Sompong had perspired through his shirt, and his hair was damp. He bought us bottles of water and drank two himself without stopping. He accompanied us onto the temple grounds but politely declined to enter any of the complex's buildings. He was happy to wait as long as necessary while Rachel and I explored.

Rachel tried to reason with him, but the man was vehement. For today his eyes were full. He did not care that the temple was a mix of Burmese and Lanna styles. He did not want to see another Naga staircase. He did not care about the teakwood temple, no matter how fantastic. He lived nearby, so he could return another time.

I understood how he felt, but I was still pretending to be the model tourist. I followed Rachel long enough to find out how wealthy Burmese immigrants had thanked their adopted city. I didn't rebel until she reached the onsite museum that boasted a gazillion Buddha statues. Although she encouraged me to join her inside, I claimed I had too many new blisters. Then I went out to sit with Sompong.

I found him reclining under a shade tree. He nodded when I sat beside him, but he seemed so tired I assumed either Rachel or I would have to drive back to Chiang Mai. He wasn't used to killer tourism, but I'd had a couple of weeks to get up to speed.

"Is your sister always so enthusiastic?" Sompong asked.

"Pretty much."

"Can she remember what she has seen?"

"She takes careful notes so that she can label her pictures."

"I see. Do you take notes as well?"

"Why bother? At the end of the trip, she'll give me a copy of hers."

"She is quite practical, your sister."

"She's learned from experience. She's been through half of Europe and most all of Greece, but this is the first time I've had a chance to do any real traveling myself."

Sompong smiled at me. He'd been doing so all day, but I hadn't decided what it meant. I couldn't tell whether he was being kind to us out of guilt or whether he was honestly enjoying himself or whether he was fond of me. I also hadn't decided exactly how nice I wanted to be in response.

"People come from all over the world to visit Thailand," he said, "but I do not understand why."

"They want to trace the past, study the religion."

"But these temples are not your past or your religion.

Why should you be interested?"

"What's fun is seeing a new country with different customs. Believe me, this place is nothing like Arizona. And temples are nothing like churches. That's what makes Rachel so crazy to see everything."

Sompong wiped his forehead; he was still sweating while sitting motionless in the shade. "I can imagine that it is interesting to visit a place that is so unfamiliar. But why did you choose Thailand over all the other Asian countries?

I didn't want to offend Sompong by admitting that our destination was an accident, so I offered a few platitudes before asking about his university studies.

We'd waited less than a half hour before Rachel joined us; she'd run out of space on her final memory card and had to sit down and delete a few pictures before she went on.

"Are you enjoying your visit?" Sompong asked.

"This site is outstanding! Are you sure you don't want to take a quick look?"

"Another day," said Sompong, "but I am pleased you admire our temples."

"They're wonderful! All over the entire country. And to think we began our visit in Thailand by visiting Wat Pho. By the time we went to The Grand Palace, I was sure I wouldn't see anything finer. Then I went to Doi Suthep!"

"That is why you chose to visit Thailand, I suppose, to see all the temples."

I rolled my eyes wildly, but Rachel didn't notice.

"Gina won a contest. Didn't she tell you?"

"What kind of contest?"

"She—"

I maneuvered so that Rachel could see my face. Then I rolled my eyes until they hurt.

"She—graduated first in her high school class," Rachel said, trying to follow my signal.

"Not possible. She told me about her grades in physics."

162

"You're right. She was third, but the first two winners chose Disneyland instead."

"No," he grinned. "I do not believe you. She also told me of her grades in biology."

Rachel was nonplussed. "Actually, Gina won a church raffle."

Sompong scrutinized us. "She said she appreciates some concepts of Christianity but only attends church for special ceremonies."

"Okay, okay," Rachel said. "It's a little personal. Southwest Sun and Fun was holding a contest for its favorite swimsuit models, and —"

I burst into laughter at the thought of my body parts falling out of a skimpy swimsuit. Sompong laughed too until he had to stop and dab tears with his shirttails.

"You have no reason to laugh," Rachel said. "You have not seen my sister in a swimsuit."

He held up his hand and pulled a handkerchief from his pocket. "I am not laughing about that, but I have always read that the American families are not united."

"And?" Rachel demanded.

Sompong shook his finger at Rachel. "Such outrageous lies come only from love."

Rachel shrugged. "Guilty as charged."

"So, now, will you tell me?"

"I won a contest sponsored by a Tucson radio station," I said. "I correctly guessed the night of the season's final freeze. The prize was a trip for two to Thailand."

Sompong rocked slowly back and forth like a street sign wavering in the wind. "I see that you do not yet want to tell me. I can wait until you are ready."

"That will be a long wait," Rachel said.

"I do not mind. I have plenty of time."

Throughout the day Sompong had made quick calls, ostensibly to check on his grandfather. As it turned out, he was giving Nui cooking directions. By the time we walked into the house that evening, spices filled our nostrils. In the dining room, a shrimp curry awaited us along with plates of *ba meen*, egg noodles.

Our host went to see if his grandfather was awake enough to join us for dinner. As Sompong led the man into the dining room, both were cheerful. Somchai greeted us with a small wave of his hand as he slowly shuffled into the room.

"Does he recognize us?" I asked.

Sompong hesitated. "I do not think so. His short-term memory is almost gone, but when he thinks he is supposed to remember, sometimes he pretends." Sompong struggled to seat the old man properly, but when his foot caught on the chair leg, I bent under the table to help out.

Rachel pointed to the man's hand. "Is he clutching what I think he is?"

"Grandfather has not let go. Nui had to trick it out of him when it was time for his bath."

"Amazing."

"That is how I realized the elephant is an object of special importance. It is lodged in his memory in a very strong way."

"Do you think he's remembering it all the way from childhood?" I asked.

"I do not see why not. Unfortunately, I cannot ask him about it."

"I'm sorry," I said. "I'm sure it's difficult for you."

"For a long time I refused to believe that his mind was deteriorating. When I finally believed it, I started asking questions about family history. I wrote down the details, but after a while the stories no longer made sense. Then he had a stroke, or perhaps a series of mini-strokes." Sompong tapped his head. "I had to admit to myself that he was already gone."

Somchai pointed to the curry, and Nui dished out a small amount in his bowl.

"By now I have accepted the natural order of things," Sompong continued. "I must accept his condition."

Nui fed Somchai a spoonful, and he eagerly savored the result. If nothing else, he still appreciated a sense of taste, but what other pleasures could he possibly enjoy?

Despite Somchai's sad circumstances, I enjoyed every noodle. Nui had surpassed herself compared to our earlier visit by using more spices and preparing larger quantities. She beamed as Rachel and I accepted seconds and finished every morsel on our plates.

We should have known better. Sompong was crestfallen when we claimed we didn't have room for dessert. When he explained that he'd made homemade coconut ice cream a few days before and was anxious for us to try it, we had to recant and accept small portions.

The ice cream was as delicious as the noodles and the curry. The small strands of coconut melted in our mouths along with the rest of the sugared cream. By the time we pushed back our bowls and swore we couldn't eat another bite, I calculated that we'd consumed enough calories for two days. This was not our fault. Given the long day of chauffeuring, we were obliged to be grateful guests.

"Shall we go to a club?" Sompong asked. We had finished post-dessert tea, and Nui had led Somchai back to his room. "There are several near here."

We didn't respond.

"Perhaps you are tired?"

Rachel stated what I was thinking: "You don't seem like the club type."

Sompong slid his fingers up his forehead, into his hair, and over his head. "It is true that I am not a good dancer, but my friends say that Ecstasy is a fine club."

We absorbed the information, not sure what to do with it.

"What do you normally do in the evening?" Rachel finally asked.

He looked between us as if guessing what the correct answer would be. Then he gave up and confessed. "Mostly I spend evenings at the computer."

I understood the general feeling. College had dictated a change in my own lifestyle as well. Neither Patty nor Jason had understood when I'd given up nights at the movies or parties to study instead. By the end of the spring semester, both were struggling to keep a 3.0 whereas I'd managed a 3.89.

"Let me guess," I said. "You spend your evenings designing websites."

"Right."

"I thought that was your day job," Rachel said.

"Sometimes I start quite late."

Rachel shook her finger. "Sompong, you must do something besides stare at a screen."

"When I cannot concentrate, I take a walk."

Rachel and I stood simultaneously. "What are we waiting for?" she asked. "A walk would be splendid."

He pointed to the ceiling fan that was working full blast. "Are you forgetting that it is quite hot outside?"

I was on the verge of sweating anyway. The room was about as toasty as Lampang had been in the sun.

"It's hot in here too," Rachel said. "What's the difference?"

Sompong still seemed hesitant, but when we stepped outside, the night air greeted us with a hint of breeze. As our host led us along his dark, gentle residential street, we strolled leisurely, chatting in the rhythm of a relaxed pace.

"You do not have any other siblings?" Sompong asked.

"You asked the same question five minutes ago," Rachel said. "I think we tired you out today!"

I wouldn't have mentioned it, but I too had noticed the repetition. "It's bothering you, isn't it? The stuff about Janjira."

We turned the corner and started down a similar street.

"My mind keeps going in circles because I cannot figure out what might have happened," Sompong said. "As he was raising me, my grandfather never told me much about his family. I did not think to ask. I suppose as any young child, I took everything for granted."

"You couldn't have known which questions would be important," I said.

"Yes, I realize this. But I am surprised that I was not even curious."

"Usually people like to talk about their own history," I said. "Our grandmother is constantly telling us about this relative or that relative."

"In this respect Grandfather has always been private."

Barking dogs startled us as they rushed the metal fence marking the boundaries of their yard, but Sompong calmly walked past.

Rachel moved to the side of the street farthest away from the dogs. "Don't take this the wrong way, but maybe Janjira was a black sheep."

"I have been considering that angle."

"Wouldn't anybody know the whole story?" I asked.

"Perhaps Vaitnee, my aunt who is Grandfather's second daughter."

"What about his other daughter?"

As we reached the busy highway, the familiar one Rachel and I had braved as stranded pedestrians, Sompong quietly guided us around a wide corner that headed us back towards the house. "Kai is quite a bit younger. She was so small when my mother died that she barely remembers her. Vaitnee is more likely to know the family history."

"You haven't talked to Vaitnee about the elephant?" I asked.

Sompong paused so long that I turned to catch his expression, but the night masked his dark eyes. "I avoid talking to her. She always has some new complaint. Even her voice makes me tired."

I had similar relatives, including an annoying aunt in Durango. In person I could never speak to her in full sentences because she always cut in with her own calamities, of which there were thousands. On the phone she was worse; I had to listen for ten minutes before explaining that I'd called about a birth or a funeral.

"The second problem is that my aunt does not easily part with information," Sompong continued. "Instead of giving me a straight answer, often she pretends not to know."

"A control issue," Rachel said. "Like a professor who wants you to fail."

"Yes. I used to ask her questions about my parents. I have realized that if I want to know something, I must trick her into telling me."

"Can't wait to meet that one," I said. I remembered that she lived far away.

Sompong slowed his pace as he turned to us. "I treat our communications as a game. You will think I am too calculating, but I have to know exactly the right question to ask. If I can throw her off balance by pretending to know the answer, I have a better result."

"Did you want to call her tonight?" I asked.

"I need to be more prepared. I will have only one chance."

"She's too conservative, so you can't tell her about us," Rachel suggested.

"Perhaps. But I will start with some ridiculous story about a friend of a friend."

"So you'll call in the morning?" I asked.

"Generally I am more effective in person. She cannot dodge me when I am standing in front of her."

"Let's visit her together," Rachel suggested. "That way we can create enough confusion to catch her off guard."

Sompong's steps became slower and more deliberate. "She loves to have dinner parties, and she becomes nervous because she hopes everything will be perfect. You are right.

We should visit her together, but there is a small problem. She lives on Ko Samui."

I'd heard of the small island off the east coast of the peninsula. Tourists we'd met in Patong had described its lovely beaches with such detail that Rachel and I had considered heading straight there, but we'd been thwarted by the long distance.

"For months Vaitnee has been telling me to bring Grandfather for a visit," Sompong continued, "but he is so difficult to travel with that I have delayed."

"And now it's the rainy season," said Rachel.

"Ko Samui is on the east coast, so its monsoons will come a little later."

It took Rachel half a second to realize the implications, and for once I was ahead of her. If we traveled to Ko Samui, we could spend our last precious days in Thailand on the beach. With any luck we could also avoid any more temples.

"You need our help to travel to Ko Samui," Rachel said cheerfully. "By all means we must accompany you."

"I could not ask you to trouble yourselves," Sompong said. "You do not have much time left in my country."

"I've known people like your aunt," Rachel said. "They can be quite difficult."

"There is no doubt about that."

"To butter her up carefully enough, we'd best plan on visiting the island for several days."

Rachel was thinking "beaches" so hard she could already taste the salt water, but Sompong didn't understand her sudden attentiveness.

"You have already done too much traveling on my behalf," said Sompong. "Another long trip is out of the question."

Rachel stopped walking. "We brought a mess of history into your life. Naturally we should help you find out more."

Sompong had no idea he was being taken for a ride by a fanatical tourist who was an even more dedicated swimmer. He assumed Rachel's offer came from the heart. "Truly you would not mind traveling to Ko Samui?"

"We are prepared to make a small sacrifice," Rachel said. "Could your uncle find us cheap tickets?"

"This is correct. Since Uncle Manat is a pilot for the airline, he is allowed to purchase standby tickets for family members for a small fee."

I put my arm next to Sompong's. "Unless you're color-blind, we don't look like family."

Sompong grinned. "This is Thailand. Sometimes it is enough to have friends among your co-workers."

Rachel smiled broadly. "Thailand is just like Mexico. No matter what happens, keep your uncle on your good side!"

"Manat has always treated me as an important member of the family. More so than Vaitnee." Suddenly our companion sounded sad and far away. I couldn't imagine his situation. While he didn't have easy access to his own history, I knew more than I wanted to about mine. Maybe I would learn more than I wanted to about his as well.

"Would it be hard for all of us to fly standby?" Rachel asked.

"At this time of the year there is rarely a problem. Still, it is a long and tiring trip, so I do not want to force it on you."

"I can handle it if my sister can," said Rachel.

"Are there any famous temples?" I asked.

"I am afraid not."

"In that case, when's our flight?"

"We shall see," Sompong said softly.

By the time we returned to the house, Nui and Grandfather were asleep. I was half asleep as well. Sompong hurried around double-checking that Rachel and I had towels and drinking water and fresh sheets, that we knew how to adjust the fan, and that the windows were open the right amount.

After he bade us good night, he returned three times to see if we wanted to use the Internet or the phone or whether we needed midnight snacks. By the fourth interruption, I met him at the door, opening it a crack so that he wouldn't see Rachel undressing.

"Gina, I want to thank you. Sincerely."

I slid out into the corridor. "You're the one who showed us around all day."

Sompong leaned against the wall. "You know what I mean. Thank you for giving me a second chance."

Gently I set my hand on his shoulder. "I understand why you were so worried. I know that your grandfather is important to you. If I were you, I'm sure I would have reacted the same way."

He wiped hair from his brow. "You are merely trying to make me feel better. Still, I appreciate your efforts."

He smiled as he turned and vanished down the hall.

Chapter Twenty

"What do you think we should do?" I asked Rachel. We'd been awake for a while, but we'd stayed put because the house was quiet, and we didn't know Thai protocol for overnight guests. I studied the room, noticing the baseball cap from an unknown team, the row of science fiction books, and the poster of an old British rock group.

Rachel closed her laptop. She'd nearly worn her fingers out transcribing notes from all the temples we'd seen the day before. "Let's venture out to the kitchen. If Sompong's gone out, he may have left a note."

We got as far as the dining room. Cardboard boxes of various sizes had replaced the dirty dishes from the night before. The boxes held memorabilia of all kinds: books, papers, an old pencil sharpener, a beat-up hammer, a faded prize ribbon. Some of the miscellaneous items had been dumped on the table and pushed to one side to make room for stacks of photos which, because of the overhead fan, had been weighed down with metal utensils.

Sompong slept at the table, his head cushioned by his right arm and unruly clumps of hair. He reminded me of university students who dozed at the library on top of piles of unengaging books except that he seemed peaceful. Sleep was relief rather than escape.

We tiptoed to the kitchen where a warm pot of coffee awaited us. Presumably Nui had prepared it before going out with Grandfather and Chubby. We helped ourselves and retreated to the veranda, where we could sit comfortably and listen to the birds.

Next door a short gray dog barked, came as close to the fence as the chain allowed, and returned to a strip of shade.

"Your boy had a busy night," Rachel said. "No wonder the house was quiet."

I sneezed twice in a row. "Talk about a crash course in family history."

"It was probably his first class. Did you see the dust on those boxes?"

"Why do you think I'm sneezing? You'd think he would have been curious before now."

Rachel stirred her coffee. "Not really. When you're young, you're too busy acquiring basic skills to have time for anything else. Relatives are part of the scenery. When you're a teenager, who cares about family? All you care about is other teenagers."

"When you're in college, you focus on studying."

"And once you have a real job, you realize how easy you had it in college!"

I put down my cup. "I wonder if he learned anything."

"Not yet. He fell asleep before he found what he was looking for."

"Maybe he arranged tickets for Ko Samui."

"He probably should think twice."

"You don't want to fly down to the island?"

"No, I mean, I'm worried he might be disappointed if he travels a long way but doesn't find answers to his questions."

"Maybe there's not much of a story."

Rachel shrugged. "Secrets are kept for a reason. Otherwise Sompong would already know the details."

The thought sobered me. My own relatives were so easy. My maternal relatives couldn't have kept secrets if they'd been paid to do so. My paternal grandparents had loved talking about family, and what my dad kept quiet about, his siblings recounted. I'd always had access to whatever I wanted to know, whether out of idle curiosity, for a school project, or to complete medical records. I was glad I wasn't in Sompong's position.

Rachel dived into a guidebook, eager to review her preferred plans for the day. She asked what I wanted to see, but I was a poor tour consultant. I didn't care what we saw. I would have been content sitting around the house all day relaxing, something Rachel would consider a sinful waste of time.

When I went inside to check on Sompong, he was still a sleeping bear. Randomly, I chose a stack of photos and brought them back out to the veranda. The grainy black and white images depicted family gatherings with bunches of people who all looked alike, pictures of temples where the visitors were so small they were distant specks, and generic miniatures of bald newborns.

"Anything interesting?" Rachel asked.

"Mildly," I said, passing her half the stack.

"Oh, good grief," she said after she'd flipped through a few dozen shots. "Check this out." She held up a picture of a young boy and a beaming woman who stood behind him, her hand gently gracing his shoulder in a sign of proud love. Her eyes were dark, her stature small.

I took the picture. "This could be Sompong."

"What about the woman?"

"His mother, I guess. Nitya was her name. She looks happy."

"Does she remind you of anyone?"

I scrutinized the picture under differing amounts of sunlight. "She reminds me of Janjira, or at least what Janjira would have looked like fifty years ago." I handed the photo back to Rachel.

"I'd say they look almost exactly alike."

I studied the picture again. I'd only seen Janjira a couple of times, but I'd thought about her constantly since our dinner with the Tamarins. "It wouldn't be unusual for a niece to resemble her aunt."

"What if she's not her aunt?"

"Who then?"

"Someone even closer."

In the next stacks of photos, we isolated three more shots of a woman who looked uncannily like Janjira.

"Good morning," Sompong said quietly when he finally joined us. "I am sorry I was such a poor host this morning."

I held up a picture. "We found plenty of ways to amuse ourselves. I hope you don't mind."

"Of course not. Family shots are always quite interesting." Sompong rubbed his eyes. "What did you find?"

"We don't want to meddle," I said.

He sat up straight. "What is the matter?"

"Nothing," Rachel said. "Don't worry."

"Tell me."

She held up the first picture we'd examined. "Is this you with your mother?"

"Shortly before the accident. She was beautiful, was she not?"

We nodded.

"Sompong—" I started the sentence but couldn't finish it.

"What is wrong? You are beginning to alarm me."

"It's nothing bad," Rachel said hurriedly.

He pushed his bangs off his forehead, but they came right back. "What is it, then?"

I leaned towards Sompong. "Your mother looks a lot like the woman we know in Tucson."

"Oh! My mother looked like my great-aunt. Why did you not say so? That is often the case. Sometimes family characteristics can be traced through several generations." He pulled on his hair. "This stuff, for example, is from my father's side of the family. If you look at their family album, every one of them has unmanageable hair."

"Sompong," I said as softly as I could, "We don't think

Janjira is your great-aunt. We think she's your grandmother."

He started to speak and then closed his mouth. Slowly he looked from me to Rachel and back again. Then he started to get up but thought better of it. "That is not possible."

"It's a theory," I said. "We were playing around with some ideas."

"The woman you met was very old. She might have changed a lot over the years. It is hard to guess what she might have looked like as a young woman."

"True," I said. I didn't want to press.

"Besides, my grandmother died when my mother was in her twenties. The woman you met could not have been her."

Rachel and I sat quietly. We'd discussed the issue between ourselves for an hour, and we hadn't come up with an alternative version.

Sompong shook his head mechanically as if it were a metal crane. "You said that the woman in Tucson asked you to take the elephant to her brother."

"That's what we thought we heard," Rachel said. "She wasn't so easy to understand."

Sompong shook his head. "The elephant had an effect on my grandfather because it brought him back to his childhood. By now that is the only thing that registers."

"That's what we assumed too until we saw the picture of your mother," I told him. "She and Janjira are like twins."

"But you told me that my grandfather's sister —"

Rachel frowned. "We told you what made sense to us at the time."

"You are changing your story?" Sompong asked loudly.

"Now we have more information."

"You are only making a guess!"

For a moment I was afraid we'd have to hitchhike back to Chiang Mai again, but this time Sompong wasn't angry. He merely disbelieved us.

Rachel placed her elbows squarely on the table. "Let me give you an example. I have an awful time pronouncing words in Thai, right?"

"You are improving. You need more practice."

"Conversely most Thais have trouble pronouncing English words."

"Of course they do. That is only natural. It is only easier for me because I had the good fortune to start learning English when I was very young."

Rachel continued, undaunted by the difficulties of getting through to our host. "Thais have an especially hard time pronouncing English Rs."

"I believe in my own case, my Rs are quite intelligible."

"Yes," she sighed. "Yours are perfect."

"I fail to see why this matter has any relevance."

Rachel took a deep breath before trying again. "When a Thai person tries to pronounce the name 'Robbie,' it comes out closer to 'Lobbie.'"

"I suppose."

"And a name like 'Roger' would come out as 'Logel.'"

"Roughly."

"And Vs are also difficult?"

"I never thought about it."

She patted his shoulder. "Janjira told us to take the elephant to her 'lothel.' Draw your own conclusions."

Chapter Twenty-One

Sompong didn't believe the woman we knew was his grandmother. Since the concept was so revolutionary to him, we didn't expect him to. "You have made a mistake," he said politely but incessantly all through a tasty breakfast of sweet breads. "Your theory is not possible." He was as discombobulated as a first-year student on the first day of college. I wished I had some way to assist him. Instead I watched helplessly as he fed fruit slices to Somchai and repeated the same command: "Come on, Grandfather, tell me about your sister. Tell me about Janjira." The man's answer was an open mouth and a grunt. Then Sompong turned his attention to us, repeatedly asking us to describe Janjira. Finally Rachel popped Sammy an email requesting a series of pictures showing Janjira over the years.

Finally Sompong declared that we shouldn't waste the day and asked where we wanted to go. He was taken aback when Rachel outlined a detailed plan that included her recommendation for the best way to reach Inthanon National Park, which was an hour or so away, but he tried not to show it. Instead he complied as if we were doing him the favor. During the drive he was hauntingly pensive, but once we reached the park, he tried to be pleasant. He dutifully accompanied us to the waterfall, the chedis, and the rhododendron grove. He took our pictures and occasionally posed with us, but he'd left his mind behind on the dining room table with all the other memories. Even when he heard our occasional questions, he answered absently. Unrest about his past had beaten him down.

By the time we returned from our excursion, Sammy had sent a dozen pictures. Sompong viewed the pictures for less than a minute, but when he came to the closeup of Janjira holding Sammy as a toddler, his eyes filled with tears. All day our host had been in denial, but now he was ready to give in and consider an alternate view to his own reality.

I tried to dissuade him, but he enlarged the pictures, printed them out, and took them in to Grandfather. Initially Somchai showed no reaction. After Nui dragged out the magnifying glass and held it over the colored printouts, the man showed discomfort. Unable to hold still, he fidgeted, alternatively focusing and turning away.

Sompong pointed to the closeup. "Janjira," he said.

The old man tried to form the word, gave up, and clutched the photo to his chest. Then he struggled to his feet and headed down the hall. Sompong walked the old man to his room, where they sat together in the silence of loss and pain.

"You think I am overreacting," Sompong said.

"Not really."

Sompong and I were sitting side by side on the veranda. Nui and Grandfather had gone to bed, Rachel had retired to the dining room to label her photos, and the neighboring houses were dark and quiet. Though I knew better, I felt that we were the only two people still awake in all of Chiang Mai.

"Of course it would be unnerving to think you knew your family history and then find out you didn't," I continued.

"My own mother lied to me. Can you imagine that? Grandfather didn't tell me the truth either. By now he is unable to do so."

"Maybe they were trying to protect you."

"Through dishonesty?"

I was dishonest about little stuff every day, such as

how slim my friends looked, but that didn't give me a way to counsel Sompong given such a difficult situation. I scooted my chair closer to his until I could smell the excess shaving lotion. Even under the dim glow of a single light bulb, he looked sweet and innocent and vulnerable. "Maybe your mother didn't know."

The idea didn't register for several long seconds. Then Sompong leaned towards me. "Do you honestly think my grandfather would have kept the truth from her as well?"

I shrugged. "Maybe your grandparents weren't married."

"Why would they not have been? How did Janjira wind up in America?"

"Sompong, take a step back. What do you know about your great-grandparents on your grandmother's side?"

He closed his eyes and frowned at the sky. "Nothing."

"Maybe we have to start there. Maybe your grandmother got pregnant and her parents didn't want anyone to know about it."

"Such a secret would be silly."

"We're talking decades ago. A lot of things have changed."

Sompong shoved his hand through his bangs several times in quick succession. "What do you think I should do?"

Ever since Rachel had planted the idea in my head, I too had the growing worry that Sompong might not find the answers he sought even after a long trek south. I was more afraid that he might find answers he didn't like. That was the problem with investigating your own history. It was the same as someone telling you the plot of a movie. Once you knew the essential facts, you couldn't go back and imagine a different outcome.

"Why do anything?" I asked.

"What? You come here stirring up family histories and now you tell me to ignore them? Grandfather and Nui and I were doing fine until you came back from Phuket. We could have continued to live our lives how they were."

I started to get up, but he reached for my arm and gently pulled me back.

"Gina, no, please do not go inside. Stay for a while."

"I'm not going to listen to you complain about me."

"Please, please, sit here with me. I am sorry. I do not mean to sound angry. Truly I do not know what to do."

"I'll stay if you promise not to raise your voice."

"Gina," he said softly, "please understand that nothing in my life has prepared me for such a situation as this one."

I leaned back against the chair and stared into the night. In contrast I'd spent little time worrying about my own family. On the rare occasions that my father returned to Tucson, my mother was sure to be out of town, leaving Rachel and me to handle the situation ourselves. The result was awkward, but it wasn't confusing. Hence I could appreciate that Sompong had been thrown into a dragon's den without a fire extinguisher. Had the roles been reversed, I'd have been going through the same emotions he was: denial, anger, disbelief.

"If I'd known we were bringing you a Pandora's box, I would have tossed that elephant off the plane mid-Pacific. Now you're at a crossroads."

"Who is Pandora?"

I tried not to laugh. Why had I assumed Sompong would know Greek mythology? When I tried to explain the reference, I realized I needed to brush up on the ancient myths myself. I vaguely remembered that Pandora, whoever she was, shouldn't have opened the box that contained whatever it did. I couldn't explain any more than that.

"You have an inkling of your family situation," I finally continued. "You have to ask yourself whether or not it's important to know about your past."

"Shouldn't I want to know?"

Again I started imagining the worst: Sompong was an abandoned orphan or the son of a serial killer. Maybe he wasn't even Thai. "Forget that Rachel and I came here. Let your grandfather carry around the elephant and be done with it."

The plan was logical in a cold, unfeeling way, but Rachel and I were convinced he wouldn't leave the mystery alone. We'd taken bets: Rachel said we'd be leaving for his aunt's house on Ko Samui within a day; I thought it might take a little longer.

"I do not know what to do." Sompong spoke so softly I had to ask him to repeat himself twice.

"Can you take a few days off work?"

"As you have seen, I do not punch a time clock. As long as I finish my current project in a timely fashion, the company will not be aware of the difference."

"We fly home in a week. In the meantime we'd be happy to accompany you to Ko Samui. Certainly your aunt can tell you about your past."

"Even so, I am not sure I want to hear the story from her."

"Sompong, you don't have many choices for storytellers."

He peered into my eyes as if they were wells. "I wouldn't mind so much if it were you telling me."

Lightly I put my hand on his. The moment felt romantic, but I didn't want to push at the wrong time. I wanted to make sure Sompong knew I was his friend. For the time being he was too confused for anything more than that.

"What's the big deal about your aunt?" I asked.

"She hates me."

"What?"

"She does not like Grandfather either. She pretends she wants us to visit, but she is always relieved when we do not come."

"I'm sure she doesn't hate you."

"You have not met her. You will agree once you do."

"How could anyone possibly hate you?"

Finally he cracked a little smile. "I believe you did, the

night we met."

"Sompong, that was way different! It was a big misunderstanding. But this is your aunt. Your mother's sister."

"Yes. That is why the situation is painful."

"But you said your uncle is nice. And what about the children?"

"They are all fine. We have a good time together as soon as she leaves the room."

"Sompong, you must be mistaken about your aunt."

"Sadly, I am not."

"In that case I'm sure I want to go to Ko Samui."

"To see me feel unhappy?"

"To prove you're wrong. What will you say about Rachel and me?"

"The truth. That Janjira claimed she was a friend of the family and asked you to deliver the package."

"You know that's not quite how things happened."

"For now that is close enough. It is wrong to give her too much information."

"When you visit, do you stay at her house?"

"Hers is very big, so she has to accommodate us. Otherwise it would be embarrassing. But Gina, I am also worried about your sister. I see that she is a dedicated tourist. She has already changed her plans for me once. I am not sure she would be content to do so a second time."

"Are you kidding? I broke my fingernails prying her from Phuket. She'll be delighted to visit a new beach as long as you can prevent it from raining the whole time."

"The heavy rains shouldn't start for at least another fortnight. But what about you? I want you to enjoy your time as well."

"I'd be thrilled to sit around and do nothing on some beautiful beach. If I have to see another temple this trip, I might start hallucinating Buddhas in my sleep. No offense."

"None taken! My legs are still sore from yesterday. But I would have to be an outstanding tour guide to make this trouble worth your while."

I swatted at a bug, missed, and swatted again. "So far you've done a wonderful job."

"Chiang Mai is my home. Of course I know where to take you."

I did not mention that once we'd reached the outskirts of Chiang Mai that morning, Rachel had to correct Sompong three times to keep him on the right road to the national park.

"You'll be a wonderful guide down south as well."

He suddenly brightened. "On Ko Samui I have a friend who runs a small travel agency. I am sure he can make suggestions for the best places."

"That sounds wonderful. But don't forget what I said about the rain."

Chapter Twenty-Two

It's so warm on Ko Samui that the airport consists of a cluster of thatched buildings. We were thankful to see such a welcoming area; the long trip with Grandfather had made us irritable. On the flight from Chiang Mai to Bangkok, he kept trying to leave his seat even though we'd firmly buckled him down. On the flight from Bangkok to Ko Samui, he'd fallen asleep but snored so loudly that he disturbed everyone within five rows of ours.

Our luggage beat us off the plane. We didn't have to drag our suitcases through the swirl of arriving tourists because Manat was waiting for us. Sompong's uncle was a medium-sized fifty-year-old with tufts of black hair that resisted being combed and a wide, brown face. He wore khaki shorts and a loose T-shirt that bore the logo of a sports team. He greeted us cordially, ringing Sompong's hand before embracing him and extending Somchai a similar greeting. When Sompong introduced Rachel and me, he repeated our names carefully, taking our hands in his. He grabbed our luggage before we could protest and herded us to his car.

The white sedan was so small that it seemed more like a sports car for two rather than a family car. My first instinct was to call for a cab, but Manat expertly fit all our bags into the trunk.

Then Manat carefully guided Grandfather into the backseat. Without observing the stop sign, Manat lunged onto the highway and headed for his house, which was a couple of kilometers southeast of the airport.

"I am sorry my English is weak," he told us in a heavy Thai accent before bursting into his native language. He and Sompong joked as if they were buddies instead of relatives. Manat winked and pointed at me; Sompong shook his head and pointed at Grandfather. I didn't need to understand Thai to realize that Manat and Sompong enjoyed an easy and relaxed relationship. I should have expected as much since Manat had so enthusiastically arranged for our last-minute tickets. The man was so kind and friendly that when he pulled up in front of his white-washed house and said "Welcome," I knew he meant it.

The house featured a thatched roof and big picture windows. It had a wide porch with wooden slats and a yard full of tropical plants. Forgotten toys were strewn throughout the yard. As we approached the front door, the dwelling seemed innocent and cheerful, an example of an older time.

Manat easily communicated his enthusiasm for seeing us, but it was clear within moments of our arrival that Vaitnee didn't share his sentiment. Although Sompong called out loudly as we reached the screen door, no one came to answer it. While Sompong steadied Grandfather, Rachel and I opened the door so we could herd the elderly man inside. We passed through a short hall into a living room with a couple of worn couches that had been recovered with a striped print. Before we could sit down, Vaitnee swooped into the room.

The woman bore no resemblance to the gentle beauty that had been Sompong's mother. This woman had an angular nose that leaned to one side and a mouth that was too large for her face. Her black hair was confined to the top of her head with a confusing array of pins. Beneath a spotless (meaning, unused) white apron, she wore a yellow short-sleeved blouse and a flowing blue skirt that only partially hid a soccer ball of a stomach.

She gave her father a brief hug and nodded at Sompong. "It's so late that you'd best come straight to the dining room," Vaitnee said with a distinct British accent. "We've been waiting on you for dinner, and by now the children are starving."

Vaitnee grabbed her father's arm and dragged him across the hall so quickly I was afraid he would fall. When we reached the dining room, Somchai headed for the nearest chair, sighing as he sat.

The room was decorated with a feminine touch at odds with the tension in the air. Floral watercolors dotted light green walls. Ruffled curtains hung at the windows. A lavender tablecloth covered the table.

"You let my father become too tired. You should know better than that," Vaitnee said as she herded us into the room.

Sompong showed no emotion. "It's a long trip."

"Much too tired. I'm surprised I've let you take care of him all this time."

"I am too."

"Sit, sit," she told Rachel and me. "It's late enough as it is. Pour yourselves some water. I don't have enough hands to do everything. Children!" she shouted.

We did as we were told. Rachel reached for the pitcher that sat on a transparent plastic tray.

Manat frowned. "We don't start with one drink in the living room?"

"It's too late, too late," Vaitnee replied. "What took you so long to come from the airport?"

None of us saw fit to answer. Rachel nudged me from under the table. Despite Sompong's descriptions, my sister and I were both surprised at her raw unpleasantness.

Two children entered sheepishly. I guessed the boy to be around eight years old and the girl to be around three.

Both took their places silently.

"Say hello to your cousin," Vaitnee told them.

They greeted Sompong in soft voices as the maid poured water into their glasses. The baby cried from a back room, and Manat went to fetch it.

"So here you are in Thailand," Vaitnee said to us. "And you came to my country for no reason?" Sompong's aunt was only in her forties, but the room's bright light illuminated the wrinkles around her eyes.

"No reason at all," Rachel said.

Across from me Sompong bristled. He stared at the water pitcher as if its contents could extinguish the fire in his eyes.

"I don't understand why you would travel all this way without a concrete purpose," the woman continued.

Manat returned with the baby. He must have heard what his wife had said, but he was shielded by the fact that "Aviator English" didn't require much everyday conversation. He simply pretended not to understand what she said.

"We Americans do the craziest things." Rachel drew out the word "craziest" as if she were in love with it.

I immediately relaxed. As a rule my sister avoided confrontation. If provoked, she defended herself more fiercely than a tennis player rushing the net for a final slam. I was glad we were playing on the same team.

"Americans are known to be practical," said Vaitnee. "For this reason they are willing to give up their family traditions and move around the country to take different jobs."

"The way you gave up your own traditions when you moved to Ko Samui?" asked Rachel.

"We had no choice. My husband was going to lose his job if we didn't move."

"Manat, I thought you took the job down here because it was a promotion," said Sompong. He repeated himself in Thai.

Manat managed half a word before Vaitnee cut him off. "Do you think we could have continued on his old salary with a family of five? No. Our case is different." She made a production of settling back down in her chair.

"Ours too," Rachel said. "Our mom had her same job for thirty-five years. With one exception, our relatives live within five miles of one another. It's easy for us to keep our traditions if we choose to."

Rachel didn't mention that we were the exception, that all of our maternal relatives lived in the same town of Durango, Durango, Mexico, except for us and Grandma. Dad lived a solid eight hours from Durango, but we didn't usually include him when reckoning family statistics.

"Easterners and Midwesterners often move around," Rachel continued, "but that's mainly so they can enjoy a better climate. Where did you find your information about Americans? I'd like to think that we're practical, but I'm not sure I believe it."

Vaitnee shrugged.

"Come on," Rachel said. "You had to gather your information from somewhere."

Suddenly our hostess sat up straight. "I saw a documentary on the public channel."

Rachel studied her water glass, which was decorated with the smudges of a small child. "Filmmakers rarely hide their biases. Who directed the film?"

"I do not remember," Vaitnee said weakly. She knew she'd lost the round, but she hadn't realized that she would need more expensive boxing gloves. "You still haven't explained your reason for coming to Thailand."

"I already told you," said Sompong. "They won this vacation. They did not spin a globe and set down a finger and say, 'This is what we choose.'"

The maid, a young girl with a serious face, came in with plates and silverware.

"My dear nephew." Vaitnee repositioned her glass as if to improve the taste of the water. "You do not have to accept everything that is offered to you. Between the two of them, they have lost six weeks' wages. Where is the logic in sacrificing so much money for something arbitrary?"

"They have more interest in the architecture of Chiang Mai than I have," said Sompong loudly. "I had never truly seen Lampang before last week. The girls wanted to see the famous temples."

"Instead of working, you are now a tour guide? Sompong, you are usually more rational."

"Haven't you heard anything I have told you?" Sompong asked. "Naturally I wanted to escort Rachel and Gina around. They went completely out of their way to do a favor."

"They brought some trinket from some acquaintance who happens to have connections to Thailand? They haven't many things to do with their time, it seems."

"They were asked to perform a special favor."

"In that case I hope they were compensated."

"Sometimes the compensation lies in helping someone out."

"Yes, they have done a small favor, but since they had no real touring plan, what difference did it make where they traveled to?"

Rachel wiped her hands on a napkin and dropped it on her empty plate. "Sompong, I've had enough criticism for one day. Where's the nearest restaurant?"

Vaitnee drew a hand to her mouth. "I was not criticizing. I only speak my mind. You can hardly blame me for that."

"Hardly," said Sompong, standing.

"Stop overreacting and sit back down. I have made countless efforts to prepare dinner. It is impolite to run away moments before the meal is served." She sounded casually authoritative, as a boss might sound when firing a long-term employee.

"Ignore her," said Manat, waving Sompong to sit down. "Melee!" he called back to the kitchen. "Soup!"

As if on cue, or maybe because she'd heard the rising

voices, the girl brought out a huge pot. The steaming broth contained onions, basil leaves, and various green shoots. Prawns floated on top. Melee made a show of warning us to sit back as she plopped the near-boiling liquid into our bowls; perhaps she knew she was the commercial break to a real-life soap opera.

The change of pace broke the tension. For several minutes we blew on the soup, ripped apart our prawns, and spit out vegetable husks, all the while wishing we could spit them at one another.

I expected that the rich meal might have a calming effect, but for Vaitnee the food served as fuel. Sompong's aunt hadn't finished her bowl before she deliberately set down her spoon. "Sompong, you have not told me what you intend to do now that you have finished university."

"You already know. I create websites for Infoteck."

"You need a proper job."

"I have one."

"You need a job that pays benefits. You will find more competitive opportunities in Bangkok."

"I do not care for the capital, and Grandfather is happy where he is."

"You cannot afford to put your life on hold for him."

"Should I leave him here with you?"

"Of course not. Leave him in Chiang Mai. What's the girl's name?"

"Nui."

"She can take care of him."

"I would not like to be so far away."

"Stop being so stubborn. You are a young man and now is the time to establish yourself. Otherwise how will you find a decent wife?"

Sompong set his fists on the table. "I am not sure that I want a decent wife."

"What does 'decent' mean?" asked the eight-year-old.

Vaitnee ignored the child. "What about Mrs. Rodchue's daughter?"

"Do not be telling me about her."

Grandfather awoke from a semi-doze and started shuffling his feet. Sompong immediately rose to escort him to the bathroom.

"My nephew is brilliant in some ways," Vaitnee said as soon as Sompong left the room, "but of course he's quite immature."

We said nothing. Rachel gathered comebacks under a silent scowl, but I couldn't react. Usually when people were rude to me, I'd done something to deserve it. Vaitnee was so overboard that I couldn't take her seriously. Instead I dived into the delicious beef curry.

"Silly me!" said Vaitnee. "I've gone and left the bombers off the table."

In Thai Vaitnee shouted at Melee, who brought out a dish of what looked like oversized *jalapeños* floating in roasted olive oil. These peppers seemed to be a specialty. Manat put three on his plate right away. The children took one apiece. Rachel and I did too. Evidently the diners were so used to Vaitnee's tirades that they never let her spoil their appetites.

"No!" Sompong shouted from the doorway as I bit down. Because he startled me, I choked. Rachel patted my back, but since I continued coughing, Manat came around and pounded on me.

Awkwardly I spit a bite of half-chewed vegetable mass to the floor. I started to bend down to clean it up, but Melee beat me. While I regained my composure, Rachel refilled my water glass. Manat stood nearby in case he needed to pound on me again. As I took slow sips, Sompong knelt at my side.

"I am so sorry," Sompong said, "but you should not eat such things."

"I already did," Rachel said, worried.

Sompong went blank. "You ate a bomber?"

Rachel nodded slowly as she sat back down.

Sompong returned to his place as well. "Your mouth is not on fire?"

"Back home we eat *chiltipines*. Same difference."

Manat smiled broadly as he forked another bomber for himself. I forked into the remains of mine, chewing off the end while Sompong and Vaitnee stared at us.

"Relax," Rachel told Sompong. "We're Mexican. Half-Mexican anyway. We were brought up on hot stuff."

"Sompong said you are American," said Vaitnee.

"We're part Italian too, but I'm not sure that counts."

Rachel had to ask for the curry dish twice before Sompong managed to pass it.

Vaitnee was so disappointed we'd conquered her bombers that for her next tactic she chose Thai. Her English was fluent, but her Thai streamed out in torrents. She must have been giving Sompong all the gossip on all their relatives. He listened, bored. I tuned out and joined in the game of table soccer Manat had created to keep the children entertained.

No wonder Sompong felt isolated. His parents were dead, he had no siblings, his grandfather was helpless, and his aunt was overbearing. I appreciated my mother more than ever. She stayed out of people's way. That was why she and Dad had first separated. When he wanted to leave, she helped him pack. When I wanted to visit him that first summer, she helped me buy a ticket. Monterrey was so hot and humid that I never felt like doing anything, and every night the mosquitoes attacked me as if I were their blood bank. I never went back.

"We're leaving," Rachel said loudly, dragging me from my chair. "Now."

Vaitnee had risen and was trying to put herself between Rachel and the front door. "You didn't understand. I was merely talking to Sompong about — "

"*Mai dee marayat*," Rachel said in a low tone. "'Bad manners!'"

I didn't understand.

Vatinee chased after her. "I meant that under normal circumstances, it's unusual for unmarried women to stay at a house where a young man also sleeps—"

Rachel extended her hand so quickly that she startled Manat, who shook it. "Pleased to meet you. Goodbye, children."

I followed her lead.

"I apologize for her," Manat said. "Come. I give you my car." He preceded us out of the dining room.

"It's ridiculous for you to leave," Vaitnee proclaimed, following along. "There are so many tourists on the island that you'll never find a place to stay at the last minute."

Sompong and Rachel paid no attention, so neither did I. He gathered our bags from the hallway and went out to the car. Manat had already opened the trunk for us.

"I am so sorry," Manat said. "These last weeks she is not herself. I think it is the woman's change of life."

"For your sake I hope it doesn't last long," I said.

Sompong slammed our bags into the trunk. "I will be back later. I cannot tell you at what time. Will you see to Grandfather until I return?"

"Yes, yes."

"Call my cell if there is any problem."

"I will."

Sompong revved the engine, and we roared off.

Suddenly calm, Rachel scooted to the middle of the backseat and spread her arms along the shoulder rests. "Sompong, I thought you were exaggerating when you described your aunt. I was wrong."

"She surpassed even herself." His voice was low and cold.

Rachel took out her guidebook. "Should I look for a list of guesthouses?"

We whizzed past a jungle forest and headed for Chaweng Beach.

"No. I will call my friend. You will be comfortable

staying with him." Sompong pulled out his cell phone and dialed from memory, one hand on the steering wheel. "Norm, we have had a serious problem with my aunt. Can we come to your office?"

Norm's cheerful invitation boomed through the phone.

"What did Vaitnee say that was so mean?" I asked. "I didn't catch a word."

Rachel leaned over the front seat so that I could hear her better. "I caught just enough. *American girls. House. Bad manners.*"

"You stunned her," said Sompong. "It was beautiful."

"It helped that she kept repeating herself."

"It's improper for us to stay at her house?" I asked.

"That is not true," said Sompong. "It is only her excuse."

"We wouldn't have slept well there anyway." Rachel sounded unconcerned. "I was happy for the excuse to leave."

"You sounded very angry," said Sompong.

She sat back, prepared to enjoy the scenery. "I'm a teacher. Half my job is acting."

Sompong slowed as we took a wide curve. "You are very good at your work in that case. I thought perhaps you would take a swing at Vaitnee. I was hoping for it."

Rachel rolled down the window. "Human nature is predictable. The hypocritical ones are always the most indignant."

"Gina, can you forgive me for my horrible family?" Sompong asked.

"Sure," I said. "As long as that friend of yours lives near the beach."

Chapter Twenty-Three

Norm, whose Thai name was Narong, ran a travel agency next to Coral Bungalows on Chaweng Beach. The pleasant building had large picture windows and bright lighting. The front door was propped open, making the establishment even more inviting. Inside were two small round tables flanked by chairs and sprinkled with tourist information. Posters filled the walls with views of hotspots around the island and a menu of daily excursions. A desk with a large computer screen filled the back corner.

Norm was seated at one of the tables. He was trying to explain to an elderly British client how to check email on her iPad. At the other table, a trio of younger tourists leafed through brochures.

Norm had short black curly hair and a scraggly moustache. He was as dark as Sompong but taller, his roly-poly stomach partially hidden by a plaid shirt. He was older than Sompong but younger than Rachel, who regarded him favorably as they were introduced.

Norm and Sompong were natural soulmates, computer programmers because they were inherently good at it. They'd first met in a tech chat room complaining about relatives who didn't understand why they sat behind computers all day. In Norm's case, his parents were old school, and his older siblings had blue-collar jobs. Norm knew his relatives couldn't understand his fascination with technology, so friends like Sompong were a buffer. Since meeting in person at a conference, the two had kept in close contact.

Norm advised the woman to repeat the maneuver several times until she felt comfortable with it. Then he gathered four plastic chairs so that we could huddle together as Sompong related our dinner entertainment.

"That's lovely about the bombers," Norm said. His English had a twinge of Australian; he wintered with cousins in Sydney. "Your aunt expected her guests to gag first and die second. Very clever."

"Perhaps we should return to Chiang Mai straightaway," said Sompong.

Rachel playfully punched him in the arm. "Nothing doing. I'm staying right here. Wait. It's almost dusk. Mind if I—" She fished her bikini out of her purse. "Got a bathroom?"

Norm nodded appreciatively. He had noticed my sister's muscular limbs.

"It is not safe to swim in the dark," Sompong said.

"That's why I have to hurry." She'd already spotted the sign for the bathroom and didn't hesitate to head in that direction.

I was hot myself, but I was glued to my chair. Even though I'd been trying to imagine the players in Sompong's family, Norm knew a lot more about the chess pieces than I did. I hung on every word, trying to sort through Vaitnee's nonsense.

"The worst part is my embarrassment," Sompong said. "I bring two guests to the island, and my aunt makes the worst possible impression."

"Sompong, we've gone over this before," Norm said. "Your aunt resents you for whatever reason. You don't need to ruminate about it."

"Today she tormented me."

"What does your aunt do for a living? Nothing. She has three kids and one maid. Didn't she train for something?"

"She worked briefly as a pharmacist, but she stopped

after she married."

"Your uncle didn't want her to work?"

"No. She decided she did not have to."

"You see?" Norm asked. "She could have had a career, but she threw it away. She has three kids who don't need her and a husband who is successful in spite of her. She needs something to control. A younger relative is a prime candidate."

"I shouldn't have come to the island. Perhaps it is wrong to learn about my past."

"Gina, have you managed to talk any sense into him?" Norm asked.

I grinned. I could tell that Norm not only cared about Sompong, but also about his friends. He gave me credit for having more influence than I did. "I keep trying. My position is that since Sompong has traveled all this way, he might as well learn as much as possible."

"Exactly. Sompong, at least you should know your bloodline. It's useful from a medical point of view."

"Since she hates me, Vaitnee might be determined to hide the truth."

"She doesn't care about her father either," Norm said. "Look how she's ignored him all this time. Does she like anybody?"

Sompong frowned. "Maybe her husband or her children."

"See? You're not even sure."

"No matter what she thinks of me, she had no right to act so rudely."

"I'm sure you'll have the chance to repay the favor." Norm glanced over at his customers. "Give me a minute?"

Norm returned to the English woman. She had managed to send an email to her daughter and thanked Norm heartily. She promised to return the next day to discuss a short cruise. Norm's other tourists signed up for excursions, so Sompong and I waited while Norm finished all the paperwork.

"Your sister!" Sompong cried. "We should make sure she is all right."

"She's a fish. Does Norm have a coffee machine in back?"

He did. We'd barely taken a sip when Rachel returned, exuberant, pronounced Chaweng the best beach in the world, and proceeded to berate Sompong for not coming to the island more often.

"If I had a friend who lived in this nice a place, I would visit all the time," she winked.

"I thought that was why you were going to Greece," I said.

"Oh, right! So I'm smart enough to take my own advice!"

"I'm glad somebody takes advice," Norm said as he joined us. "But I've had enough work for today. Shall we adjourn to my house?"

Norm turned off the lights and led us outside where an old motor scooter had been parked under a tree.

"Anyone want to ride with me?" he asked Rachel as he mounted. "It's not very far."

She immediately jumped on behind him. "I don't care how far it is!"

Sompong and I followed by car, but we only drove for a few minutes before reaching a residential area. Norm zipped up a curvy driveway that led to a huge house with a veranda that would have held twenty people. We kicked off our shoes and followed inside to a spacious living room with high ceiling fans and maroon throw rugs. A pair of old couches with bulky cushions faced an entertainment center. A desk with a laptop filled a corner. The other areas hosted an assortment of potted plants, including a palm tree that stretched above our heads.

After Norm plopped into the cushions, we did the same.

"Surely you don't live here alone?" Rachel asked.

Two of the walls had windows, but the other two had doorways leading into other rooms. "You're right. But my parents have gone to visit my sister, who's working in Malaysia. They won't be back for two weeks."

"I can see you've been having huge parties each night," Rachel joked. Even though the room was full, the furniture was neatly arranged. The coffee table before us held a single magazine and a water glass.

"This is it! The biggest party I've had all week!"

Norm proceeded to make small talk about the house and the neighborhood. Then he fetched beers and chips. It wasn't until he offered to show Rachel the garden that Sompong and I could finally talk alone. He stretched against the couch and rested his feet on the coffee table.

"This has been the most difficult day I have had for a long while," he said.

"Right. Since the night we went to your house and you went ballistic."

"At least that trauma only lasted a few hours!" Cautiously he took my hand. "I apologize that my aunt was so impossibly rude."

"Don't worry about it. We had fair warning."

"I never expected such behavior. Perhaps Manat is right. Perhaps the change of life is making her crazier than usual. Most of the time she is merely unpleasant. I am sorry you paid the consequences."

"Don't think we're scarred for life. My sister enjoyed herself immensely. As long as Norm doesn't mind, we're better off here anyway." I crossed my legs, accidentally rolling closer to Sompong.

"Gina, I cannot thank you enough for helping me. I could not have faced my aunt without you."

"Without us, you wouldn't have needed to!"

"I have postponed a visit for a long time."

"Your grandfather is stressful to travel with. You did a great job with him today."

He set his arm over the back of the couch. "It is easier

facing problems with somebody's help." He rested his fingers on my shoulder, sweetly unsure.

I loved the warm feeling, but I didn't want to rush anything. I sat quietly, letting the conversation lapse into silence. To avoid a next step, Sompong was forced to invent small talk, so he told me all about a famous politician's court charges and the soccer trials for the World Cup, topics I cared nothing about. I wasn't bored because I was concentrating on the shape and proximity of Sompong's lips rather than on a single word they formed.

When he finally kissed me, it was by closing his eyes and brushing against me. Afterwards he seemed startled and backed away.

Still, it was progress.

Sompong was so crushed by Vaitnee's behavior that for the next days we avoided speaking of her altogether. He slept at his aunt and uncle's house, but each morning he would bathe and dress his grandfather, drop Manat off at the airport, and come for Rachel and me. We'd have a late breakfast of fruit shakes at The Coral Bungalows Café. Then we'd go exploring. We scampered up the Big Buddha temple, photographed the famed phallic rocks called Hin Ta and Hin Yai, got rained out kayaking in Angthong National Marine Park, and hiked to the Na Muang waterfall. One day we drove all the way around the island because we felt like being on the road.

By early afternoon we would hit the beach at Chaweng or Lamai. Both were beautiful because of the wide shelf leading out to the sea, the rows of palm trees on the beach, and the gentle way the water kissed the horizon. Best of all, we could use the time on the beach in our own ways. Sompong let nature blank out his thoughts, and Rachel swam laps while reviewing the Greek lyrics she'd need on Amiros. When I wasn't trying to put myself into Sompong's shoes as he delved into his past, I imagined his next romantic moves and how I would feel about them. Several times I asked if he'd pressed Vaitnee for information about his past, but he said he was waiting for the right time.

Rain interrupted each afternoon. We'd leave the beach and dash for shelter, sometimes huddling with the hawkers who'd been temporarily thwarted from selling their snacks and trinkets or offering massages or tattoos. We'd watch the heavy drops of rain tumble down, laughing at their efforts because they hadn't spoiled our day.

Evenings consisted of choosing a restaurant, difficult only because Chaweng had so many, and then strolling up and down the strip doing mild shopping. We weren't set on buying anything, but the horrendous number of stores made window shopping an unavoidable activity. If we weren't too full from dinner, we stopped for crepes made by Muslim couples at their portable stands. We'd watch hungrily as they flipped the batter over the hot metal stove and deftly rolled dough with pieces of banana or coconut. Then we would walk slowly enough that we could eat our dessert as we wandered along.

After Norm closed his office, he and Rachel would disappear; they'd formed an immediate and uncomplicated rapport. Sompong and I would have a little time to ourselves. Mostly we meandered. For a while he would take my hand, letting loose after he became embarrassed by his sweaty palms. I didn't mind the sweat, but I kept waiting for something to happen. As my departure date neared and he failed to make a move, I wondered if any man could really be that shy or polite. Then I reminded myself that Sompong had to spend each night at his aunt's watching over Somchai in a hostile environment. I worried that while he catered to me, he wasn't interested in romance. Either his responsibilities overshadowed his sense of desire or I wasn't the woman he was hoping for.

On our fourth day on the island, we dropped by Vaitnee's house after our session at the beach; Sompong had forgotten a change of clothes and didn't want to wear his swimsuit to dinner. Manat was nervously pounding the driveway with heavy feet. "I want to call you, but your phone off!"

"Grandfather!"

Manat spoke rapidly in Thai. Even during the disastrous dinner the night of our arrival, Manat had never raised his voice nor altered his composure. Now his voice quavered and he was nearly as pale as I was, never mind that he was naturally brown instead of white. He hopped in the car with us and we zoomed off. "Somchai is at the hospital," Manat explained as scenery flew by on either side. "He had a massive stroke. Perhaps fatal. The ambulance came a few minutes ago."

Since I was sitting behind Sompong, I placed my hands gently on his shoulders. I couldn't stop trembling, and he was shaking worse than I was.

At the hospital the staff was waiting for us. A concerned intern escorted us to the emergency room where a nurse was checking Somchai's pulse. The man was lying in bed, eyes closed, as if the most he could do was concentrate on his own breathing.

Vaitnee emerged from the corner. "It was horrible! We were still at the dinner table, and —"

None of us paid attention to her. Besides, I already knew what she would say. The stroke wasn't an act of nature. Somehow it would be Sompong's fault.

The petite nurse discreetly stood to let Sompong take her place at the patient's side. Sompong squeezed the thin hand as hard as possible. "Grandfather!"

The old man opened his eyes for a brief second. He mouthed a word I couldn't hear, and smiled, and passed.

Chapter Twenty-Four

Sompong, Rachel, and I spent the evening sprawled over the couches at Norm's paying blind attention to the TV without noting the difference between news reports and cop shows. Occasionally Sompong would interject with stories about the time Grandfather taught him to put on a tie or Sompong's futile attempts to explain the mechanism of a computer mouse. Sompong's fondest memories about growing up all included his grandfather.

When Norm arrived from work, he tried to buoy our spirits by complaining about a few of the evening's clients, such as the Italians who wanted a room next to the "say-uh," which Norm finally recognized as "sea," and the two Brits who wanted to go home early since the island was so damned hot.

Norm had also brought home a case of Chan beer. I didn't care for it, but eventually I downed half a can. By then we were merely hoping for a way to make it through the night. Finally Norm and Rachel went out for a motorbike ride — the quiet mourning was too much for them — but I stayed in with Sompong, thankful for each minute that passed and put Grandfather's death farther into the past. When Sompong fell asleep against my shoulder, I didn't wake him up.

Suddenly I heard a strident, clanking sound. Sompong's keys had fallen from his pocket, bouncing off the throw rug and onto the floor. In the still house, the result sounded like a bomb.

"I am so sorry!"

I peered at him through the dark; evidently Norm had come home and turned off the lights when he'd found us both asleep. "What time is it?"

Sompong held his wristwatch to the window to catch the beam of the streetlight. "Four a.m."

"Is something wrong?"

"No. Go to the bedroom. You will be more comfortable."

"Do you have to leave right now?"

"I should have returned to my aunt's house earlier."

"She'll be mad if you sleep here?"

"I do not care how she feels. I do not want her pawing through Grandfather's things when I'm not around."

"Surely she wouldn't steal anything."

"Only the elephant."

He kissed me and slipped from the room.

"Think Grandma will like this?" Rachel asked, holding up a purse decorated with a sequined elephant. She was in the final stages of packing, but the first time she'd tried to zip the suitcase, it only sealed on one side. She'd emptied the entire bag and was packing more carefully, utilizing every inch. I gave her as much advice as possible. I knew she would make me cart home anything that she couldn't fit into her own bag.

I watched her from the only chair not covered by her stuff. "You already bought something for Grandma. That miniature spirit house."

Rachel patted a package wrapped in a piece of red and gold silk. "I'm not sure I can part with it. Besides, it might not arrive home in one piece."

"I'm sorry you have to leave."

She wrapped a clay elephant in a sock. "I'm on my way to the Aegean! Don't feel too bad."

"At least we could have travelled back to Bangkok together."

"The flight's less than an hour. And I'm glad you're staying with Sompong."

Originally we were scheduled to fly the same day — Rachel to Athens, me to Arizona — but when Sompong asked me to stay an extra week and help him through the cremation ceremony and travel back to Chiang Mai, I agreed. "I'm not sure I can help him."

"Everybody needs moral support. This is a big shock for him no matter how much he was expecting it. Was he able to take some time off work?"

"He has to finish a couple of projects, but they will only take a few hours. Then he's allowed five days for bereavement. His boss is aware of Sompong's close relationship with Somchai."

"He'll need the extra time. You'll have to make it fun for him." She winked. "That shouldn't be hard."

"I'm not sure. Once Sompong recovers from the shock, he's going to be terribly upset. Somchai wasn't physically sick." I snapped my fingers. "Then he was gone."

"The man was ninety-one. Nobody lasts forever." She slid a book among her shirts so that it wouldn't get bent. "Thanks for bringing me on your trip. It's been swell. Most of the time."

"Without you, I wouldn't have come."

Rachel folded her jacket and rolled it into a pocket of space. Over the years she'd become an expert. I needed to study every move; when it came time for my own packing, I'd have the same problem. Despite myself I'd collected at least two dozen elephants, many of which would be destined for Mom's living room whether she liked it or not.

Rachel searched for another spare gap, one big enough for her socks. "Visiting Thailand hadn't occurred to me because I hadn't gotten around to thinking about Asia. Plus I used to think you couldn't have fun in a place where you couldn't speak the language. Luckily that's not true, or we wouldn't be able to visit many countries in one lifetime!" Fondly she regarded the cheerful cover of her Thai language book. "You noticed how bad my Thai is, but all the studying was worth it for the moment of faking out Vaitnee. Who knew that the one phrase I would really need would be *'bad manners'*?"

"You'd think Vaitnee would learn to keep her mouth shut."

"Nah. You know how some people have their stomachs stapled? That's what Manat ought to do to her mouth. Can you imagine having a fight at the hospital?"

"What do you mean?"

Rachel flattened three more tank tops into her suitcase. Luckily for her, the hot temperatures in Thailand were about the same as the ones she'd be facing in Greece, so she'd only needed to bring one wardrobe.

"Sompong hasn't said anything?" Rachel asked. "I guess he wouldn't have. Anyway, Norm told me."

"What?"

"If you remember, as soon as Somchai died, we went downstairs to the waiting room to tell Manat and the kids."

"Sure."

"Vaitnee started arguing with the nurse. There was some problem about the insurance."

"That's what she was worried about?"

"That's what she chose to make a scene about." Rachel reached into a plastic sack lying on the bed and brought out four porcelain elephants which she rolled into narrow strips of *Ko Samui News*.

"What happened?"

"Sompong told her to calm down. They got into such a loud argument that they scared the patients. Doctors came running. The head administrator ordered them outside."

"That's awful!"

"Maybe not. Ill will has been growing between Sompong and Vaitnee for years."

"Our lovely dinner didn't help."

"They were already on the brink of a fight. The hospital scene merely pushed them over the edge. Poor Manat. I feel sorry for him. I wonder if he had any idea what he was getting into when he married Vaitnee."

"I'm sure he was clueless. Otherwise he would have run away."

"I'm sure he wishes he could run somewhere now."

"At least Manat is used to his situation. Imagine Sompong, dealing with the loss of Grandfather and battling his aunt at the same time."

"Maybe the battle is good for him." For the third time, she unzipped an inside pocket of her backpack, checked for her passport, and zipped it back up.

"To take his mind off Grandfather?"

"To give him enough strength to take control."

"He needs work on that."

Rachel chuckled involuntarily. "I hope you're not talking about your relationship."

I must have sounded disappointed. "Only a little."

"Don't worry. It's the circumstances, not you. Try to put yourself in his shoes."

"I guess."

She handed me a stack of postcards. "Do you mind taking these home with you so that they don't get all beat up?"

I took the heavy bundle. "I'll show them to Mom and Grandma."

"Great! I'm sure they'll be anxious to hear all about our trip."

"Do you think I should tell them about Sompong?"

"Tell them what? That he caused us to hitchhike through Chiang Mai at ten at night or that he almost got arrested in a hospital brawl?" Rachel folded an empty plastic bag and tossed it on the floor with others she'd discarded. "You'll have to tell them about Sompong. What excuse did you give for changing your ticket?"

"I explained about a friend's grandfather, but I kept it vague."

Rachel smiled knowingly. "How do you feel about Sompong?"

I sank back into the chair. "I'm not sure. I can't compare him to anyone. He might be messed up in some ways, but he's still more together than most of the guys I know back home. Look at how he took care of Somchai."

"He seems Mexican. He's not afraid to show kindness as well as emotion. Personally, I find that attractive."

"Exactly," I said. "Not all guys are willing to put such a high premium on family."

"And those who do aren't usually open about it."

Rachel managed to close the last section of her backpack. Fortunately, most of her purchases only had to travel as far as Amiros, where she would surprise her friends with a variety of silk products decorated with elephants. "You never answered my question. How do you feel about Sompong?"

I couldn't tell her exactly because I hadn't figured it out for myself. "I like being with him."

She handed me what was left of our bug repellent. "You'll need this more than I will. Okay, so you like being with him. And?"

"He's special. Even though we've known each other a short time, I feel as if we have a close connection."

"After all our adventures together, you couldn't avoid having a close connection. But anyway, that's a good start."

I straightened the edge of my blouse. Hand washing hadn't been conducive to fashion. By now every shirt I had was limper than the last. "What would you do if you were me?"

She paused. "Do about what?"

"About Sompong. I don't know how to think this through."

"What are you concerned about?"

"I'm not sure if he wants a romantic relationship. Even if he does, I'm not sure I should want one with someone who lives as far away as Thailand. Maybe I should just forget about it."

"Certainly distance is a factor." She patted her suitcase, which was so fat it was about to give birth. "I guess I'm ready to leave."

"Do you think he just wants a fling?"

She hugged me. "It sounds like you haven't achieved fling status."

"Not exactly."

"Do you love him?"

"I don't know."

"You feel much stronger about Sompong than you did about Jacob, right?"

"Jason."

"Whatever."

"You're right. The situations don't even compare."

Rachel set her hands on her hips. "You don't talk about Jason and Sompong in the same way."

"I don't?"

"When you talk about Sompong, your eyes go soft. You feel a kind of *cariño* for him."

Dictionaries defined the Spanish word as "affection," but the translations missed the most important sense of the word. It was more like a feeling of sweetness. You felt *cariño* for someone who was super special to you, such as a small niece, but it went deeper than love to include something like tenderness crossed with joy and hope and pride.

Rachel was right. I felt *cariño* for Sompong. Whether we ever got past friendship wouldn't change how I felt. He was the gentlest young man I'd ever met. He wasn't afraid to show vulnerabilities, or to cry, or to confess that he was at a loss. He had shown great love for his grandfather and done his best to care for him. Sompong couldn't have asked any more of himself, and I couldn't have asked any more of him.

"He's special, Rachel. I felt that from the beginning."

"Uh huh. That's why when the three of us are together,

you don't hear anything I say."

"I'm sorry!"

She laughed. "I don't mean it like that. I mean that when he's in the room, there's a sort of sparkle between you. It's like nothing else matters."

"Oh." I felt my face getting red.

"¿Lo quieres, verdad?"

I nodded. Somehow it was easier to admit to loving someone in Spanish. At least I thought that's what I was feeling.

Rachel set her bags near the door. "I hate to give advice, and I'm not much on getting it either, but if you want my two bahts' worth, you're onto something with this guy. Believe me, good men are hard to find no matter what country you're in."

"I haven't even known him a month. That's scary when I come to think about it."

"So don't think! Listen, before you can decide anything, you need more time together. But first he needs to make it past all this family stuff. He needs time to grieve. You can't hold him to his emotions for the moment because they're all over the place."

"That might be true, but I'm here now."

"So invite him to visit."

"You mean in Tucson."

"Sure. Why not?"

"But—"

She gave me a bear hug, nearly squeezing the life out of me in the process. "Invite him so strongly that he comes."

Chapter Twenty-Five

I missed Rachel as soon as Manat and I waved goodbye to her at the airport. Since Sompong was busy with funeral arrangements and work deadlines, Manat dropped me off in Chaweng, and I spent the day by myself. As I walked around, I imagined what Rachel would comment on. I thought a lot about her parting advice, but for the time being I couldn't imagine Sompong in Tucson. I couldn't be sure that he wasn't an invention, a fantasy that would dissipate as soon as I left Thai soil.

Sompong caught up with me at the beach behind Coral Bungalows in the late afternoon. He was relieved they'd made progress: Aunt Kai was flying in from Bangkok with her family that evening, so the cremation could take place the next day. Since Grandfather's friends were deceased, the customary several days of visitation could be cut short, which would make the situation easier on everybody.

Even though Sompong was fully clothed, he sat next to me on the sand. "What shall we do tonight?" he asked.

"Shouldn't you spend time with Kai?"

"Perhaps. They are staying with friends of her husband's who live on the island, so we could visit over there. After the fiasco with Vaitnee, I was not sure you would agree to meet other relatives."

"I thought you liked this aunt."

"For the most part. She has never been deceitful to me that I know of, and she is always pleasant although perhaps not under these circumstances."

"I wouldn't mind meeting her if you'd like me to," I lied. He was right; I didn't want to meet any more of his relatives.

"Thank you. Then we will pay a call."

A young man in a straw hat walked by hawking fruit slices. I watched until he laboriously made his way out of view.

"Sompong, you came down here to find out about your history. Don't you think it's time to start asking questions?"

"I have been too irritated with Vaitnee to speak to her."

"Would Kai be able to help you?"

"I don't know. She's much younger than Vaitnee. She's actually closer to my age than Vaitnee's."

"You might ask." Given Vaitnee's general demeanor, a younger sister could hardly provide a more toxic option.

"The time is not right. She is grieving as much as I am."

I dug my feet into the sand. "Fine. Don't find out anything about your past. It's your history, not mine."

"Gina! Please do not be cross with me."

"I'm not. I'm trying to help you. Vaitnee is a total witch on a broom, so target her sister instead. No matter what Kai thinks, she probably won't lash out at you in front of friends."

"Perhaps I will ask a few questions."

"No, Sompong. You will ask. Do you know why?"

"Why?"

"Otherwise I'll do it for you."

We arrived at the tiny residence before Kai and her husband did, but Decha and Lawana made us feel right at home. The jovial, English-speaking couple showed us their house and launched into explanations about the island. They showed pictures of different beaches and suggested short excursions, all the while plying us with drinks and salty snacks.

They made me feel completely at home, but the feeling was enhanced when Kai and her family arrived. Sompong's aunt and uncle were thoroughly congenial and seemed happy to see both of us. They were worn out from their journey, but they'd driven all day long with a baby and a toddler.

I could guess why Kai and Sompong enjoyed a kinship. Both had suffered under the shadow of Vaitnee because they didn't make waves. Kai's temperament fit her looks. She wore a sky-blue pantsuit that was becoming but not showy. Her rounded features gave her grace while her smile made her attractive. She spoke energetically as if she weren't sure how long a conversation would be allowed to last. When Sompong recounted his life in Chiang Mai, his aunt listened, asking pertinent questions that showed she was digesting the information rather than judging it. I liked her because she felt like an ally.

Her husband, Bunsom, was well suited to her. The short, quiet man spoke no English but never interfered with our conversation. Instead he watched over the two-year-old son and the infant daughter, responding when they required attention and joking with our hosts when they didn't. We had cocktails in a pleasant, relaxed atmosphere, which was much more than I'd hoped for. Instead of being on the edge of my chair in case I needed to dash from the room, I could relish the uniqueness of being a foreign guest in a Thai home. I appreciated every minute of such an opportunity. Rachel would have approved.

When we adjourned to the dining room, it was clear that Decha and Lawana had made careful preparations. The table was set with fine plates and silverware. The salad was carefully arranged. I enjoyed the homey atmosphere, but by the time we reached the main course. I felt antsy. When the children started shouting at the same time, I leaned over to Sompong. "When are you going to ask your questions?"

"Soon."

"Soon we'll be going home."

"Do not rush me, Gina. I will wait for the right moment."

During the whole drawn-out main course, that moment never came. The subjects ranged from soccer to politics, back to soccer, to child-raising, to Tucson, and to Sompong's job in Chiang Mai. Each topic steered carefully away from the deceased. When our hosts brought out a colorful ice cream dessert, I gave up on Sompong and took initiative.

"After people pass in the U.S.," I said, "we like to tell nice stories about them. Since I only met Somchai last week, perhaps you could tell me about his younger days."

The silence suggested I'd made a cultural gaffe.

"I remember when Bunsom met Mr. Swoonswangs," said Decha. "He was so nervous he called me three times that morning!"

Kai patted her husband on the knee. "He was afraid that Father would send Bunsom away and tell me not to marry him!"

"Was your father strict about your boyfriends?" I asked.

"Not at all!"

Everyone laughed, even Bunsom, who had guessed the content of the story.

"That's well and good," I said. "But how about a story from Somchai's childhood?"

"That was a long time ago," said Kai.

"Or what about when he was a young man?"

I felt Sompong's foot on mine. Since I was wearing sandals and he wasn't, this was not a fair exchange, but I knew what it meant. He wanted me to stop poking around.

"You are talking seventy years ago," said Lawana. "I don't think anyone here can remember back that far."

"Perhaps Somchai had friends from college, for example."

Again I felt a foot on mine, one that pressed down urgently.

"My father didn't talk much about himself," laughed Kai. "Although he was a sweet man, he was also private."

"He must have been hiding many secrets," Decha said. "But never mind old history. Who wants a nightcap?"

Any potential questions were drowned out in orders for liqueurs. Soon after, Kai started yawning, She made her excuses to leave, so Sompong and I did the same.

"She knows something," I told Sompong as soon as we climbed into our borrowed car.

"What makes you say so?"

"I can't tell you exactly. It was a feeling."

"You asked so many questions! They will think you are nosy."

"I don't care what they think. But something bubbled underneath the surface. Didn't you feel it too?"

Sompong started the car and headed back towards Norm's. He was so quiet I thought he was angry with me. Sure, I'd stepped over the line, but he'd forced me to do so. He hadn't been able to step over the line himself.

"Maybe I'm wrong," I said as we hit the main road. It was nearly midnight, and the traffic had died down to a trickle.

"Gina, all my life there has been something unsaid, something that lies beneath the surface."

"Between you and your aunts or between you and your grandfather?"

"I never noticed it with Grandfather. But with my aunts, always it was the same thing. I would enter the room, and they would suddenly stop talking."

"As if they'd been talking about you?"

"Exactly."

"You didn't question them?"

He kept his eyes on the road even though we had every bit of it to ourselves.

"I refused to believe that there was a problem. I convinced myself that they were having girl talk. Or, if they were talking about me, I liked to think that they were trying to decide which school I should attend or which friend of the family they hoped I would date."

"You never thought any deeper than that?"

He swerved, but the object in the road was an empty sack. "No, Gina. I suppose I was too afraid. I know that sounds silly."

"Not at all."

Regardless, Sompong refused to discuss the situation. The emotional drain had caught up with him. Norm was still at the office doing paperwork, so we retired to my room and watched a silly TV show. Sompong fell asleep on my bed, fully clothed. When his breathing sounded deep, I rose and donned a night shirt. Then I pulled off his socks and lay beside him in the dark, unable to sleep. Instead I kept imagining a young Somchai and a young Janjira meeting for the first time.

I imagined that the moment was wonderful.

By the time we arrived at Wat Chaweng, preparations were well under way. The coffin pyre had been set up in the funeral temple, which was like a small gazebo. The temple was complete with wreaths of flowers, blinking lights, and pictures of Grandfather as a handsome young man only a bit older than the man in Janjira's photo. Morning prayers followed. After lunch was served to the monks, they waited for an auspicious moment to set Grandfather free.

In the meantime Sompong and I alternated between visiting the funeral temple and sitting on the plastic chairs before it. Whenever friends of Vaitnee's approached or I felt vaguely in the way, I wandered around the temple complex. The main features were two wats, a yard full of chedis dedicated by wealthy relatives, and an old bell that hung from a wooden frame.

This wat paled after Chiang Mai's selections because none of its features were unique. The Buddhas of the main temple were like others I'd seen, and the altar background of dark blue and silver stars was harmonious rather than striking. The atmosphere was comforting though because the complex was brimming with life. Dogs scavenged for scraps, monks traveled between buildings, townspeople enjoyed the shade of leafy trees that had dark berries the size of olives, and motorcycle-taxi drivers in beige vests luxuriated in naps between fares. The rustling of the wind among the palm leaves provided background music.

The complex included an elementary school. Dozens of children swarmed around in disheveled white shirts. The boys wore khaki shorts held by brown belts while the girls wore skirts of navy blue. Most ran barefoot in the coarse, sandy dirt that carpeted the complex. They chased each other, tagged each other, and fell down. They competed for their instructors' attention, jumping and hollering to achieve it. Their shouting was a constant and welcome reminder of life.

Although I teared up from time to time, my rational side knew that Grandfather was at peace. Sompong was more emotional, lapsing into tears that he quickly brushed away. He tried to apologize for grieving, but each time I cut him off. "You weren't there when my Aunt Milena died," I told him. "Italians grieve better than anybody. You've never seen such a mess." He seemed to understand my analogy. More importantly, he needed a simple show of support. During the cremation, as we tried to follow custom by focusing our thoughts on spiritual lifting, he locked his fingers through mine and squeezed.

Chapter Twenty-Six

That night we couldn't avoid dinner at Vaitnee and Manat's. I urged Sompong to go alone, but he claimed that by now I was part of the family. He said that I had learned to care more about Grandfather in a week than the man 's daughter had in the forty-some years she'd known him. Dinner was only tolerable because Vaitnee was vacuous and subdued. Kai and her husband added levity. They hadn't been present for the Disaster Dinner nor had they been debriefed, so they didn't recognize underlying tensions. They would have assumed that for a post-funeral function, everything was going as well as it could.

Sompong barely ate. Usually he had a healthy appetite, but he picked at the noodles and only tried a few bites of the beef and oyster sauce before pushing back his plate. I was afraid he felt ill, but instead he was distracted. As soon as the maid cleared the dinner plates, he stood and clanked his knife against his water glass.

"By now Grandfather is gone. Our words cannot hurt him. But I am sick of mysteries and half-truths. Who will explain to me about Janjira?"

Inside I cheered. From somewhere deep inside, he had finally managed to take the initiative. The effect was remarkable. Just like the moment in a horror movie when the Victrola gives out and the music whines to a halt, conversations stopped and all eyes turned to Sompong. Even the children sensed that they needed to be quiet.

Quickly I looked from Kai to Vaitnee to catch their reactions, but they had frozen into garden gnomes.

"I am tired of not knowing," Sompong said more loudly. "I am fed up with your deceptions. And if you think I will leave this house tonight without finding out, you are wrong."

"You know as much as you need to," said Vaitnee. She wasn't watching Sompong. She was fingering the edge of the tablecloth where the seam had started to pull apart.

Sompong walked over to her. "Who is Janjira? Tell me now!"

His words echoed in the silence. Vaitnee pretended not to hear.

"Janjira!" he shouted.

Vaitnee finally turned to look at him. "Where did you hear that name?"

"Janjira is the woman who gave Gina the package to bring to Grandfather. Tell me who she is!"

In hushed tones Kai translated a few words to her husband while Vaitnee stared angrily ahead.

"What secret is so awful none of you can talk about it?"

Silence. Outside, birds chirped.

Sompong returned to my side. "Why is the past so sinful? Was Grandfather a criminal? A drug dealer? A murderer!"

"Don't be stupid," said Vaitnee.

"You have always treated me as ignorant except for when you were deliberately ignoring me," Sompong told Vaitnee. "Maybe it was my mother who did something wrong. All the time she has been dead, you have never managed to say a kind word about her. You have never wanted to tell me about my past. It is time I claimed my own history. Who is Janjira!" He spoke so loudly that Vaitnee's children completely abandoned their table soccer. Kai's son, who was in a high chair next to her, started to cry.

Kai had grown visibly agitated. She stood briefly but sat back down. When she started to speak, Vaitnee stopped her. Subtly Kai signaled to her husband that it was time to leave, and Bunsom immediately helped her gather the children's belongings. Then he picked up the squirming two-year-old.

"We had better be going," Kai said. "The children are restless." She started a round of farewells. She shook my hand, saying she was pleased I had joined them. Then she hugged Sompong gently. "Father told us never to tell you while he was alive. Janjira is your grandmother. Your mother was our half-sister. We didn't know it until after she died."

"Why not tell me?"

Kai sighed. She'd held up well until now, but her eyes were moist, and her breath was short. "Father wasn't trying to be mysterious. Vaitnee convinced him that the information would make you feel bad. Above everything else, he didn't want you to be hurt. I know it's hard to accept this, but some day, when you have children of your own, you will understand. Do not hold this against his memory."

As Bunsom picked up the infant's carrier, he waved. He held the door open for his wife and son and they disappeared into the night, leaving a painful vacuum behind.

"Feel better?" Vaitnee snapped as the door closed behind them and we all sat back down again.

Sompong showed no expression. "What she said I already knew. What else have you hidden from me? And why?"

Vaitnee turned away, but Manat looked on helplessly, as if he could atone for his wife's mistakes if only he tried hard enough.

"How can it be that my know-it-all aunt has nothing to say?" asked Sompong. "And she is supposed to be the smart one!"

For twenty seconds, perhaps the longest of my entire life, no one spoke.

Finally Sompong turned to me. "Kai had the right idea.

Let's leave. There is nothing for us here."

I stood and grabbed my purse. I'd been ready to leave before we'd entered the house.

"I will come for my things tomorrow morning," Sompong said. "Then you will never have to see me again. But do not think you can fool me. I know why you refuse to tell me my own stories. You are ashamed of your own selfishness. Someday, you will pay for it."

Manat hurriedly accompanied us outside, glad for the chance to leave the room. He spoke with Sompong in Thai—I caught something about the airport—before hugging us goodbye.

"At least you stood up to Vaitnee," Norm said. "You have to give yourself some credit."

We had retired to Norm's living room. Six empty beer cans adorned the coffee table, not a one of them mine.

"I do not see why I had to scare the information out of them," Sompong complained. "I do not understand why it was such a big deal."

"Janjira's parents didn't approve of Somchai. They tried to shut him out, but by then Janjira was already pregnant with your mother," said Norm. We'd gone over the story ten times already, trying to figure out explanations for the secrecy, but we were too drained to be imaginative.

"They made her stay far away so they could claim she was dead and no one would find out," I said.

"Normally a child would have remained with its mother or been sent to an orphanage," said Sompong. "Why not this time?"

Norm and I shook our heads. We were fed up with hearing the questions because we didn't have any way to answer them.

"Everything would have been different had my mother grown up in America," said Sompong.

Norm shook his head. "It won't do you any good to think along those lines. Had your mom been raised in the

U.S., she wouldn't have met your dad. I don't know who you'd be, but you wouldn't be you."

"If my parents had been in a car accident in America, they would have received medical treatment right away, and one of them would have survived."

Norm pretended to agree by popping open another beer.

"There's no use blaming yourself," I said. "You were too young to know what was going on."

"Gina, at first I was too young. But I've always known there was something wrong. Something shameful."

"You can't be sure."

"I knew from the way Vaitnee and Kai always hushed when I entered the room. Chat, chat, hush. Every time. Sometimes I sneaked up on them, but they were wary, as if they anticipated my interruptions. At first I kidded myself that their topics were not suitable for a little boy's ears. But I always knew better. And I was afraid. I thought something was wrong with me, that I had some terrible disease they would not tell me about. So I protected myself from knowing the truth. What a fool! You have to confront yourself sooner or later the way we all confront death in the end. Like Grandfather. So now he is gone and the stories have gone with him. Had I insisted, he would have shared. I put the past out of my mind never thinking that someday he would be gone. The things I should have asked about my mother are lost to me forever. I feel guilty that I never helped Grandfather share the pain he held behind that quiet mask. Now he is dead, and Vaitnee is dead to me too. I can never forgive her. What I do know is that I will not live my life the way Grandfather did, meaning the way somebody else wants me to. I vow to both of you that I will not repeat my ancestors' mistakes. I will live my life my way. If I ever have children, I will encourage them to do the same. Grandfather suffered and so did Janjira. But it all ends here."

Sompong rose and took his keys from his pocket. "I

must take a drive. Alone. Please do not wait up for me. I am not sure how far I need to go."

Norm and I watched numbly as he left the room.

"Think we should follow him on my scooter?"

"That's sweet of you, Norm. But I don't think it's necessary. He just needs some time."

I retired to Sompong's room, but I was too wide awake to do anything that came close to sleeping. Instead I searched through my suitcase. I'd brought along a deck of cards for the occasional evening Rachel and I would spend relaxing. That time had never come, which was why I had to dig pretty far to find the cards.

I laid out the seven rows to play Solitaire and reviewed the evening in my mind. How dare an aunt hide so much information from a younger, vulnerable relative? I assumed it happened often, which made me feel even more appreciative of my own family. If I wanted to ask something, I did so.

But come to think of it, I didn't always want to. I'd avoided the subject of my parents' separation with the excuse that the event was clear cut. Dad wanted the job. Mom refused to live in Mexico. No doubt there was more to the story. Dad's job might have been an excuse. Maybe at ten years old I'd been too young to notice undercurrents. I vaguely remembered our waiting on him for family dinners. Like as not he would turn up an hour or so later, and by that time Mom had all the leftovers wrapped up tight. She never seemed angry on those occasions, however. Instead she seemed relieved.

I lost the game, shuffled, and started another. Come to think of it, what had brought my parents together? They'd met in college when they were both juniors. Mom said that Dad had started flirting with her. At first she'd resisted. She was supposed to stay in Arizona long enough to attend the university before hurrying back to Durango. Instead they married after they finished school and stayed together a quarter of a century. Maybe that was long enough to be with anybody. Lots of my aunts and uncles had been married for twice that long, but did they ever notice whether or not they were happy?

Sompong had no way to know whether his grandparents would have stayed together and enjoyed a fairytale marriage or not. Such a relationship was possible, but was it likely? And honestly, couldn't the young lovers have found a solution if they'd really, really tried? Sompong hadn't considered such contingencies. He wouldn't want to.

After losing four games in a row, I shuffled the cards a few extra times. As I did so, I realized that the current lesson might as well be for myself. No matter how strongly I felt about Sompong right now, we were the same age as his grandparents when Nitya was conceived. If we'd been in that same situation, would we have made a smart decision?

I wanted to think so, but I didn't have any proof. Then I proceeded to lose another seven games.

Chapter Twenty-Seven

We were at Vaitnee's by eight the next morning. Our goal was to retrieve Sompong's suitcase and Grandfather's personal belongings. Manat had assured us that if we left early enough, we would find standby flights to Bangkok and then on to Chiang Mai.

The woman who answered the door was different from the one I'd first met. Vaitnee had aged overnight. Her hair was as unkept as if she'd fallen out of bed without thinking about herself. She looked dazed, not because she'd recently woken up, but because her eyes were so puffy they barely fit on her face.

The terrible appearance served her right. I suddenly hoped we would have time to take some family portraits.

"Good morning," she said in a crackly voice. "Please come in. Won't you have coffee?"

"We are in a hurry to start our journey," said Sompong.

"Manat is still in the shower."

Sompong looked at me, but I shrugged. In the background I could indeed hear that the water was running.

"One quick cup," I said.

"Then we must leave without delay," said Sompong.

Vaitnee led us into the dining room where the children were finishing bowls of cereal. They greeted us before they slunk off. The maid was conspicuously absent.

"Wait here." Vaitnee quickly went into the kitchen and came back with a plate of sweet cakes, which she set in the middle of the table. "I am sorry I have been a poor hostess."

She'd been a hostess at all?

"You have many things to be sorry for," Sompong said. "If you have anything to say, do so quickly."

"Sompong, I need you to hear me out."

Vaitnee took her time pouring us coffee. When she offered us the sweet cakes, Sompong shook his head, but I took the fattest of the bunch.

"We are waiting," said Sompong.

"I knew this day would come," she said softly, looking down at her lap, "but I fought it all the same. You and Father were so far away that I didn't have to think about you. Manat suggested that I visit, but instead I made excuses. I didn't want to talk about your childhood, Sompong, because then I would have to talk about my own."

Sompong stood. "Now you are talking in circles. Come, Gina. We will wait for Manat outside."

"No! Please. Listen."

Sompong frowned, but I took his hand and pulled him back down.

"Five minutes," I said.

"The truth is that I didn't want to believe your story about an old friend sending Father a present." She spoke so quietly I had to strain to hear her. "As far as I knew, Father didn't have any friends in America."

"You assumed I lied to you," said Sompong.

"I thought you'd made up the tale to explain how you suddenly found an American girlfriend. It never occurred to me that the 'friend' might be Janjira. Is that what she told you, Gina, that she was a friend of the family?"

"Not in so many words. We all misunderstood. We thought she was Somchai's sister. After Rachel and I saw some old photographs, we put things together."

Vaitnee fingered a tissue that was half-concealed in her palm. "Why didn't you tell me what you knew about Janjira when you first reached Ko Samui?"

Sompong crossed his arms over his chest. "You have

always hidden information from me, Aunt. Instead I had to bait you as a mouse in a trap. If it hadn't been for Kai, you'd still be denying that you ever heard Janjira's name."

Vaitnee placed both elbows on the table and supported her cheeks with her hands. "Please understand that your announcement last night came as a shock. Because we hadn't heard Janjira's name in years, we had forgotten about her. We thought Father had too."

"I am quite sure you had not forgotten. Will you tell me the story or not?"

"Are you sure you want to hear it?"

"I will not beg. Tell me or not. Your choice."

She shrugged defeat. "The story started more than eighty years ago. I'm not sure how well I know the details."

"I am waiting."

Slowly Vaitnee took a sip of coffee, frowning because it was still hot. "Father and Janjira grew up on the same block south of The Golden Mount. By the time they were in high school, they were practically inseparable."

"So?" asked Sompong.

"Janjira's parents disapproved of Father because his family was barely middle class."

"Hers was better?"

"No, but they expected her to marry into money."

"That's terrible," I said.

"Yes," Vaitnee said. "To our modern ears it is shocking. But we are speaking of many years ago. People were desperate. They found resources any way they could."

I knew such stories were common. My aunts had hinted about similar situations in Mexico, where oversized families became equally frantic.

"My great-grandparents were monsters," said Sompong.

"Sompong, at that time people assumed they knew what was best for their children, and children were to be obedient. Father's parents didn't approve of Janjira either. They said she was too high on herself."

"So Janjira and Somchai saw each other secretly?" I asked.

"They did."

Manat popped into the room. He looked around anxiously before asking if we needed anything.

"Is the baby sleeping?" she asked.

"Yes."

She pointed to the pot. "Perhaps you could prepare more coffee?"

He nodded silently and left the room.

"Janjira's parents introduced her to potential suitors, but she turned them down one after another, claiming various defects in character. Then the perfect suitor came around, a good-looking businessman with a cheery nature and a secure future. He was a decade older than Janjira, but her parents said she would marry and set a date."

"Poor Grandfather! How did he stop them?"

"He was lucky. Janjira's mother came down with a severe case of pneumonia. The wedding was postponed. The suitor was called off to business in England. I'm not sure if he returned to Thailand or not. While Janjira's father was preoccupied with his wife's health, Janjira and Father sneaked off and married."

"That was their only option," said Sompong.

"They thought so. They had a private ceremony and ran off to live with some of Father's friends on the outskirts of Bangkok. When Janjira's parents found out, they were furious. They denounced Father's family, demanding to know where the couple was staying. For weeks the two families argued back and forth, but nobody knew the newlyweds' whereabouts. After a few months Janjira's parents hired an investigator to find the couple. Eventually he did. Even though Janjira was pregnant by then, they dragged her home and reported Father to the police, claiming the marriage had been illegal."

"Grandfather's crime was to love!"

"Janjira's parents had a relative who worked for the police. Father was ordered to stay away or face arrest. Janjira's parents would have sent her to another city, but by then she was too pregnant to travel. She gave birth before they could figure out what to do."

"Is that why they gave my mother to Grandfather?"

"Not quite. Their plan was to give the child up for adoption so that Janjira could start fresh."

"And forget about her own child?" I asked.

"That was the theory. I know it's wrong, but they still carried through. They had the marriage annulled and prepared to marry Janjira off to a diplomat."

"She did not protest?" asked Sompong.

"Perhaps she had given up, but she was determined to get Nitya to Father. How they managed to communicate, I don't know. I suspect they had help from the maid. At any rate Father went for your mother in the middle of the night. He had no idea of the work involved with a baby, but perhaps he would have chosen the same path anyway."

"Somchai rescued the baby but not its mother?" I asked.

"She'd been locked in her room for days. She slipped Nitya out a narrow window. Father went into hiding with the child because he feared repercussions, but there weren't any. Janjira's parents were glad to be rid of a problem. Soon after it seems they shipped Janjira out of the country. Her second marriage took place abroad, presumably in England. Father found out second-hand, and by then he had no way to track her."

"Shortly after that Grandfather moved to Chiang Mai."

Vaitnee stirred her coffee. "That's where he finished school. He liked living in the northern city because he was anonymous. He could claim his wife had died, and in some ways she had."

Sompong pushed his bangs from his forehead. "Why all the secrecy?"

"Don't blame me. It was Father who wanted to bury

the past."

"I'm sure he felt awful that he couldn't rescue his wife," I said.

"That was part of it," Vaitnee concurred. "His parents never forgave him for the whole episode. They never spoke about it when we were around, but Kai and I sensed tensions."

Sompong sat back against the chair, making it creak. "So Grandfather struggled for a couple of years before falling in love with your mother."

She turned her chair towards the window as if hoping to escape through it. "You're wrong, Sompong. Father was never in love with her."

For several seconds none of us could speak. Manat came in with more coffee, filling our cups silently before sliding away.

"That's the tragedy of it," Vaitnee said. "That's why it was best kept a secret."

"You are wrong, Aunt," said Sompong softly. "Grandfather was devoted to your mother. I'm sure he loved her very much."

She rubbed away another tear. "He loved her, yes. But he was never once in love with her."

"Why did your mother agree to marry him?" I asked.

"She assumed he'd fall in love with her eventually."

I could imagine a hopeful young woman with a broken but gentle man. The picture wasn't a pretty one.

"How did they meet?" Sompong asked.

"She was a waitress in a noodle shop near Father's apartment. She admired Father because he was a professional, yet he had a sense of humor." Vaitnee smiled for the first time all morning. "She used to tell me about the first time she saw him, how he was sitting by himself in the corner, how his shirt was clean and ironed, but buttoned wrong. He seemed awkward, and that endeared him to her."

"Somchai asked her out?"

"Eventually. Every time he came into the noodle shop, she'd fight off the other waitresses so that she could wait on him. She'd quiz him about his many girlfriends, but he didn't like to talk about anything personal."

"She must have known he had a daughter," Sompong said.

"When he finally brought Nitya to the restaurant instead of leaving her with the maid, Mother was enchanted. Even at three years old, Nitya had a sparkle to her, an inner beauty." Vaitnee sighed. "She brought out the best in almost everybody."

"Never in you," said Sompong.

"No. Mother fell in love with her on the spot, just as she'd fallen in love with Father. She invited them to her parents' house. They liked Father's humble nature and the tender way he cared for his daughter. They felt sorry for him because he told them his wife had died."

"Grandfather did not change his story."

"He'd been in Chiang Mai for several years by that point. He had no reason to think that he'd ever see Janjira again. He had a good job, but he was isolated. He needed Mother, and when she offered to join their lives permanently, he accepted. It was a reverse proposal. They married and were relatively happy together. Especially Nitya. She grew up secure in the love of her father and the woman she assumed was her mother. She was an only child until she was ten, which is when I was born."

"But you never liked her," said Somchai.

"I've always lived in Nitya's shadow. She was always so perfect, so kind, so smart, so funny, so pretty. How could I hope to compete? And there was no one to help me. Mother was oblivious. When I told her I was unhappy, she didn't listen."

Sompong slowly nodded. "You have always been resentful of my mother because you assumed Grandfather loved her more than you or Kai."

The oldest child peeked in from the doorway, thought better of it, and backed away.

"No." Vaitnee started tearing again. Abruptly she stood and fled the room.

"Now what?" whispered Sompong.

"Now we wait," I said.

Chapter Twenty-Eight

We listened intently as several slow minutes passed. Faintly we heard the sounds of someone trying not to cry. Then we heard flushing.

Vaitnee returned and sat down, eyes freshly irritated. She sat on the edge of her chair and faced Sompong straight on. "Sompong, I resented your mother because my mother always loved her best too."

Vaitnee's face became a dark cloud about to burst. For several seconds she held her emotional turmoil inside; then it poured out in streams of tears that fell to the floor with audible plops.

No wonder she'd woken up looking like such a wreck; she'd spent the night going through what most people don't solve in a decade of therapy. We couldn't help her. Sompong was too stunned, and I was too unfamiliar with the protocol. Finally I couldn't stand it anymore. I scooted my chair next to hers, and when I tried to comfort her with a hug, she squeezed me like a snake. Awkwardly we rocked back and forth until she calmed down.

Manat entered the room, kissed the top of his wife's head, and asked Sompong if we were ready to go. We were more than ready, but Vaitnee spoke quick words in Thai, and Manat retreated.

"You can't leave me now." She used a paper napkin to dry her face. "You must hear it all. Isn't that what you wanted?"

Sompong nodded.

Vaitnee twisted the napkin into a pretzel. "Father assumed that if he tried hard enough, he could make the past go away."

"So he never told Nitya about her real mother," I said.

"He wanted us to be a happy family. If awkward questions came up about family resemblance, he laughed them away. His silly answers satisfied us because they were entertaining."

Finally Sompong succumbed to a sweet cake. He placed it on his plate as if it might break. When he spoke, he was still looking at it. "How did you find out differently?"

"Father's relatives knew the story, of course. There wasn't any way he could have hidden it from them. And they respected his decisions to keep things quiet. Then Mia came to visit. Do you remember her?"

"Who?" asked Sompong.

"Father's brother's niece. You've met her before."

"I vaguely remember, but I have not seen her for years."

"There's a reason for that. Anyway, Uncle Hatna and his wife wanted to take a short vacation by themselves. Mother had offered to babysit Mia, so they shipped her up to Chiang Mai. I was in paradise because I finally had someone my age to play with. Your mother was too old to be any fun, and Kai hadn't come along yet. Mia and I were alone in the garden. We got into a fight, and I taunted her about the fact that her parents had gone on vacation but didn't want to take her along. I don't know why I did it. But you know how children are. If you're mean to them, they're mean right back. Mia started making fun of me. She said that my family was fake and that I didn't have a real sister. I became angry. I think I punched her. After Mia went home a few days later, I followed your mother around, comparing her features to mine and asking if she were my sister or not."

Vaitnee closed her eyes. The past was more vivid than

anything recent, and the grooves around her eyes had deepened into shelves. I still disliked her, but I was beginning to imagine her childhood.

"Nitya ignored me even though I kept pestering her. I ran to my parents asking if I'd been adopted."

"They told you the story?"

"They refused to admit to it. They wouldn't budge. For the next few days, I worked on each of them separately, trying to trick them into admission. They were stronger than I was. That's where I made a tremendous mistake." She sighed with her whole chest. "I took in my anger and didn't let loose of it. I pulled away from my parents and your mother too. At least that's what I thought. Instead I was pulling away from myself. I grew into a horrible teenager, always testing my parents' will against mine. I don't have to bore you with that part."

I could imagine the scene already, the rebellious teenager who married young to get out of the house and whose husband and children were her sole identity. No wonder Rachel and I had threatened her. We could have never guessed her desperate sense of territory, but her story was stupid enough to be completely believable.

Sompong pushed his coffee cup towards Vaitnee, who filled it. "You learned the truth at your mother's funeral?"

"No. She only lasted three days after the aneurysm. We were so shocked that we didn't have time to prepare. Her funeral was a whirlwind, and I was taking exams at the time." Vaitnee bowed her head. "I learned the truth when Nitya died. I went around asking the older relatives. They ignored my questions, telling me how sorry they were about my sister's death. I wasn't even listening. I became more stubborn. By that night Father was too brokenhearted to care. I asked him straight out if Nitya had a different mother. He blinked. That was his answer. Up until then Nitya had been his ray of hope. I'm sure he kept praying, but since he never expected to see Janjira again, after Nitya's death he had nothing left of her."

"He still hadn't told you anything," I said.

"No. But I was stupid enough to hound him. After a couple of days he caved in. He said he'd had another wife, but she'd gone away. That's all he ever told me, but I was like a detective on the worst cop show. I haunted all my other relatives until, piece by piece, I knew the basic details."

"How did Grandfather link the purple elephant to Janjira?"

"That part no one told me about. I've never seen anything like it."

Sompong stretched. "I guess that is the whole story, then."

Vaitnee shrugged. "You should probably know that Father tried to kill himself."

"What?" cried Sompong.

Vaitnee took a sweet cake, but she didn't bite into it. "Father was sad after my mother died. He mourned her loss as any spouse might, but in time he bounced back. He moved us forward with our lives, and he moved forward himself. After Nitya died, he lost control. Night after night he sat by himself, staring into space. Kai and I were so busy taking care of you that we didn't pay attention to Father. Before we realized it, he'd lost fifteen kilos. He was hospitalized for dehydration after fainting at a niece's wedding."

"Still," Sompong said stubbornly, "that is hardly killing himself."

Vaitnee grabbed a floral napkin and dabbed at her eyes. "That came later. On a hot afternoon Kai and I had offered to take you to the pool. Father stayed home with the excuse of doing some gardening. As we drove towards the pool, you spotted an ice cream shop and started nagging that you were hungry."

"I do not remember."

"This particular shop was the most popular in the neighborhood, so we didn't mind waiting in the long line of customers. But by the time we'd purchased our treats, clouds had gathered overhead. We were deciding whether or not to continue to the pool when the rain started. So we went back home. Father was lying on the bed curled into a ball, but we could tell something was wrong with him. We called for the neighbors. They took one look at him and called emergency. Interns whisked him through the hospital and pumped twenty sleeping pills from his stomach."

"I never knew about this," Sompong whispered.

"He wouldn't have wanted you to. Afterwards he was ashamed. He was aware that you had lost even more than he had. After that he tried to recover. I give him credit for it. He spent time with me and Kai. He pretended to be happy, but we knew he was acting."

Sompong shook his head. "I feel awful. I would have never guessed."

"You're the one who cured him. It started by accident one day when Kai and I crossed our signals. The maid was sick, and no one was around to take care of you. We left you with Father. Kai and I were both at work all day, so we worried he would be irritated by the time we arrived home. Instead he was smiling, and you were asleep on his lap. Over the next months he was only cheerful when he was taking care of you. After a while we left you with him on purpose."

"Then you married Manat. I have some memories of the wedding."

"And Kai married a few months after. By then we all agreed that you should stay with Father. Kai and I were both newlyweds. We needed our privacy. Father needed you."

"No wonder I have always felt a strong bond with him," Sompong said.

"From time to time Kai and I wondered whether we should invite you to live with us, but there was no point. No matter what you did, Father was happy about it. When you did something wrong, he smiled and said that you

were a child growing up. Then you went to school and ex-
celed in math the way that he had. The older you got, the
prouder he became. I could never measure up. Neither
could my children. I didn't have the personality of your
mother, and I didn't have a knack for the things that Father
most cared about. What did that leave me with? When
Manat had the chance to move south, I insisted he take it. I
lied about that too. He didn't take a salary increase. He took
a slight decrease. I didn't mind the sacrifice because I wanted to be far away where I could put the family history out
of my mind. Now it has ricocheted back in my direction.
This was something I knew would happen, as I have said.
But I didn't believe it would. Not really. I prayed I'd never
have to confront the situation. Now I have no choice. For
that I am suffering. Someday I will be thanking you and
Gina for forcing the issue. Eventually I will appreciate that a
weight has been lifted from my shoulders. I have carried
this weight for so long that I still feel its pain. In time it will
lift. When it does, I will be able to talk to my children about
their family history. I may never have a happy relationship
with you, Sompong. I realize that you will resent me for a
long time to come. I could expect nothing different. But I
ask that, eventually, when you can, you give me a chance. I
appreciate that you have always treated my husband and
children with kindness even though I have not returned the
favor. For this, and for many things, I am deeply sorry. But I
cannot change the past any more than I can change Janjira's
history with Father. Instead we must go on."

We fell into the silence of the past. As if he'd been listening for an appropriate moment, Manat reentered the
room. "They should try for the midday plane," he said softly. "Otherwise they will have to wait until three o'clock for
the next possibility."

Vaitnee nodded, worn out. She was too hard a woman
to give in to her emotions easily, and now that she'd
dropped her guard, her strength had drained. We hugged

her briefly but left her at the table lost in a past she'd spent most of her lifetime trying to forget. I was thankful I didn't quite know how she felt.

Manat was able to slip us onto the next flight. He sat with us until boarding time, making small talk under the thatched roof designated as Terminal One. Sompong kept trying to apologize for his rude behavior to Vaitnee, but Manat repeatedly shook his head. "Always she has inside this monster who strangles her. Now that the monster is on the outside, I can fight too." Affectionately, he hugged us goodbye.

As soon as the flight left the ground, Sompong kissed my hand. "Gina, I would not have survived Ko Samui without you."

I nodded, watching as the trees turned into miniatures and the plane shot over a calm sea of blue. I was well aware that delivering Janjira's memento had triggered a painful cascade of events. At the time the task had seemed delightful. Deliver a package. Greet a friend's relative. Easy.

Once Ko Samui became a dot, I turned around. "Your history all makes sense now, doesn't it?"

Sompong nodded. "I knew Grandfather loved me in a special way. I could not have guessed why."

"Do you remember your parents at all?"

"I only remember my mother and from only one occasion. Or perhaps I remember the picture of it. For my fourth birthday, we had a party at Grandfather's house. In the photo, my mum is holding me, and I am squirming. Grandfather is trying to light the candles on my cake, but he can't because I am thrashing my legs. He and Mum are laughing so hard that they have their eyes closed. That is the most I can remember."

I nestled my head onto his shoulder so that he wouldn't see my own tears. He rested uneasily as we entered a system of angry clouds that shook the plane.

Chapter Twenty-Nine

Steady rain marked our return to Chiang Mai. On our way home from the airport, we stopped for dinner at an open-air restaurant at the night market. Over shrimp soup we watched bargain-hunters dart in and out of the storm. Sompong ordered with relish but ate little. I could guess why. The turmoil we'd faced on Ko Samui was bad enough, but now he feared going home to an empty house. I was nearly as spooked as he was. I picked at the salty noodles even after I was full so that we had the excuse to stay put. When the rain accelerated, Sompong ordered more beers.

We left when the waiters started going home themselves. Except for the *plop, plop* of the rain on the windshield, we drove in silence all the way from the river past Shinawatra. As soon as we turned down the soi leading to the house, Sompong pulled over and stopped the car.

"I need a minute."

"Take deep breaths," I suggested. I did the same. When he reached for my hand, he squeezed it until his nails dug into my skin and I involuntarily pulled away. "It'll be okay."

Chubby welcomed us enthusiastically, oblivious to our reluctance. Nui had left on a light for us, but we'd returned to an empty shell. The entrance hall was the same, the dining room was the same, but one glance at Grandfather's empty chair was enough to drag us down.

"Let's go outside," I said. "It's too hot in here. We need some fresh air."

At least from the veranda we could look up at the night and think beyond ourselves. We took turns petting Chubby. We practiced small talk, but uncomfortable lulls broke up our petty topics.

"Grandfather did his best," Sompong finally said. "I see now that he made a lot of mistakes."

"That's human nature. At least Somchai acted from the heart."

"Rather than from the head?"

"Or out of self-centeredness. Like my dad."

"You rarely mention him."

"I rarely see him. Talk about making a mistake."

"By taking a job out of the country?"

"By assuming Mom would go along with his decision."

"He wanted to move to her home country, right?"

"Yes. And I love being in Mexico for short periods of time. The country is progressing. But it's still sexist. Women are paid less than men and given little respect."

"The men are not faithful?"

"The problem is the double standard. When men cheat, they're macho. When women cheat, they're whores."

"Certainly the women don't stand for this."

"Many of the older ones do. Things are changing with the younger generations, but Mom didn't want us growing up in a place where she had struggled. Dad has never understood that."

Sompong angled his chair towards me. "He must have received a special job offer."

"That doesn't change a whole country's attitude. Now he's got a girlfriend, but for years he lived alone, hoping my mother would follow. I'll never forget the scene. It was a Sunday night, and Rachel was over for dinner. We were having dessert when Dad announced he was taking a job in Monterrey, which is several hours south of the border. I screamed that I wouldn't go, thinking I'd have to leave my school friends. Then Mom calmly said, 'If you're going without so much as consulting the rest of the family, you're going by yourself.' That was it. No argument, no discussion. For a moment Dad was shocked. Then he asked for a second piece of cake."

"Why did he take the job if your mother wished him not to?"

"He assumed she'd come around."

"Why did she permit him to leave?"

"She wasn't about to keep him against his will. She believes in letting go."

Sompong hung his head. "As I must let go now?"

"It's really not the same thing."

He scooted towards me and lay his head on my shoulder. After a few minutes I stood and pulled on his arm. "Let's lie down," I whispered. "It's been such a long day it seems like tomorrow."

He followed me to his bedroom, where stale air greeted us. Sompong opened the windows and turned on a ceiling fan. After he turned off the light, he removed his shirt and lay it over the desk chair. While he changed from long pants to shorts, I slipped out of my Capris and blouse and into a nightshirt. I pulled down the sheets and crawled onto the bed. A moment later Sompong lay down on the far side.

The room was vaguely illuminated by electric lights from the backyard. I turned sideways so I could watch Sompong's reactions as he stared at the ceiling. "Do you want to tell me what you're thinking?"

"You should sleep," he said. "The last days have been heavy."

I took his hand and pulled it close enough to graze my cheek. He rested it between us.

"If you'd rather talk, I'd like to listen," I said.

He turned towards me. "I do not know what to say. I feel odd, you know?"

"Of course."

"I need to rethink everything I thought I knew. For

example, I assumed no one liked my aunt because she was unpleasant by nature."

"No need to rethink that part."

"What if, from her earliest memories, she felt inferior?"

"You're giving her way too much credit."

"Such a feeling would make a difference."

"Characteristics are preprogrammed. Take Kai. She grew up under the same circumstances as Vaitnee, but she's so different that they barely seem related. She's good-natured. So are you."

"Are you sure?"

"You work hard and you're kind. You're usually in a good mood. You see the positive side of things."

"I have trained myself to do so."

"You've made a choice," I said, ruffling his hair. "Vaitnee has made a different one."

Once more I felt thankful to be from a family of independent women who made reasonable, healthy choices and stuck to them. Between my mother and my grandmother and my sister, I'd had reasonable training for living my own life. It was impossible for me to imagine growing up in any other way.

"Do you know what I am still wondering?" Sompong asked. "I want to know if Manat knew about this family history before they married. If I had been in his place, I would have become intimidated. I would have run off."

I ignored his comment. When I stretched my hand to his waist, his eyes flickered. I slid my fingers along his waistband and let them rest there. Eventually he reciprocated.

"On the plane," he finally said, "I thought about this too."

"And?"

"I did not know what to think."

"Who says you're supposed to know?"

With his free hand, he took mine, gently rubbing his index finger over my wrist. "If you were a Thai girl, I would know the parameters. With you I do not know the rules. I am afraid of doing too much or not enough."

"I could say the same," I said. "I'm not trying to push you into something."

He let loose of me and rolled onto his back. "I so wish you would."

I decided against waiting for a second invitation. I started by slowing kissing his lips and traveling south. Eventually he reciprocated until the hot room became even hotter. We took off one another's clothes, slowly, one piece at a time, and lay naked on the sheets as we went through the unfamiliar motions of touching one another.

He was more nervous than I'd expected because he'd never slept with a woman before. I decided not to mention that I knew more about it than he did.

Sompong awoke with a smile and a new outlook. For the next few days we relaxed into one another as I helped him through the stages of letting go. While I cleaned or straightened, he went over insurance policies and banking papers and gave away clothes. Other mementos he stashed in an assortment of boxes. Sompong claimed that he would go through them slowly, making careful decisions about what to keep. I doubted he would get around to it, but so what? The house had plenty of closets. Perhaps he would put aside some things for his nieces and nephews; at some point they too would wonder about their history.

In the evenings we sampled native cuisine at Sompong's favorite restaurants before taking long walks around Chiang Mai. Instead of suffering Rachel's Energizer Bunny style of tourism, we lingered over any detail that took our interest. Then we hurried back to Grandfather's house and practiced the lovemaking all over again.

In this area Sompong was both patient and kind. He would start by taking my hand, kissing it, luxuriating in the feel of my skin. I would reciprocate, running my fingers softly up and down his limbs. It wasn't simply a matter of desire. It was the slow, meaningful communication that takes place when two bodies come together in layers of softness. Even if I felt impatient as he massaged my back or tickled my ears with his tongue, I encouraged him to take his time.

After a couple of hours we would decide we really ought to sleep, but then we would start talking, sharing the most trivial details about our lives. We recounted adventures from high school and childhood dreams. I told him about life in the desert, and he explained about all the modernization that had happened in Chiang Mai. In the height of sharing I even told him about Jason; I suppose it was a kind of test to see whether he would get angry or show a jealous streak. Instead he merely said, over and over, how happy he was that I hadn't taken Jason's advice about canceling my trip. And although he admired my sister's enthusiasm, he was thankful that I made a better genealogist than a tourist.

After making love to me on our final evening together, Sompong rolled over me to turn on the light. "I found some interesting tidbits among the bank papers." He opened the nightstand drawer and pulled out three envelopes. When he held up the first, I could see it was crusty. Gingerly he pulled out the letter written on the kind of thin paper people used to buy to save on postage. He translated from Thai: "'I'll walk by your house every morning. Put a yellow flower in your window if you can see me that day. Put a red one if you can't.'"

"Somchai's code," I said.

"We knew they communicated somehow. I suppose they had to pay attention to every small clue."

I had a sudden flash of a Pedro Infante movie in which the star had to sneak past his girlfriend's parents. Finally I realized what I should have understood from the start, that my Mexican background helped me understand Sompong much more easily than my American one did. Mexico and

Thailand were conservative and passionate, outdated and romantic. The trick to a happy life wasn't to live one way or another but to fuse together the best of all worlds.

Sompong handed me a second envelope with a torn corner. It was addressed to Nitya Swoonswangs in bold male script.

"It is my father's writing," said Sompong. Again, he translated: "'Honey, I know you were upset last night, but you shouldn't have been. Blood doesn't matter. It doesn't dictate feelings or character. I love you for you, and I love you with all my heart. And your stepmother always loved you as if she were your mother, didn't she? If not, how could she have kept the secret all these years?'"

Sompong set the letter on the sheets. "Sweet, is it not?"

"Fabulous! So your mother knew."

"She must have found out shortly before she married. Everyone tells me my father was a wonderful man. I have to take their word for it."

I took Sompong's hand and squeezed it. "Maybe you'll find more letters."

"I am sure I will in time, but I am not obsessed about my history. I needed to know the basics. I had never seen my father's handwriting before, for example. Now I can start to complete the picture. It is a comfort to me. Before you arrived in Thailand, everything was blank because everything I wanted to know was taboo. Now I can be at ease with myself."

"Thank goodness," I said, reaching for him as he switched off the light.

Chapter Thirty

On my last morning in Chiang Mai, we both woke early as if we wanted time to feel as melancholy as possible. I had an evening flight to Bangkok, so we would have to suffer through the whole day as an extended farewell. We agreed to sleep in a little longer, but lying awake was painful. The happily chirping birds annoyed me. So did the sunshine. So did everything.

Sompong put on tea and set out sweet breads. Instead of whistling as he normally did, he was silent. He sat across from me in the dining room and took my hand. "I do not want this day to end, but at least I want to remember it."

For the hundredth time I considered changing my flight, no matter the extra fee or even summer school classes. Once again I decided that the airline had no right to another change fee. Save the funds for another trip, I told myself. There is no other trip, I answered. I was getting tired of myself.

Sompong knew I was miserable and kept me company by feeling miserable himself. He kept asking what I wanted to do because he couldn't think of anything else to say. I finally gave up and gave in. "Would you take me to Doi Suthep?"

"Doi Suthep?"

"The temple on the top of the hill or the mountain or whatever. Maybe I didn't pronounce it correctly."

"You said it the right way."

I pushed back my cup. "We don't have to go if it's too far. I don't really care."

Sompong stood and pulled me to my feet. "I would love to take you! It never occurred to me that you had not already visited our most famous temple. That is a real twist. But I will fire your sister. She is not a good tour guide after all. No traveler to Thailand should miss such a beautiful temple. Doi Suthep is vital to our heritage. You see — "

"While Rachel went to Doi Suthep, I visited CMET and met the French lady."

Lorraine and I had been exchanging furious emails. She'd been so delighted by my progress that I was sure the whole staff at CMET knew about it. We hadn't met up because she'd already left for a vacation in France, but I had a standing invitation to visit.

"I am stunned that you have not visited the temple," Sompong said. "Without it, your Thai experience would be incomplete."

"Then why are you just sitting there?"

"I am your chauffeur, waiting for your command."

"Let's go!"

He raced me to the car, but since he slipped on the grass, I beat him hands down.

Doi Suthep is perched on top of a mountain overlooking Chiang Mai. From the edge of town, a serpentine road of steep curves leads to the bottom level of the site. We parked the car and, since I insisted that taking the funicular was cheating, tackled the long staircases that led to the temple. Surprised at my latent tourist impulse, Sompong followed behind, mandating a few rest stops along the way.

As directed, we left our shoes with the smiling female clerks and passed through the gates into a courtyard of shiny floors where a golden chedi reached for the sky. Golden Buddhas reclined in positions that corresponded to days of the week. Imitating other visitors, we sat in the shade on the edge of the courtyard, breathing in the scene.

Newcomers crossed the threshold to the temple, gasping at the huge chedi they recognized from every advertisement about Chiang Mai and most of the ones about Thailand. The majority of today's visitors were Thai or Japanese, but there were Westerners as well. Most of the latter had arrived at the temple in short shorts, which were improper; for a small fee the wayward tourists had borrowed scarves from the shoe ladies and fashioned their silk rectangles into awkward skirts. I had known to wear Capris.

"Everyone comes here," Sompong said. "It's the most famous pilgrimage in the country."

"Do you often visit?"

When he didn't answer right away, I turned towards him. His mouth couldn't decide between a grin and a frown.

"I have been here once. When I first received my driver's license, I celebrated by driving up here."

"Alone?"

"With friends from school. We made a day of it, bringing our lunch, buying trinkets on the way up to the temple, eating ice cream on the way down."

"This place holds pleasant memories for you."

"Now it is different. My memories will be of you."

I must have turned red, which was the regular curse suffered by someone who was too pale to tan.

He patted my arm. "My memories will be perfect."

A noisy Thai family passed before us, the parents herding a quartet of small children.

"You'll have to visit often," I said.

Sompong squeezed my shoulder until it hurt. "I will. When I feel the most alone, I will come loaded with lotus blossoms, and in that sense you will still be with me."

I feigned intense interest in the young family. On today of all days, I didn't know how to listen to Sompong's romantic comments. I'd heard similar ones during summers with my cousins in Durango, but the Mexican teens had been easy to read: say nice things, get laid maybe.

A white cat sprawled on a shaded stone near us. A brown patch of fur marked its left eye. When I scratched the slender head, the cat purred.

"If they weren't so hard to take on airplanes, you would have adopted six or seven cats by now," said Sompong.

"No. They'd get into fights if I adopted too many. I'd only take two or three. Why don't you take a few yourself?"

He hesitated before answering. "I no longer have a home. I merely have a place to sleep."

He didn't have to say what we were both thinking: Tonight, for the first time, he'd be sleeping at Somchai's house alone except for Chubby. Again I wished I could stay longer and extend the dream, but no matter how many times you hit the snooze button, eventually you turn off the alarm clock and drag yourself out of bed. As it was, my classes would start two days after I reached Tucson, so I would have the pleasure of starting summer school with jetlag.

Sompong stood and pulled me to my feet. Leisurely, almost reluctantly, we joined the crowd milling around the temple's outer square.

Confused, I pointed to a see-through glass cage on an outdoor altar. "Isn't that—"

"Yes. A copy of the Jade Buddha you saw in The Grand Palace. I suppose you know the story of the relic?"

"Rachel told me about it."

He grinned. "Do you remember what she said?"

"I know that the monks started building their temple where the elephant stopped."

"Correct!"

"Do I pass the test?"

"Not until you visit the temple."

Worshippers packed the main hall so tightly that it was hard to breathe. Sompong and I knelt beside the others as a bald monk sat before us with crossed legs. As he waved drops of water into the air, he chanted nonchalantly in Thai. The locals nodded as he went along; the rest of us listened politely even though the monotone suggested boredom rather than inspiration. After the monk finished his prayer, the throng slowly approached the front of the room.

Men and women formed separate lines to give offerings. In return they received plain string bracelets. The monk tied bracelets around the men's wrists while a red-haired assistant tied them around the women's.

The bracelets weren't merely good luck charms. The idea was that a bracelet allowed you to take your training with you no matter how far away you went. In this case my teacher would be Sompong. Without ever trying to, he had taught me to be thankful for the beautiful life I'd enjoyed so far.

Sompong and I got lost among the throng, but we met back outside wearing matching white strings. He ran his finger along mine. "You passed the test."

For a moment I felt a wave of emotion. Then I shut off an impulse to cry. I'd come all the way to Thailand to find a simpler version of myself that had been locked up inside.

We walked behind the complex where we could view the city from under the shade of a huge bougainvillea that protected a wide terrace. Hand in hand we walked along the white handrails. Down below, Chiang Mai's structures rose gently as if the earth had been tapped with a magic wand.

"Gina," Sompong said in a strong tone as he pulled me towards him, "I must ask you something. Would you marry me?"

I must have looked horrified. He took a step away, then two, and then turned towards the view and set his hands squarely on the railing. "I am so sorry. I spoke without thinking. You are not ready to make such a decision. I am not ready to make such an offer."

I was ahead of him in that I'd thought about the possibility countless times, but I hadn't gotten past the question of where we would live. I placed my hands on his shoulders and gave him a brief kiss. "Can you put that thought on the back burner for now?"

Sompong was so stunned by his own question that he was unsure what to do. He opened and closed his mouth several times without saying anything. He indicated his watch. "Should we go on back?"

"Not yet."

As I held out my hand and we continued along the railing, we focused on the view so that we could avoid each other's eyes. The distant rooftops were a sea of small orange and beige patches. Once in a while the sun caught them enough to make the twinkle.

Sompong's words still weighed down the air.

"Anyway, why wouldn't I marry you?" I asked.

Sompong stopped so abruptly that the couple behind us, heavyset tourists with old-style Nikons, bumped into us and set us stumbling.

The man grabbed my wrist, which prevented me from landing on my rear. "Pardon me!"

"Goodness, my dear! Are you all right?" asked the woman. They were in their 60s and primed for rambunctious sightseeing. I guessed it was their first or second day abroad.

"No problem," I said, glad I'd only lost my balance, not all my dignity.

"You're from the States too!" the woman exclaimed. She roped me into a conversation before I saw the leash. The couple was from Nashville. This was their first trip to the Orient. They'd struggled to put their kids through college, and now they were determined to see the world. Thailand was their first stop, so their story poured out like water from a garden hose.

"Tell us about yourselves," said the woman. "Have you been married long?"

Sompong took a deep breath, preparing to impart our

story, but I was too quick for him. "Not long," I said. "This is our honeymoon." I took out my cell phone. "Would you take our picture?"

The woman was delighted at the suggestion. She handed her own camera to her husband and took my phone. She directed us a little closer to the left, then to the right, and then took several shots in case we didn't like the first ones. As I reciprocated by taking their photo as well, I wondered if this could possibly be what Sompong and I would look like in another forty years.

Except for the polyester, maybe it would be.

"Come on, honey," I said. "Your brother is probably waiting for us by now."

We shook the tourists' hands and wished them a good trip. Sompong followed my lead, and we headed off.

"You are very smooth," Sompong said as we headed for the long, stone stairway leading back to the parking lot. "Do you always tell outrageous stories to strangers?"

"My stories are true in spirit," I said smugly. "That's what counts."

His color may have protected him, but down deep, I knew that Sompong was blushing too.

Chapter Thirty-One

I pushed away the empty plate. We'd reduced the leftovers to three strands of noodles. Sompong had offered to take me out, but I'd opted for a quiet, intimate bite at the house and a last-minute shower that was supposed to keep me fresh for the long overseas trip.

He stretched his hand across the table and I stretched mine to meet it. "That thought we put on the back burner," he said, "how long does it have to stay there?"

Behind me, I heard the wall clock tick. I pondered the irony of sitting slouched around a table of dirty dishes when considering a decision that would change my life. I felt as if I should be standing up, wearing my best clothes, dancing on the table. Instead I looked into Sompong's bright eyes. "I probably wouldn't make a decision like that until I finished college."

"I would not blame you. School is the most important thing. We can agree on that."

I stirred my tea. "On the other hand, I'll need three more years to complete my degree, and that's if everything goes well."

"Life requires patience. If you rush, you cannot make the right decisions."

"Tucson is a long way from here. A very long way."

"I realize that." He placed his chopsticks beside his plate and bent his head. "What would your mother think of me?"

I walked around behind him and put my hands around his neck. "She'd like you fine." After the words left my mouth, I realized that "fine" was a weak endorsement. He reached his hand to meet mine, and I laced my fingers with his. "Actually, a lot."

"What would she think if we became serious?"

I pulled my chair closer and sat beside him, wrapping an arm around his waist. "She'd worry about cultural differences. She's been through them herself."

"Now your parents live apart."

"My dad is stubborn and my mother is independent."

"And you are both."

I laughed nervously. "I'm not sure that's a good thing."

"Of course it is." He patted my cheek with the back of his hand. "That is what led you to find me."

The next two hours were excruciating. The airport was bustling with activity, but Sompong and I dragged our feet. We chose the longest check-in line. Once I had a boarding pass, we shuffled to the uncomfortable plastic chairs in the lounge closest to the security gate.

Sompong sighed heavily. "I am not a Catholic."

"I'm barely Catholic myself. That's not a problem." I curled and uncurled my toes. After all the walking Rachel had mandated, I was surprised my Tevas had survived, though by now both heels were worn.

"There is a problem?"

"I don't know if I could live in Thailand."

He kissed my shoulder. "It is hard for people to give up what they are used to. For example, how could I ever give up my grandfather's house? How could I allow it to belong to somebody else?"

I'd wondered myself. But the house was too big and empty for one person, so how could Sompong cope with living in it?

"I'm sure Arizona is beautiful," he said.

"Come visit me?"

"When?"

"Whenever you want."

"That would be tomorrow." We sat hugging for a few minutes until he checked his watch and escorted me to the security line. "I will email you before you reach home."

We shared a noisy kiss. If people were watching, I hope they took notes.

The flight was sardine-style full. I had a window seat, but I was stuffed beside an elderly couple with no understanding of a carry-on. Their bundles took up half my leg room, but I felt too sorry for myself to say anything. The woman was writing postcards while the man, who sat between us, supervised.

"What the hell is a wat?" he asked. "I never did figure it out."

I picked up the in-flight magazine and pretended I was interested in it.

My mother and grandmother rescued me from Tucson International. They expected a full account right away, but as soon as we reached the house, I threw down my bags and plugged in my dead device. I didn't have time to explain. How could they have understood that my life was riding on an electronic screen? I sat in the family room, nervously tapping my fingers as the tablet kicked into life.

I didn't have one email from Sompong but six. Most of the messages were short: He'd found another letter written by his father, they'd had another rain storm, he'd asked Nui to help with extra cleaning. The final email proposed dates I'd like him to come visit. He could get the best price if he left on a Tuesday and came back on a Wednesday, so could I handle him for nine days or even eighteen? He needed a few weeks to catch up with his web work, but would it be all right if he came to visit in August?

August is not the time to invite visitors to Tucson if you want them to like the place, but September isn't much better, and October can be hot too. "Come as soon as you can," I wrote back.

I meandered to the kitchen and attempted to be normal rather than airborne.

"Tell us all about your trip," Mom said as she set a bowl of salad on the table. My grandmother had already sat down.

"I hardly know where to start."

"What was Bangkok like?" asked Mom.

"What did you like the most?" asked Grandma.

"The country is full of temples," I said, deciding that I would need to explain about my fantastic trip in small raindrops rather than deluges. "We saw them everywhere. They were magnificent, full of rich decorations and intricacies I can't even describe. Wait! I'll show you some of Rachel's postcards. I brought them home for her."

It only took me a moment to rustle through my backpack to find the stack. I spread the cards out over the table, including on top of the empty plates and the napkins. "This is The Great Palace," I started. "This is Doi Suthep. This is—"

Grandma picked up one of the cards, but her eyes glazed over. "Your temples are lost on me, dearie. Tell us about something else." My grandmother didn't care about foreign buildings. Besides, she hadn't bothered to locate her reading glasses.

"The people were very friendly, always trying to help you find your way around town."

My mother set a bottle of salad dressing on the table and sat down. "Could you understand them?"

"Most of the time. A lot of people spoke some English. People in the tourist trade have to be able to communicate."

"What about the cooking?" asked Grandma, helping me restack all the cards.

"The food was delicious! Lots of noodles. With spices and hot sauces. Very tasty."

"What was your favorite dish?" Mom asked as she offered me a slice of cheese.

"I'm not sure. Maybe *pad thai*—that's a noodle dish with a sweet peanut sauce. But we had lots of curries. I'll have to learn to make one so that I can give you the idea."

Mom and Grandma exchanged long glances.

"You?" Mom asked. "Make curry?" She was probably wishing she was recording me. Up to this point I had a clean record on cooking. I hadn't much tried it.

"An easy curry," I explained. "I bet you can buy the sauce ready-made."

"She must be delirious," my mother told my grandmother.

"Yes. You'd best check her temperature. Plus there's jetlag."

"Don't be silly!" I laughed.

"You've never offered to cook dinner before," Mom said.

"I don't mean I'd cook a whole meal. I would just try a curry!"

"Think there was something funny in the water over there?" Mom asked her mother.

"Don't they have jungle diseases? Maybe she caught something."

"You must have had some trip," Mom concluded as she filled her water glass.

I couldn't fool them. Without meaning to, I laughed nervously. "I guess I don't have a good way to explain myself. But really, the whole trip was wonderful."

"You'll have to call and thank the radio station. And by the way, they want to know when to expect their article."

The article! I'd forgotten all about it. But I knew one thing for sure. I wouldn't write about a gazillion temples or museums or even the rain. I'd write about Thierry and Lorraine and Norm and Kai. I'd describe how life in Thailand was for its inhabitants, not its tourists, and I'd explain how visiting The Grand Palace on my first day and Doi Suthep on my last was a kind of cultural closure that I wouldn't have been able to appreciate without all the steps in between.

"Tell us some of your impressions, at least," said Mom. "What did you do in Bangkok, for example?"

I could hardly think back that far. "I suppose the trip was a bit overwhelming at first. A new country, new language, that kind of thing."

"And all the sightseeing," Mom added.

"I don't think she saw many sights," Grandma said as she crunched into a cracker. "She was too busy chasing boys."

What?

"Rachel sent us a long email from Greece," Grandma said. "She mentioned something about a boy. Isn't that the reason you stayed all that extra time?"

I felt hotter than I'd ever felt in Thailand. How much had Rachel told them, and how much were they reading between the lines?

"Rachel and I went around to several places with Sompong," I said.

"What's a Sompong?" Grandma asked.

"Janjira's grandson."

They looked at me blankly.

"You know, Janjira. Sammy's aunt."

"Now I remember," said Mom. "You're talking about that nutty relative the Tamarins took in."

"She's not completely crazy."

"Last week she went out for a walk and they couldn't find her. Had to call the police to track her down."

Well, she was a little nutty after all.

"I hope this friend of yours spoke some English," said Mom.

"Nonsense," said Grandma. "You know what they say. *De noche todos los gatos son pardos.*"

At night all cats are brown. On the surface the sentence was innocent enough, but the sexual connotation was so blatant that I must have turned red. My relatives laughed conspiratorially. Grandma was relentless, asking about Sompong's parents and his car and his looks and his career. I didn't mind. Grandma only grilled me about things that were important. She was even less interested in tourist sights than I was.

I'd slept a couple of hours before I awoke to moonbeams shining in my face. They sneaked in for a few hours whenever there was a full moon, and I'd been too exhausted to think about closing the blinds. My back itched; I'd fallen asleep in my shirt and bra. I unzipped the top layer of my suitcase and felt around for my nightshirt.

A small package had been tucked inside the shirt, probably when I was taking a shower. Twine guarded its contents. After a dozen jabs with my fingernail clippers, the twine gave way. I unrolled several layers of wrapping before encountering a note that said "Open carefully" in Sompong's script.

The wrapping revealed the familiar velvet maroon pouch that held Janjira's elephant. At first I assumed Sompong had merely sent it back with me, but now a second elephant, black with purple specks, had been added to it. I also found a note:

Dearest Gina,

By now I hope you have arrived safely. I have enclosed a souvenir I know you will appreciate and another I found among Grandfather's things. I am sure he would want you to have them both. Pairs should stay together, should they not?

Love, Sompong

P.S. I will think only of you until we meet again.

I picked up the two elephants and held them side by side. They were the same height, weight, and shape, but they were opposites. Janjira's was purple with black, this new elephant black with purple. Janjira's had its front left leg raised, this one its right. Like mirror images, when scooted together, the elephants' raised legs graced one another's while their trunks gently kissed. I set the statues in the moonlight of the windowsill. Then I focused on their fused image until I fell into a deep sleep.

Undoubtedly, I dreamt of elephants.

Campanello Travels

Amirosian Nights

Haunting melodies, moonlit nights, and one handsome bouzouki player make for a musical challenge!

Rachel Campanello travels to the island of Amiros to stay with friends she's met in Tucson. Her summer turns into a "workation" when two of the local band members have to leave at the same time and Rachel offers to fill in. Such a challenge helps her grow as a musician and grants her a fine opportunity to practice Greek. It also gives her the chance to spend evenings with the town's star bouzouki player, a songwriter so handsome and mysterious that she can't help falling for him . . .

Carillon Chase (forthcoming)

A suspicious co-pilot, a carillon festival, and a fearless musician liven up a Midwest road trip!

Gina Campanello is excited when Happy Travels Press offers her a summer internship. Gina envisions traveling to Europe, South America, or even Asia! When she's assigned to cover the route between the capitals of Arizona and Illinois, she curses her bad luck. She cajoles her Thai friend Sompong into accompanying her, but they are also saddled with babysitting two pre-teens who can think of nothing but vampire comic books. Gina pouts all the way through New Mexico. She's cheered up by thoughts of attending the international carillon festival in Springfield, Illinois, but when the star musician skips his first concert, they realize that the Midwest is a lot more complicated than they expected . . .

Andy Veracruz Mysteries

Mariachi Meddler

A troubled woman, a guilty conscience, and a mariachi band in jeopardy turn Andy Veracruz into a meddling mariachi player!

When the death of a fellow musician threatens his mariachi, Andy Veracruz must risk everything to find the killer even if evidence points to Yiolanda, the boss's flirtatious wife. The more Andy learns, the more trouble he gets into. A sleuth by accident, he would much rather devote spare time to working on new songs. Instead he spends sleepless night walking around town in search of Yiolanda. He goes to his brother Joey for advice, but, unfortunately, Andy doesn't listen!

Island Casualty

An island paradise, a lost engagement ring, and a midnight Vespa chase sabotage a memorable vacation!

When Andy Veracruz flies to a Greek island for a holiday with Rachel, he expects to spend afternoons swimming and nights making love. After all his troubles in *Mariachi Meddler*, he deserves a break! But at an outdoor café, he meets a fellow traveler who accidentally leaves behind a package. Before Andy can return it, the man disappears. Andy tries to enjoy his vacation, but after he and Rachel are run off the road by a determined motorist, the musician starts doing undercover work by playing in a bouzouki band. After further "accidents," he realizes that he's not safe anywhere on the island, and neither are his friends . . .

Dizzy in Durango

Missing women, abandoned children, and one crazy mariachi fan drive Andy dizzy in Durango!

Once again Andy finds himself in the thick of things! The jobless musician travels to Durango, Mexico, to visit Rachel and her relatives, but after a fellow traveler disappears, Andy can't concentrate on vacationing. When he tries to investigate, instead of finding one woman, he loses another! Before he can discover more about the women's connection, he's saddled with two children who aren't his, an angry would-be girlfriend, and a self-appointed younger brother who is more reckless than he is. No wonder he's dizzy!

Substitute Soloist (forthcoming)

A dazzling concertmaster, a determined conductor, and a priceless violin save the concert!

When Andy takes a job with the symphony orchestra in Tucson, he worries about keeping up with the more experienced players and their fancy instruments. After a board member has a deadly fight with the concertmaster, however, Andy takes control. Impressed with his quick thinking, the conductor recruits Andy for a reconnaissance mission, but neither expects a European concert tour to lead to . . .

When D.R. Ransdell first traveled to Asia, she had visions of being stuck in a police station at two in the morning while trying to explain her way out of a terrible misunderstanding! Instead her wonderful visit to Japan inspired additional trips to Asia. She admires Thailand in particular for its friendly, fun-loving natives. She also appreciates its archaeological sites, colorful temple complexes, and all those lovely beaches! However, on future visits she will be careful to avoid the monsoon season . . .

Author Site http://www.dr-ransdell.com

Facebook http://www.facebook.com/dianereneeransdell

Pinterest http://www.pinterest.com/drransdell/boards/